DISCOVERING THE REVELATIONS OF GOD

NINE WITNESSES TO GOD'S EXISTENCE

THOMAS IDLER

DISCOVERING THE REVELATIONS OF GOD
Copyright © 2024 by Thomas Idler

All rights reserved. Neither this publication nor any part of this publication may be reproduced or transmitted in any form or by any means, electronic or mechanical, including photocopying, recording or any information storage and retrieval system, without permission in writing from the author.

Unless otherwise indicated, all scripture taken from the New King James Version®. Copyright © 1982 by Thomas Nelson. Used by permission. All rights reserved. Scripture quotations marked (KJV) taken from the Holy Bible, King James Version, which is in the public domain. Scripture quotations marked (MSG) are taken from The Message, copyright © 1993, 2002, 2018 by Eugene H. Peterson. Used by permission of NavPress. All rights reserved. Represented by Tyndale House Publishers. Scripture quotations taken from the (NASB®) New American Standard Bible®, Copyright © 1960, 1971, 1977, 1995, 2020 by The Lockman Foundation. Used by permission. All rights reserved. lockman.org

Soft cover ISBN: 978-1-4866-2511-6
Hard cover ISBN: 978-1-4866-2519-2
eBook ISBN: 978-1-4866-2512-3

Word Alive Press
119 De Baets Street Winnipeg, MB R2J 3R9
www.wordalivepress.ca

Cataloguing in Publication information can be obtained from Library and Archives Canada.

I would like to dedicate this book to my dad,
who taught me how personal, loving, and revealing God is
in every aspect of life.

CONTENTS

FOREWORD vii
PREFACE ix

PART ONE

CHAPTER ONE
THE EXISTENCE OF LIFE 3

CHAPTER TWO
DEFINING OUR CONCEPT OF GOD 12

CHAPTER THREE
THE ABSOLUTE TRUTH OF GOD 22

CHAPTER FOUR
THE GENERAL REVELATIONS OF GOD 32

CHAPTER FIVE
THE REVELATION OF GOD'S WORD (THE WRITTEN WITNESS) 42

CHAPTER SIX
THE REVELATION OF JESUS CHRIST (THE LIVING WITNESS) 54

CHAPTER SEVEN
THE REVELATION OF THE HOLY SPIRIT
(THE TRANSFORMING WITNESS) 63

CHAPTER EIGHT
THE GOD OF THE MOMENT (THE SPECIAL WITNESS) 73

CHAPTER NINE
THE GOD OF THE PERSON AND GOD OF THE FUTURE
(THE PERSONAL AND PROPHETIC WITNESS) 82

CHAPTER TEN
THE GOD CONNECTION 92

CHAPTER ELEVEN
THE SPHERE OF TRUTH AND THE CIRCLE OF FAITH 102

PART TWO

CHAPTER TWELVE
THE EXTERNAL WITNESS — 117

CHAPTER THIRTEEN
THE INTERNAL WITNESS — 128

CHAPTER FOURTEEN
THE HISTORICAL WITNESS — 140

CHAPTER FIFTEEN
THE WRITTEN WITNESS — 152

CHAPTER SIXTEEN
THE LIVING WITNESS — 169

CHAPTER SEVENTEEN
THE TRANSFORMING WITNESS — 183

CHAPTER EIGHTEEN
THE GIFTS OF THE HOLY SPIRIT — 194

CHAPTER NINETEEN
THE SPECIAL WITNESS — 200

CHAPTER TWENTY
THE PERSONAL WITNESS — 209

CHAPTER TWENTY-ONE
THE PROPHETIC WITNESS — 221

CONCLUSION
KNOWING THE WILL OF GOD — 237

BIBLIOGRAPHY — 241

FOREWORD

IN THE MIDST of today's confusion about God, Tom Idler disentangles the mesh of false notions about God's existence. He provides a fresh look at the foundation of the Christian faith: the revelation of God Himself.

In this book, Tom gives us some invaluable teaching that allows us to look at God's existence in a way that will benefit all of us. Woven together with solid references, personal experience, and testimony, this volume engages us in a thoughtful and meditative way on a subject that is critical to our faith. His section on how people view God is an important read in emphasizing the need for personal revelation and the need for intellect to be enhanced by spiritual understanding. Tom's own life experience of personal revelation is eye-opening and thought-provoking.

Throughout this volume, I have been pleased to note a consistent and clear outline of the gospel. The existence of God and His purposes in salvation are profound and the truth of the gospel is masterfully woven into the narrative of each chapter.

The comparisons of absolute and counterfeit truth are certainly worthy of further study and understanding, recognizing that the truth God has established is permanent and eternal.

I have known Tom Idler for many years and it is my joy, pleasure, and privilege to recommend *Discovering the Revelations of God* as a scholarly, well-written work and pray that its contents will confirm your faith, challenge your heart and mind, and deepen your understanding of the reality of God's existence and who He really is. Be blessed as you read it!

—Rev. Colin R. Wellard
President, Oasis Christian Ministries International
Abbotsford, BC, Canada

PREFACE

WHAT AN AMAZING journey it is to be able to understand who God is. This book will explain God's astounding traits of creativity and power through His creation of the world, solar system, and universe. We can also marvel at the fact that He created us individually with the ability to enjoy a personal relationship with Him through a conscience which contains all the divine qualities He possesses. History will also show that God passionately guided humanity in His truth from the past to the present, and He will continue into the future.

The revelations of God are profoundly explained and fulfilled through His Word, through His Son, and through the Holy Spirit. These Immanuel revelations reveal how personal God is and His willingness to show us His truth in person. This book will explain the amazing ways in which God displays His love, His plan for us, and His truth, which gives us the greatest hope. Without Him revealing His redemptive plan for us, we wouldn't be able to see these revelations in their most intimate and wondrous ways.

The most profound revelations are those that affect us personally, especially when God meets with us in person. These God-moments are astonishing and make us wonder how He can single us out and make us feel so special that He would want to chat with us one on one.

The book also explains my own encounter with God, my own God-moment, where he met me personally, face to face.

Please know that you can experience a one-of-a-kind God-moment in which He gives you a unique and special encounter with divine purpose. It will be a life experience you'll never forget.

As our Abba Father, God is continuously watching over us, looking out for our best interest. Even though it doesn't seem like it sometimes, the circumstances and struggles we face on a daily basis make us wonder where God is. Please understand that He knows about everything we go through. He allows us to go through these circumstances for His own reasons, which will be fully understood when we get to heaven. This mystery must be part of our faith and trust in God.

When you study the nine witnesses of God discussed in this book, you will test them through your own eyes of truth. The world will try to persuade you that God is not involved in these revelations, but please know that this book shares the absolute truth of God's honest, personal witness to us. He is revealing Himself. He wants us to get to know him in a real way.

Read this book and find out how amazingly your life will be affected by the revealing witnesses of God.

PART ONE

GOD HAS REVEALED, and continues to reveal, both Himself and His truths to us through nine general, unique, and intimate witnesses which we can experience personally.

It begins with our existence. Since God is a revealing God, we understand our existence through these revelations. He seems to be ever-present, walking alongside us to make us aware that He is truly with us in every respect. We can observe this in a general sense as well as experience it firsthand.

The first part of this book will focus on seeing these revelations through God's eyes. It's all a matter of perspective, because we each have our own opinion about God and the reason for our existence. We either experience our lives with God in mind or we don't. We interpret God by what we observe and experience. This determines the lifestyle and truth we want to live by. Therefore, it is important to interpret these revelations of God correctly, so we can live our lives with a truth that's worth living for.

We will systematically look at how God has revealed Himself to us. These revelations are logical, simple, and easily understandable because they are right in front of us. They offer proof of His existence and demonstrate that He is a provisional and personal God.

Encounter these witnesses with an open heart and mind, because they will reveal a God who loves you, wants to be there for you, and wants you to experience a personal and special relationship with Him.

CHAPTER ONE
THE EXISTENCE OF LIFE

THE FACT THAT we exist here at this moment proves that something profound happened in the beginning. When we look at ourselves, we can see how complex we are. We marvel at the intricate workings of our bodies. Even the concept of life brings us to a state of bewilderment! How could life come into existence? How is it that we are self-aware?

There are indications of intelligence all around us. We seem to have been meant to be on this earth. Everything fits. We have the necessary components for living here. Somehow we were given the knowledge and tools we need to function and live out our lives.

At some point, everyone has asked these questions: "Where did I come from? Why am I here?" To exist is to demand an answer to such questions. We have an abounding need to satisfy our curiosity and pursue truth. This truth is the basis of everything, the foundation on which we build everything else. We have an unfailing belief that if we could somehow look to the beginning, we may just find the answers we seek.

There are two possible causes for the existence of life, and they are determined by whether one believes that life has always existed or it came from nothing.

If life has always existed, we must consider that eternity is possible; the source of this eternity must be perfect and complete, without flaw or imperfection. This view leaves no room for evolution, because the infinite qualities and characteristics that define us have always been there. Nothing can be added or subtracted because everything that exists is unlimited and unchangeable. This points to an eternal, infinite Being who is the cause of all life.

If life came from nothing, if it had a set beginning, then evolution is possible. In this view, however, there would have to be some kind of mechanism that causes life to emerge from non-living substances. There must be a process by which simple organisms evolve into more complex organisms. At some point in history, there was no life, and then, for some reason, there *was* life—and it began to evolve. Many believe that this beginning was the Big Bang, a moment at which life exploded into existence and gave birth to the evolving universe and everything observable within it.

In either case, it takes faith to believe in the cause. Is it possible that life was created and designed only by a supreme, infinite Being? Or is it possible that life came about only by chance?

THE CAUSATION FACTOR

Who is the source of this life? Where did it come from? And for what purpose, if any? As finite humans, we can only assume that life had a beginning. It is beyond our comprehension to think otherwise. For the physical universe, it does appear to have had a definite beginning. All we can say is that at some point the physical universe didn't exist, and then, in an instant, everything came to be. This includes time, matter, and space, all governed by established physical laws which show that order came into the picture to bring stability to the cosmos.

The invisible realm came into existence as well. We are living beings, possessing both a spirit-nature and a soul which contains our true selves. These exist inside a physical body. There is no denying this. When a person dies, the only evidence that remains is the physical body. The invisible force which kept the body alive is no longer present, and so the body starts to decay.

This is what leads us to the question of the origin of life. Who, or what, made us alive in the first place? We therefore come to the causation factor.

We understand the law of cause-and-effect, in which one event is caused by an earlier event, which is in turn the result of something even earlier. This continues until an original cause is found. Scientists have been debating this "first cause" for centuries.

It is reasonable to assume that we can come to this first cause by working backward in time from the present to the very beginning. If we look to the beginning, common sense would indicate that there was a certain set of circumstances, occurring at the right moment with all the right components, in order to produce the first cause.

It appears that the essence of life, the initial activating agent which birthed everything, was essential in causing the visible and invisible aspects of the cosmos to become real and alive. This spark of life was either initiated by an eternal presence or it was begun by an extremely dense singularity which exploded the physical universe from the realm of nothingness.

Whether life evolved or was designed, we understand that there must exist an original cause to explain everything. We can only look at the results, visible all around us.

Since the cause is beyond our comprehension, it stands to reason that there must exist some intelligence that is beyond us, an intelligence that set the boundaries of what life would become.

THE LIMITATIONS OF LIFE

Amazingly, the body, soul, and spirit are connected to each other. Yet they are also distinct. Each part is vital not only for our sentient existence but for our development and growth into our full potential. We can mature ourselves through experience, but our physical bodies have limits.

The general theory of evolution indicates that life can develop without limits. The potential is there for us to become even more than we are.

However, it does appear that we are limited in how far we can go. Our purpose appears to be one of replication through reproduction, which indicates design. This reveals some boundaries that only God could have set.

Even non-living substances have limits, from the basic elements of the periodic table to the construction of solid, liquid, and gaseous objects. We can observe the physical laws of the universe, study the forces of nature and time. These properties of the universe wouldn't be able to function unless they, too, were limited to a given purpose. Each performs its function to maintain the foundation behind all life.

Matter, time, and space have interesting qualities of their own. Matter is essential in lending structure and substance to the physical universe. Time has the most important function of all, because it keeps everything in line; it keeps everything moving forward. Without time, we would be left with chaos.

Space, on the other hand, does appear to be unlimited. But this is necessary in order for the universe to do its work.

God is revealed in the fact that everything we see in creation is limited to a purpose. He accomplished this by planning out a design to sustain life and everything else in the universe.

If we look to the present, we find numerous proofs that life can only have come from a designed program. These include the cycle of life, the anthropic principle, and the mirror effect.

The cycle of life. Biogenesis is the process by which life emerges, *bio* meaning "life" and *genesis* meaning "beginning." This process is seen so consistently that it has become known as the first law of biogenesis.

On the other hand, the process of life developing from that which is non-living is called *abiogenesis*—*a* meaning "not," *bio* meaning "life," and *genesis* meaning "beginning." This is the idea of life sprouting from non-living substances.

When we compare these processes, we find that they correspond to whether one believes that life has always existed or whether it had a beginning. Further, this means that *biogenesis* corresponds to the eternal-source cause and *abiogenesis* corresponds to the beginning-from-nothing cause.

Greg Koukl once spoke a message at my church on the subject of why he was not an evolutionist, explaining the point of view that evolutionists believe that life happened by chance and that life began to evolve billions and billions of years ago. The first pillar for evolutionists is the belief in *abiogenesis*. At one point in history, there was no life upon the earth; at another point, through some mechanism, life began—and then it developed. This evolutionary development leads to the process of transitions, by which one organism can be transformed into another, more complex organism.

We can see that *biogenesis* is the clear-cut winner. All the evidence points to the fact that life can only come from life. There really isn't any kind of evidence to demonstrate life coming from something non-living. This process isn't seen anywhere. All we can see is the reproduction cycles of life happening all around us. Fruit trees produce more fruit trees. Flowering plants produce more flowering plants. Grasses produce other grasses. Trees reproduce trees, insects produce insects, etc.

Humans produce more humans. This process begins with a seed fertilizing an egg, which then develops at the genetic level, the cellular level, the tissue level, and the organ level until finally reaching maturation. Every living creation follows this pattern. It is happening right before our eyes. This demonstrates that the biological aspects of life have been programmed to follow a design. This reveals the existence of God as the master designer.

Every ten seconds, twenty-five thousand cells replicate themselves in the human body. Multiply this by the earth's population and you have approximately two hundred trillion cells reproducing themselves every ten seconds! In fact, a living cell can reproduce itself every thirty minutes.

The living cell is such a complex machine. One can only marvel at what it accomplishes and then wonder how a non-living cell could ever initiate the process of creating life. How could *nothing* produce *something*? This process requires knowledge and the means to accomplish such a feat. Only God has this capability.

The Bible confirms that God is the originator of the design found in all life on earth, including plants, insects, animals, and humans.

> Then God said, "Let the earth bring forth grass, the herb that yields seed, and the fruit tree that yields fruit according to its kind, whose seed is in itself, on the earth"; and it was so...
>
> So God created great sea creatures and every living thing that moves, with which the waters abounded, according to their kind, and every winged bird according to its kind. And God saw that it was good. And God blessed them, saying, "Be fruitful and multiply, and fill the waters in the seas, and let birds multiply on the earth...
>
> Then God said, "Let the earth bring forth the living creature according to its kind: cattle and creeping thing and beast of the earth, each according to its kind"; and it was so...

> So God created man in His own image; in the image of God He created him; male and female He created them. Then God blessed them, and God said to them, "Be fruitful and multiply; fill the earth and subdue it; have dominion over the fish of the sea, over the birds of the air, and over every living thing that moves on the earth." (Genesis 1:11, 21–22, 24, 27–28)

Life can only come from life. This process reveals the existence of God, through its infinite characteristic. Life is infinite because only an eternal Being could bring it into existence. God is therefore the original cause of life, and life continues to exist because it was designed to continually exist.

God intended for the life He created to last forever. This is how it was supposed to be.

However, death then entered the picture and gave us the impression that life first begins and then ends. If death didn't exist, as originally intended, life would have continued forever and revealed its own source.

It's hard to imagine a Being who was never created. God has always existed, yet He never had a beginning and He will never have an end. This makes Him self-existent.

How is this possible? The fact that we are here right now on this earth proves that it is possible. We obviously came from somewhere and it would make sense that the source of our existence is God.

We find that God is infinitely perfect, complete, and fulfilled in every aspect of His being. This makes Him immutable, or unchangeable, which leaves no room for the processes of evolution or maturation. God has always been God. He is the same today as He was in eternity past and will continue to be for the rest of eternity into the future.

Since God is eternal, He possesses an incomprehensible quality: *infinite faith*.

When we possess the will to accomplish something, we must believe that we can accomplish it. This is where faith comes into the picture. We all have a measure of faith, at the finite level. But imagine having an infinite amount of faith! This would mean that nothing is impossible for you. There would be no limit to your abilities, no limit to your existence.

Because of His infinite faith, God has the ability to do anything. This means that He is omnipotent (almighty and all-powerful), omniscient (all-knowing and infinitely wise), and omnipresent (present everywhere and unlimited by space). He is boundless and therefore eternal.

The easiest way to explain this on our terms is to say that God *willed* Himself to be eternal. His infinite faith allowed this to happen. Only infinite faith could bring eternity into reality. God has always existed because this is the only possible result of having infinite faith.

God also transcends His creation and is separate from it, beyond and above the earth and the entire universe. Time cannot contain Him because He is eternally present at all times, past, present, and future. In His foreknowledge, God already knew what we would freely choose to do.[1] Therefore, nothing that happens in the future will ever surprise Him.

Who else could be like God? No one, because everyone else was created. Only He is the glorious, eternal, and infinite God.

Having infinite faith allowed God to speak the physical universe into existence. He spoke words and breathed out stars, planets, and galaxies. He logically designed the laws of physics, including gravity, light, and energy, to govern the ways of the universe within the cradle of time.

Yet amidst all this majestic beauty and omnipotent awesomeness, He created the planet Earth in one of the billions and billions of solar systems and created us humans to dwell on it. Does this not demonstrate how powerful, creative, and personal He is?

Why would God create us in the first place? After all, He was complete within Himself, content with who He was. Yet He chose to create us and give us a suitable place to live on a planet filled with all the components we need to survive, live, and grow.

The first human to be created by God was Adam. He created Adam's physical body first, then breathed into his nostrils the essence of life. Adam thus became a living being (Genesis 2:7), made in the image of God. He was the crowning achievement of the physical universe.

From Adam, God created Eve as a soulmate and companion, devising the plan for one to carry the egg while the other carries the sperm. This gave them the ability to procreate and begin the cycle of life design. This cycle is God's signature, His fingerprint, which proves that He is the cause of everything.

When God bestowed the breath of life into Adam, He breathed into existence all of humanity. God designed each person differently, with their own characteristics and abilities and the capability to mature, develop relationships, and procreate. He thought about each individual before time even began.

Not only was the universe created for us, but Earth became our home. Life began in the garden of Eden, where God created plentiful food-bearing plants to sustain life.

---

[1] John H. Sailhamer, *Christian Theology* (Grand Rapids, MI: Zondervan, 1998), 29.

He gave our first parents the task of caring for everything. In His love and wisdom, God wanted to create beings who mirrored Him. He gave them His moral likeness. And since God can't really worship Himself, He designed humanity to be creatures of praise.

God had already created the spirit world, with angelic beings, but they were not created in His image. They were created to serve Him in whatever capacity they were designed to do. Rather, Adam and Eve were made in the image of God, after His likeness, so that they and those born after them could worship and have fellowship with God and enjoy life in all its fullness.

The anthropic principle. God intrinsically created the earth and everything on it with purpose. When He created us, He knew that He would have to create an environment suited to fulfill our needs. The earth perfectly secured that foundation.

From there, God gave us the food we needed to energize our bodies. He gave us the air to breathe, water to drink, and food to eat, fulfilling the needs of our bodies. It is amazing how well these components fit together.

This environment was designed not only to fulfill our needs but also the needs of all life. Plants and trees require water, sunlight, and nutrients. Insects and animals require the same kind of nutrients we need. There is such a delicate balance between us and the ecosystem we live in. We are interdependent on each other for our existence and survival. The amount of planning that went into this plan is incredible.

Our solar system is also a key part of this plan. Without the sun and its balanced gravitational forces, without gaseous and chemical equilibriums, we would cease to exist. Our planet is positioned perfectly, ninety-three million miles from the sun, to sustain us. Too close and we would boil, like Venus; too far and we would freeze, like Mars.

All this preparation for humanity's care is known as the anthropic principle. Stated simply, this describes the properties of the universe being perfectly established to maintain life. One must revel in amazement at how well our environment fulfills our most basic needs. Consider also the cycle of day and night. It is a marvel that we have a period of darkness to stimulate our need for sleep, in order to function optimally.

Truly, every detail has been planned perfectly, demonstrating that a superior Being created this environment just for us. Only a Being with such forethought, creativity, and ability could have designed it. Could chance or nothingness accomplish this result? That must surely be an impossibility.

The mirror effect. Since we exist, God exists, and we are therefore only alive because of Him. Those who believe otherwise can only theorize. They must conclude that we must have evolved from nothing. Which is more believable?

The easiest way to understand this is to look at yourself in a mirror. Marvel at how well you were designed. Observe your facial features, your arms, your hands, your legs, your muscles, your bones, and your skin. Every part of your body is so functional and purposeful. Does it not make you wonder how you could otherwise be created, apart from God? Could you honestly believe you came from nothing?

George Gallup, who originated a well-known polling company, once said in regards to the human body: "the chance that all the functions of the individual could just happen is a statistical monstrosity."[2] When considering the human eye alone, evolutionists have a difficult time explaining how it could have developed gradually in stages. One writer, R.L. Wysong, figured out that the probability of the eye forming by chance is 1 in 10^{266}.[3]

Indeed, the eye is an amazing feat of engineering. It's like a miracle. How would you explain the automatic adjustments that the eye continually performs on a daily basis? It aims, it focuses, and it adjusts what it sees in full color. This information is then relayed to the back of the brain via the optic nerve, information which is instantaneously recognized and understood. The designer of the eye was so ingenious that He thought about adding a second eye so that depth and perception could give us even more detail.

Only an infinite God could be responsible for this degree of planning. He designed our eyes so we could see one another and observe the beauty of our world and wonder of the universe.

The mirror effect can also help us understand our Creator, for we mirror God. All of nature mirrors God, displaying His glory. The universe is His masterpiece. All these works are a product of the thoughts and desires of a creative and loving Being.

When we create something by our own hands, we use all our energy, talent, and abilities. The final product is thus a part of us, reflecting and revealing who we are.

One only has to consider the masters of the art world and look upon their masterpieces to know the artist. Can we not do the same with God? When we look at the universe, ourselves, and the world we live in, can we acknowledge that only God could have done this and nothing else?

When we acknowledge God as Creator, we give Him pleasure. It is a form of worship. When we don't, God feels rejected, just as anyone else would when rejected by their own creation.

WHO ELSE BUT GOD?

Now look outside into the marvelous world of nature and contemplate the wonder of what you see. Who else but God could create an animal that flies? The sky would

---

[2] Cora A. Reno, *Evolution on Trial* (Chicago, IL: Moody Press, 1970), 103.
[3] R.L. Wysong, *The Creation-Evolution Controversy* (Midland, MI: Inquiry Press, 1981), 308.

be empty without the various birds which fly so naturally through it. They honor God because they were designed to fly.

Who else but God could create an animal that swims? He provided the means for these creatures to separate oxygen from water through the use of gills. This is truly remarkable. These underwater creatures honor God by swimming so naturally in their own environment.

Who else but God could design a symbiotic relationship between oxygen and carbon dioxide, forming a cycle that is so vital for our existence? This interdependent chemical equilibrium between humanity and the earth has been replenished and sustained since the beginning of time.

Who else but God could create and design our human bodies to be so self-sufficient? We each have a natural computer, the brain, that regulates and controls everything the body needs and does, yet it remains subservient to our human will and desire.

Who else but God could fill the night sky with stars that are so incomprehensibly far away? The night sky would be boring without them, yet stars fill us with wonder when we observe how exact they are in design.

Who else but God could give life to us so we could believe in Him and accept the fact that He created everything for our benefit? The existence of life is a gift of love that proves God's existence.

Something can only come from something, and this something must be eternal. Something cannot come from nothing, because nothing cannot surpass itself. It remains nothing.

No matter how we look to the cause of life, it all comes down to the fact that God is the reason for our existence. Even if one accepts the supposed singularity which birthed the Big Bang, where did it come from? No matter how you figure it, the original cause always points to God. Life, therefore, can only come from an eternal presence, and God is the only presence who is eternal.

CHAPTER TWO
DEFINING OUR CONCEPT OF GOD

THROUGHOUT HISTORY, WE have seen how those who lived before us viewed God. Some viewed Him as the God of nature, with the sun, moon, and earth being the focus of worship. If there was a drought, it meant God was angry. In order to make it right with Him, there had to be some kind of payment to bring the rain again and allow the crops to grow. People had the mentality that if they could offer God something, He would be happy and produce some kind of blessing. If we can appease God by being good, this might be enough of a personal sacrifice to satisfy Him, and thereby enough for Him to extend a reward.

Others have needed God to be a real object. Many cultures have utilized handmade idols as objects of worship. This has been influenced, in particular, by those who make idols for a living. They've crafted these profitable items to symbolize who they thought God needed to be. They couldn't grasp the idea of God being invisible, so they made Him into something that could be seen. Conceptually, they needed to confirm the old adage: "We'll believe it if we can see it."

Still others, like the Greeks and Romans, viewed Him as the chief god amongst many gods, like Zeus and Jupiter, interacting with the human race in whatever way they wanted: imposing their will, judgments, and blessings in order to teach humanity about life and death.

The Roman-Greco culture introduced a mythical explanation of how God dealt with the physical world and the human race. They intellectually understood His actions by explaining that there were many gods, each portraying a different facet of life. The idea was for humanity to focus on a concept that made God seem more human. This resulted in developing polytheism and pantheism.

He has also been viewed as the god of fertility and pleasure, with hedonism as the focus. This belief stimulated the building of temples for the fertility goddesses Diana and Artemis, where some would pay temple prostitutes to fulfill their sexual desires as a form of worship.

Others have embraced a new age concept of God, unseen and mysterious. They would practice a form of unitive meditation as a progression toward stripping away the unnecessary and obtaining only the necessary. God becomes the spiritual entity who influences His followers toward a heightened sense of self-awareness and self-truth. Spiritual enlightenment becomes the god of the higher consciousness, or "altered perception of reality,"[4] meaning that those who obtain more

---
[4] Bob Larson, *Larson's Book of Cults* (Wheaton, IL: Tyndale House, 1984), 47.

knowledge or reach a higher level of being can better understand what it's like to be God.

Stemming from this idea, others believe in a metaphysical lifeforce that explains how all living things are connected as one. God is associated with all things as the living sustainer.

Then there are those who have no view of God because they believe He doesn't exist. We are here by chance and must fend for ourselves. Our destiny is in our own hands because it's the survival of the fittest.

VIEWS ABOUT GOD

Our beliefs about what is true determine who we think God is, and they will ultimately determine how we live. They influence our way of thinking and infiltrate our way of life.

When it comes to understanding truth, however, there is the objective knowledge of revealed truth and then there is the subjective interpretation of perceived truth. Both establish the basis for developing a worldview about God.

The objective, or revealed, truth is that there is only one way toward salvation. The subjective truth involves us perceiving many ways to God, and no matter which way we choose we believe it will lead us there.

We should take a black-and-white approach to accepting God's truth: deal with sin, understand how it separates us from Him, and embrace our need for a Savior, which only God can provide. This is considered by some to be far-fetched, outdated, or ineffective.

As a result, subjectivism has led the world to embrace many different views about God, life, and salvation. Many believe that salvation must be earned and not just simply accepted as a free gift. This premise is based on the idea that only we can change our own predicament; God cannot change it.

There are five basic universal views about God.

1. God is inaccessible, giving the impression that He is unreachable. We therefore can only work on our own salvation and leave the results up to God. Islam is an example of this. For Muslims, the Shahada confession of faith goes like this: "There is no god but God, and Muhammad is the messenger of God." Followers must ritualistically obey the five pillars of Islamic faith to affirm their devotion to Allah:

- Recite the Shahada daily.
- Pray five times daily toward Mecca.
- Engage in almsgiving.
- Fast during Ramadan.
- Make the pilgrimage to Mecca at least once.

Devoted Muslims submit themselves before the one true God, believing that obeying the sacred law and fulfilling their obligations to the pillars of their religion will bring them to Paradise in the end.

2. God is all-encompassing and existent in everything. Hinduism is an example of this. That polytheistic religion has thirty-three million gods in their polytheistic view, although this is metaphorical by nature and not a definitive number.[5]

Hindus believe, "All is one. Everyone is divine. God is not out there, he is within everyone."[6] Their culture is influenced by this pantheistic belief and they live their lives accordingly. Whatever they do, they do it for the greater good because this way of life is part of the universal soul where karma and reincarnation rule. They believe that everyone is part of this oneness of God. Since everyone is ultimately god, and since sin, circumstances, and fate are mere illusions, there are no judgments, only acceptance.

3. God is non-essential or non-existent. According to this view, the self is the center of the universe; only self can achieve deification through personal devotion and achievement.

Buddhism is an example of this. Its adherents pursue the ultimate path toward nirvana, which can be explained as the state of ultimate well-being. This state can only be achieved by following the eightfold pathway of rules and regulations which can take a lifetime to master.

Buddhism promises to rid its followers of all evil, develop in them only pure thoughts, and making them indifferent toward materialistic wealth, pain, and pleasure.[7] There is no God, no consequences for sin, and no need for salvation. The truth obtained from self-deification is the only answer needed in terms of understanding what life is about.

4. God is a subjective concept, leading to secularism. Taoism is an example of this. Taoists believe that when everything is in balance, the result is peace. This is where the concepts of yin and yang come from. Yang is the positive force of good, light, life, and masculinity. Yin is the negative essence of evil, darkness, decay, and femininity.[8]

When followers live in harmony with the cosmic forces of the universe, a balance will result which leads to contentment. The only way to achieve this is to plug oneself into the *tao*, "the way," which will lead to the perfect life.

When we are united with the energy force of the universe, like the Force in *Star Wars*, perfect peace will result and we will obtain oneness with everything and achieve

---

[5] Ibid., 72.
[6] Ibid., 12.
[7] Ibid., 95.
[8] Ibid., 98.

ultimate self-awareness. God becomes nothing but a part of the macrocosmic universe, consumed in the balanced whole.

5. God is personal and provides the means to obtain salvation through His gift of grace by faith. Christianity is an example of this. Believers accept that God created us in His image so we could have a personal relationship with Him. But when our sin, through Adam and Eve, separated us from God, He planned for His own Son to pay the price for our unfaithfulness to Him through His death and resurrection. Atonement is made, and when we accept what Jesus did for us we become restored to a right relationship with God. Salvation doesn't need to be earned but simply accepted by faith.

THE TWO MISCONCEPTIONS OF HOW WE VIEW GOD

Thousands of religious and cultic groups around the world hold to a subjective concept of God. Some people become frustrated when they can't seem to understand which truth is right.

The right view is the one in which we have no doubt about who God is and have a definite understanding of His ways. Why are there so many different views and opinions about God? And why are people drawn to believe these other concepts about God?

The problem is that we must first digest these concepts through our finite intellect, our own understanding. This results in differences of opinions and conceptions of God, depending on the teachings and revelations we have been exposed to. It is therefore imperative that we search the truth of God by the revelations He has personally given us.

There are two common misconceptions about God. The first is that we think the best way to understand Him is to bring Him down to our level. This causes Him to fall far below His infinite standards. We cannot, as created beings, do this. We make Him less than He is and consequently develop a false concept of Him. This is exactly what most people do, as described earlier in this chapter. They bring Him to the human level in order to make Him more manageable.

God cannot be measured, because He is beyond measurement. We cannot comprehend His magnitude. God is separate from us and His creation. He is uncreated and infinitely perfect in every way.

We are the complete opposite of this. How can we compare ourselves to Him? How can we equate ourselves with Him or place ourselves above Him?

The second misconception is that we think that the only way to connect with God is to elevate ourselves to a higher level of being. This results in a false view of God because it presupposes that we can become like God, that we can somehow achieve godhood.

This was predicted in the very beginning by Satan, who spoke to Eve about the idea in the garden of Eden:

> Now the serpent was more cunning than any beast of the field which the Lord God had made. And he said to the woman, "Has God indeed said, 'You shall not eat of every tree of the garden'?"
>
> And the woman said to the serpent, "We may eat the fruit of the trees of the garden; but of the fruit of the tree which is in the midst of the garden, God has said, 'You shall not eat it, nor shall you touch it, lest you die.'"
>
> Then the serpent said to the woman, "You will not surely die. For God knows that in the day you eat of it your eyes will be opened, and you will be like God, knowing good and evil." (Genesis 3:1–5)

Whether you believe that you can elevate yourself to God's level, achieve a higher state of consciousness, or perceive that everything in the universe is God, the misconception is in trying to spiritualize God through human insight. We cannot manipulate God to be who we think He should be.

We can use our intellect to understand God to a certain extent. But when it comes down to it, we must use our spiritual senses to comprehend His truth. The intellect is actually enhanced by spiritual understanding, and this is how we learn more about God.

Our responsibility in regards to having a proper concept of God is to use our spirit-nature as it was designed. It is capable of discerning these revelations by helping us to know who He really is. He has personally revealed Himself to us, but this is only possible when we utilize our spiritual understanding. We cannot elevate ourselves to a higher place; we must understand the magnitude, greatness, character, attributes, and glory of God.

Another true concept of God is that He is infinitely holy. Any view that contradicts this is a lie. His entire being is shrouded with His holiness; all His other attributes are encased within it. This ensures that God will always remain true to Himself and ethically pure in whatever He does.

This should cause us to come before Him with humility and reverence, not with selfish elevation. We were designed to worship and obey a holy God. As Creator, the ways of the universe follow His design. It would make sense for us to follow it as well.

THE INFINITE PERFECTION FACTOR

When it comes to finding the right concept of God, it must first be founded upon the absolute truth. The problem is that when someone outside of God considers a truth and makes it absolute, the result can be a false view. The possibility is there for this truth to seem right in our eyes without reflecting who God really is.

How do we know the truth about God with any certainty? To answer this, we must first consider and realize that God reveals Himself to us personally as an infinite Being. This surpasses our own understanding. In order to be in a state of infinitude, we must be perfect. If one has any imperfection, a state of infinitude is impossible.

This brings us to the infinite perfection factor, the idea that one who is infinite can only possess perfect and complete qualities and thus be absolutely holy. Holiness is infinite perfection. God therefore can only be infinitely good. He can never change. There can only be one absolute conception of who God is. Since God is perfect and holy in every way, there would be absolutely no kind of evil within Him, because being good is perfection and being evil is imperfection. Anything contrary to this truth manipulates our concept of God and causes us to deviate from who He really is. Infinite perfection can only lead us to one absolute view of God.

Can we imagine a being who is infinite and also possesses evil qualities? We would see a being who is hateful, who seeks only his own desires and pleasures. We would see a being who creates and then destroys. He wreaks havoc so that life means nothing and contains no hope. There would be no possible salvation in this scenario, because such an evil infinite being wouldn't care for us, nor would he show any kind of love or mercy.

It therefore can be concluded that it is impossible for an infinite being, like God, to possess incomplete or evil characteristics.

Yet, in our world today, imperfection can be seen everywhere. The infinite world that God designed perfectly became imperfect through the introduction of finite humanity. The Bible says that God created everything good—and when Adam and Eve disobeyed God, that perfection, that goodness, became imperfection.

With His infinite knowledge, God knew that we would mess things up. Before time even began, God, in His infinite love, made a way to restore all things new. However, we haven't yet seen this complete restoration, because humanity's story must run its course. The consequences of our actions must be fulfilled.

God gives us time to understand this restoration of all things, because He planned to bring redemption to our finite world at the right moment. This redemption began when God's Son, Jesus, became human and took our imperfections to His death. When He resurrected, all things, including us, were restored—to some extent. Creation will be perfected again, when this age comes to an end. This is God's greatest revelation.

WHO GOD IS

When we think about someone we know, we consider the characteristics and qualities that define them. When we spend time with them, we begin to understand their personality. This is especially true when it's a person we form an intimate relationship with. We see all the ins and outs of who they really are, the good and the bad.

In order for this process to play out, we must reveal ourselves to one another in transparency. The same can be said about God.

We learn about people's attributes by observing them, by viewing their tendencies and seeing how they react. We become familiar with their special forms of communication—their body language and the words they speak—and even come to intuit what they're thinking. These are known as a person's *communicable attributes*.

God has given us an awareness of His communicable attributes because we were made in His image. They are familiar to us because we share these moral qualities.[9]

God also possesses *incommunicable attributes* which are distinctive to Him. We do not possess these attributes because they can only be associated with God. In fact, we are incapable of having these characteristics because we are finite creatures. Our abilities are limited. Only God can possess these qualities because they are eternal, just like Him.[10]

GOD'S COMMUNICABLE ATTRIBUTES

God's dominion. God has allowed us to have dominion over what He has created on the earth. He gave us the responsibility to take care of everything and to treat others, including all living things, with respect and integrity. However, God has the final say, which is why we are accountable to Him. His dominion over all things is sovereign.

God's will. God has allowed us to have free will. This gift to choose extends to us a sense of ownership over our lives. We determine how we live, what we should do, and how we will take care of things. It may seem like we have control—but when it comes down to it, God has absolute control. His will can be purposeful (He wants something to happen), permissive (He allows something to happen), or prescriptive (He allows us to respond to His request).[11]

God's justice. There exists an absolute knowledge of what is good and what is evil, according to God's standards. We know this because we have a God-given conscience that tells us when we've done something wrong, or when someone has wronged us.

---

[9] Sailhamer, *Christian Theology*, 28.
[10] Ibid., 27.
[11] Ibid., 28.

CHAPTER TWO: DEFINING OUR CONCEPT OF GOD

We can easily point out other people's mistakes, but we rarely point out our own.

God's standards represent absolute perfection in how we act in relation to ourselves, others, and our circumstances. God looks at our conduct, and especially at the intent of our hearts. He is just because he keeps His own standards perfectly. He knows all things perfectly.

God's faithfulness. We can be faithful by showing how committed we are, but sometimes we can become unfaithful. This happens when we become lazy, uncommitted, sinful, or simply tired. It takes great strength to be faithful, whether it be to another person, our work, or other commitments.

But amazingly, even when we are unfaithful, God remains faithful. He sets the standard of faithfulness regardless of what happens. When we are faithful to God, things get accomplished—because God is faithful to see things through.

God's goodness. When we are good to others, we demonstrate God's goodness to them. Our attitude often demonstrates that we're trying to be good, but this can be difficult due to our sinful nature. We can act badly toward others, and even ourselves.

Not so with God. He will always be good, because His nature is always good. It's impossible for anything bad to exist in Him.

God's goodness usually follows those whom He loves. David said in Psalm 37:25, *"I have been young, and now am old; yet I have not seen the righteous forsaken, nor his descendants begging bread."*

God's love. The greatest gift we can ever give is love. If we had more love, there would be less hatred in the world.

Love is best experienced when it becomes reciprocal, and the greatest act of love occurred when God introduced us to His plan of redemption by sending His Son to die for our sins, our unfaithfulness to Him. He could have left us alone in our fallen state, but instead He chose to save us, out of love, because He wanted us back. Nothing compares to His love for us.

God's grace. We often think we need to make some kind of payment to gain God's favor, but no payment can ever be enough. Our own self-righteousness is never good enough.

Grace, which is God's unmerited favor, is the only answer. Only by His grace, through the work of Christ at the cross, could payment for our sins be made in full. All we need to do is believe in what He did for us and accept His grace.

God's mercy. Mercy is an extension of love. Nothing can be greater than when one experiences forgiveness, when mercy is offered in a hopeless situation. God extended to us His mercy to give us hope and comfort. He is the master of hope of comfort, without which we couldn't live.

God's virtues. Examples of virtues are meekness, temperance, and perseverance. We need to be familiar with all these virtues because they keep us in tune with God. We can experience God through these virtues because we have been blessed to utilize them, not only for God's pleasure but for ours, and for those around us.

GOD'S INCOMMUNICABLE ATTRIBUTES

God is a boundless spiritual Being. God has no material body. Nothing can contain Him. He is bigger than the universe. This is why He can be everywhere at once. This is why He can see everything and know everything. This is why He is separate from us and His creation. This unlimitedness is beyond our comprehension. We are limited; God is not.

God is eternal. God has always existed. Psalm 102:25–27 says,

> Of old You laid the foundation of the earth, and the heavens are the work of Your hands. They will perish, but You will endure; yes, they will all grow old like a garment; like a cloak You will change them, and they will be changed. But You are the same, and Your years will have no end.

God willed Himself to be eternal. Time cannot contain Him, for He exists beyond time. Before time existed, God was there. Since time existed, God has been here. When time is gone, He will still be there.

God is the only God. God doesn't owe His existence to anyone or anything. He is self-existent. We read in Isaiah 44,

> Thus says the Lord, the King of Israel, and his Redeemer, the Lord of hosts: "I am the First and I am the Last; besides Me there is no God… Do not fear, nor be afraid; have I not told you from that time, and declared it? You are My witnesses. Is there a God besides Me? Indeed there is no other Rock; I know not one." (Isaiah 44:6, 8)

There is no other God but God (Deuteronomy 4:39).

God is infinite. All that God is and everything He does is complete and perfect. He did not evolve to this state; He has always been like this. All of His attributes are infinite. They have always been at their full potential. These attributes include His holiness, self-sufficiency, omniscience, omnipotence, omnipresence, wisdom, transcendence, immanence, morality, and sovereignty.

God is immutable. It is impossible for God to change. If He was to change in any way from who He is and what He has established, He would become less than He is. He would become fallible and imperfect.

Even though the Bible tells of occasions when God changed His mind, like His judgment on the city of Nineveh in Jonah, this was part of His prescriptive will. This does not change who He is.

In order to keep us on track, He had to provide a way to account for our failures, inconsistencies, and changeableness. God does not have to change because He is already perfect.

God is of one essence. There is only one God. He is one Being, but He exists in three Persons, each subsisting within the one essence. God wouldn't be complete unless the three were together as one. An infinite God wouldn't be infinite unless there exists an infinite relationship. The Father, Son, and Holy Spirit are the perfect composite of an infinite relationship. The three coexist in perfect unison.

CHAPTER THREE
THE ABSOLUTE TRUTH OF GOD

GOD'S TRUTH IS absolute. It does not change. It does not waver. It is permanent. It is from everlasting to everlasting and, like any constitution, maintains its authenticity. For God is the source of this truth and He has established it by His own infinite wisdom.

This was the foundation on which Adam and Eve were created. It's part of the image of God that was implanted within them. It gave them the ability to know the difference between what was right and what was wrong, through the gift of the conscience.

Before the Fall, Adam and Eve had perfect peace. After it, they knew they had done something wrong and their peace became marred. They tried to hide their physical and spiritual nakedness from God because their consciences condemned them. They played the blame game, which is the sign of knowing when you have violated God's truth. Your conscience will give you the feeling of guilt.

God's truth stands on its own. It is not chaotic or confusing, but perpetual and steadfast. It's like passing through a narrow gate. It is straight. It is founded upon by what God has ordered (decreed) and by what He has established (designed).

Once we begin to understand this truth, we begin to know who God is and what He stands for. Whether we accept His truth, however, is up to us.

GOD'S STANDARDS ARE ABSOLUTE PERFECTION

God being absolute, everything about Him is perfect and beyond imagination. It's a utopia in which nothing could ever go wrong. You would never want to leave this state of supreme wholeness and tranquility where there exists no sin, no trouble, no suffering, and no evil. Imperfections aren't even considered or seen. It's just eternal bliss and unconditional love, and this heavenly realm is where God resides.

God's truth is based on His holiness. For Adam and Eve, biting into the forbidden fruit seemed like such an insignificant offence, yet it was enough to devastate them and throw the entire world into a state of sinfulness, decay, and death. They hadn't expected such a harsh sentence for their act of disobedience. The result was absolute judgment.

Payment for such disobedience had to be made. Why? Because God's standards need to be upheld. His view of perfection needs to be maintained. Nothing can be left unresolved. The resulting state of imperfection contradicted everything God stands for. He had every right to decide what to do about it.

God's standards are absolute and He expects nothing less than perfection. This means that everything which has been created by Him has to be absolutely perfect, including us.

The dilemma is easily seen. With humanity's free will and finiteness comes the possibility of failure. In fact, God knew that we would fail before Him. He knew that Adam and Eve would disobey the one commandment He asked them to uphold.

They ended up believing in a false truth which Satan dangled in front of them. The serpent Satan used to deceive Adam and Eve was part of a clever plan through which he persuaded them to believe a different kind of truth, which he portrayed as a better truth.

There is God's truth, and then there are other truths. This is the basis for every decision we make. We must decide whether to do things God's way, our way, or someone else's way.

When God created the invisible world, He created spiritual creatures who were given specific roles. They had a purpose. At some point, after Lucifer was created with all his glorious gifts and abilities, he led a band of followers to rebel against what God had established as truth and decided to establish his own truth so he could become like God. His sin of pride led him and about a third of the angelic beings to be rejected by God.

Lucifer, once an archangel and now known as Satan, was thrown out of God's presence along with those who banded together with him. They were judged to be lost for all eternity without any hope of being saved. This is perhaps why they stand against everything God has created and established in the physical world. They have resolved to take down those who were created in God's image, in order to get back at Him for His punishment.

In a way, Satan was granted his wish because he became the prince of this world. He established his domain here, including his own truth for those who are willing to follow it.

To understand how he has done this, we will compare his truth to God's truth, for there is only one absolute truth and it belongs to God. Any other truth is counterfeit. But this is what Satan wants us to believe in. In every decision we face, Satan offers something different.

Let's compare God's absolute truth to Satan's counterfeit truth:

ABSOLUTE TRUTH	COUNTERFEIT TRUTH
Only God is God, and no one else. Deuteronomy 4:39 says, *"Therefore know this day, and consider it in your heart, that the Lord Himself is God in heaven above and on the earth beneath; there is no other."* God is the only one who is uncreated. He is eternal.	Satan declared in Isaiah 14:12–14 that he would be like God, the Most High. He is the prince of this world (John 14:30) and the father of lies (John 8:44). He also declared, when tempting Adam and Eve, that they could be like God (Genesis 3:5). A created being can never become God or be equal to Him.
God is absolutely holy. He has no sin within Himself and is set apart from every aspect of it. He possesses only absolute righteousness and perfect goodness. Isaiah 6:3 says, *"And one cried to another and said: 'Holy, holy, holy is the Lord of hosts; the whole earth is full of His glory!'"* God desires for us to be holy because He is holy (Leviticus 11:44–45).	Satan wants us to believe that God has rejected us. He tries to sabotage our holiness (our sanctification in Christ) by having us do unholy things just to make us feel that God won't want us anymore. He tried to do the same with Jesus by tempting Him in the wilderness after His baptism. Three times Satan asked Jesus to disobey His Father in heaven, tempting him to believe in his own truth (Matthew 4:1–11, Luke 22:31–34).
God is the Creator and Owner of all things. Psalm 24:1 says, *"The Earth is the Lords, and all its fullness, the world and those who dwell therein."* We belong to God and are stewards of His creation. God has allowed us to have that which we have and those with whom we interact. God's wisdom is the foundation for everything.	Satan wants us to believe in the wisdom of this world, which declares that the universe and everything within it happened without God, that we evolved from nothing and have evolved to our current state. We believe that this is a matter of survival and that what we have is ours; we have earned it, and therefore we deserve all its resulting benefits (1 Corinthians 1:20–31).
God has established His truth as relevant. His truth is perpetual and beneficial to us. God's written Word declares who He is and Jesus, His Son incarnate, becomes the living Word. Both reveal the absolute truth of God (John 1:1–18, John 14:5–7, 2 Timothy 3:1–17).	God's truth is irrelevant. Satan wants us to believe that truth is relative and that a person lives by his own truth. This relativity says that the Bible was written by imperfect men. Jesus is not deity, but a human. What the Bible says and what Jesus said are just words. We decide whether their truth is acceptable or not (Romans 1:18–23).

God's righteousness is all that matters. He chose to save us through Christ's righteousness. If we are in Him, God sees His righteousness within us because we belong to Him. We are, therefore, blameless before Him and free from all condemnation (Romans 8:1–17).	Self-righteousness is all that matters. Satan keeps telling us that we can save ourselves by our own good works. This is what the world believes. Being a good person will get you into heaven. There are many ways to get to God. Why would a loving God reject what He created? (Revelation 3:5, Revelation 20:11–15)
God is personal. God is aware of everything we need and everything that happens to us. He knows what we need materially and spiritually. He allows us to go through circumstances in life because He is preparing us to spend eternity with Him (Matthew 6:19–34, John 3:16–17, Romans 8:28).	God is impersonal. Satan wants us to focus on the personal aspects of this world, because this is more important than God. Only we can solve our own problems. It is by fate that I am where I am. I am my own destiny. If God is truly a personal and caring God, why does He allow all this pain and suffering? (Job 1:21–22, Job 2:9–10, Job 13:15–16, Job 19:25–29)

From the above, we must conclude that the responsibility for being misled falls on our shoulders. God never changes, and neither does His truth. It is always the same. We are the ones who must conform to God's standard. Since He does not change, we must change.

Why don't we believe in this perpetual truth of God? Because we have fallen into the same trap as Adam and Eve. Satan dangles a counterfeit truth before our eyes in the hopes of deterring us from embracing God's truth. Satan is our enemy, and sometimes he appears as an angel of light to deceive even the elect. Make sure that the truth you believe in is the truth that God has established.

GOD'S TRUTH IS PERMANENTLY ESTABLISHED

God has established His truth for our benefit, which is why it is separate from any other truth. Paul tried to explain this to the Athenians and foreigners who listened to him at Mars Hill in Acts 17:16–34. He explained that the "unknown God," from all the other gods being displayed, was the One who held absolute truth.

This is one of the best explanations for how an invisible God can reveal a visible truth. Once the people heard Paul's challenge about a real God who cared for them, they couldn't help but doubt their own truth. That day, Paul's conviction led some to find the saving truth of God.

These days, truth is being portrayed as being in the eye of the beholder. If we see a truth we like, we believe it. This leads to a few questions. If a chance existence evolved some kind of truth, wouldn't that truth be unreliable? Can truth really evolve? What are the chances that such a truth could be real? How can all truth be right? If a truth is founded by a finite intelligence, it becomes relative, because it depends on the individual.

There can only be one standard of truth, and the Orthodox Christian faith believes that only God can establish this absolute standard. Only He is capable of permanently establishing and faithfully maintaining it.

God has established everything in existence to be part of His domain, and throughout history He has made us aware of His established truth. He has revealed them to us in every way possible. He wants us to know about this truth and wouldn't hide it from us, because He loves us. This is why the truth of God is absolute. It will never change.

ONLY GOD IS GOD

In order to understand any kind of truth, we must first look to its source. Reporters always look for reliable sources to get to the truth. Truth breeds authenticity, meaning, and believability. People want to learn about the truth, about what has really happened. It's part of our nature. We love real stories, real people, and real situations. This is what connects us.

If only we believed in the same truth. If we did, there would be less hatred, less disunity, and less trouble. We would all be on the same page, understanding and pursuing the same goals. Conflicts emerge when different truths are imposed upon us. If we don't want to believe in something, we don't want it to be part of our lives.

Let's look to the first absolute truth: only God is God. If this is true, God must be our only reliable source to explain how everything came into existence. If God exists, He has every right to establish His own truth and impose it upon His creation. He sets the rules and conditions. If we don't believe in Him and His truth, we must accept the consequences. God has made known to us what will happen if we reject Him and His truth. The Bible makes this very clear.

Problems do arise, however, and there are many different opinions about Him. Some question how we can know that the God we believe in is the real God, the right God. To reasonably come to this conclusion, we must ask ourselves these questions:

1. Who can explain how everything came into existence?
2. Who is capable of creating and putting into motion everything that exists?
3. How does everything work together for our benefit?

We must realize that only God has the intelligence, creativity, ability, and purpose to not only bring everything into existence but cause everything to fit together harmoniously. Can chance or nothingness even be considered? Can something come from nothing without some form of intelligence behind it?

Once we realize that only an eternal God can explain everything, we begin to understand how His truths can be implemented.

Satan, our adversary, has the ability to deceive. It is his gift. The very first lie he presented to Adam and Eve was this one: "You can be like God." This resulted in our downfall. Believing this lie brought sin and death to the human race.

Satan continues to peddle his counterfeit truths because he wants to discredit God in order to establish himself. However, he is a created being who desires to become God. Therefore, whatever truths he wants to tell must be unreliable and deceptive.

This is why only God can perfectly establish truth. His sovereignty distinguishes Him as the one and only true God. He sets in place an absolute truth which is founded on his own decrees. Without this truth, there would be no reason to believe in Him. And if we don't believe in Him, we live according to a counterfeit truth. That is a disconcerting possibility, because it leads us to live without knowing who God really is, without knowing how to conduct ourselves.

GOD IS ABSOLUTELY HOLY

A reliable source must come from a place of honesty, integrity, purity, and genuineness. From this foundation emerges an uncorrupted truth which cannot be broken or altered in any way.

Have you ever told the absolute truth but people didn't believe you? Failing to believe God, including everything He is and all that He has established, grieves His heart. How can we deny the absolute truths of God when they have been permeated with His holiness? God has always been true to His nature. His holiness encompasses everything that He has done and will continue to do.

Author R.A. Finlayson expresses this holiness of God so well:

> Since holiness embraces every distinctive attribute of the Godhead, it may be defined as the outshining of all that God is. As the sun's rays, combining all the colours of the spectrum, come together in the sun's shining and blend into light, so in His self-manifestation all the attributes of God come together and blend into holiness. Holiness has, for that reason, been called "an attribute of attributes"—that which lends unity to all the attributes of God. To

conceive of God's being and character as merely a [collection] of abstract perfectness is to deprive God of all reality.[12]

God's holiness means that His actions cannot deviate. It is therefore impossible for God to sin. This is why God is separate from everything He created.

Pantheism states that God is all, and that all is God. If we are all part of God, God would be sinning when we sin. This would make God unholy, which contradicts all that He is. How can we then believe in Him and His truth? Since pantheists believe that all is God and everything else is illusion, which includes sin, is God therefore an illusion? Is His truth an illusion and therefore unnecessary?

To answer these questions correctly, we must come to the realization that God must be separate from all things. He is separate from us and everything else. If we compare our sinful nature to God's holy nature, we will understand why we can only live a certain way before Him.

God is so holy that there are conducts and behaviors which go against His nature, like how we desire to act contrary to that nature when we sin. God has standards and the Bible reveals them. Many don't seem to understand why God allows us to do those things which we deem to be okay and He does not. We must realize that God's standards are holy, just like Him, and we must accept this in order to understand who He really is and how we should conduct ourselves.

Since Satan knows that God is holy and that we can be holy in God, he tries to destroy our sanctification—our right standing and position—with God. His intent is to destroy us and keep us away from what we believe in. He will do everything in his power to deter us from what we hold so dear: our belief in an absolute holy God and our trust in God's absolute holy truth.

GOD IS CREATOR AND OWNER OF ALL THINGS

Since God is the Creator, He has the wisdom and capability to maintain and take care of everything. He has established all things for our benefit. This is why we must trust in His wisdom. Who else could have the intelligence to possess such infinite wisdom? Who would you rather put your trust in? An infinite God? A created being? Something else which gives no hope?

God has controlled everything in the universe by the decrees He has put into place. He spoke these perpetual plans into motion and they faithfully maintain themselves to fulfill His sovereign will.

The decrees of God can be described as "that eternal plan by which God makes sure that all the events of the universe—past, present, and future—take place."[13]

---

[12] R.A. Finlayson, *The Holiness of God* (London, UK: Westminster Chapel, 1955), 530.
[13] Paul E. Little, *Know What You Believe* (Wheaton, IL: Victor Books, 1987), 33.

Having established these decrees, He has implemented a universal plan and given us a purpose which we need to find. He has given us the gifts and abilities to fulfill this purpose because He wants us to feel special, knowing that we are loved and created by Him to give Him pleasure. Others, as well, can be encouraged to find their purpose and give glory to God.

This is why God made us in His image. Even though God owns everything, including us, He made us all unique and special so we could experience a one-of-a-kind relationship with Him. We are therefore stewards of God's creation and way of life. Amazingly, we forget this. We usually end up focusing on our own agenda and forget about His.

When we realize that God is the Creator and Owner of all things, we begin to see that everything we have, everything we do, and everything we say has a God-purpose. We begin to respect all things and all life. When we lose sight of this, we end up behaving in selfish, sinful ways. This usually leads to some form of destruction.

Satan wants to take God out of the picture. When we begin to subscribe to the worldly truths he wants us to follow, we end up forgetting about God. Instead of keeping God at the forefront of our lives, we end up leaving Him behind and pursuing what the prince of this world wants us to pursue.

But when we realize that God is real and owns everything, we understand that God watches our every move, especially when it comes to who we devote ourselves to.

GOD'S TRUTH IS RELEVANT
God's truth is based upon His sovereignty because there is a purpose for everything He has made and established.

There is His directive will and then there is His permissive will. His directive will is what He brings to pass, like the decrees He has established, with everything happening the way He has planned it from beginning to end. This will never change.

His permissive will is what He allows to take place. For example, God permitted but did not direct the entrance of sin into the world.[14]

It was His directive will which allowed Him to implement the doctrine of reconciliation. Since sin caused us to become separated from Him, God had to decide whether to reconcile us back to Himself or not. Thankfully, God decided that He wanted us back.

In order for this reconciliation to become effective, God had to implement the act of atonement, which was completed by Christ Jesus when He took upon Himself the sins of the world through His death and resurrection, resulting in His redemptive plan

---

[14] Ibid.

of salvation becoming permanent and available to everyone through faith—for those who lived before Christ, for those who lived with Christ, and for those who would live after Christ.

Christ's salvation must be accepted by faith because we have been saved by grace. To believe in God and what He has done for us is an act of faith. This is where His prescriptive will comes in. God allows us to decide whether to accept this saving truth. This is why His truth is relevant. We can't be saved without it. We must therefore accept God's way of doing things, not ours.

When Satan tells us that we can live by our own truth, he is saying that we don't need God's truth; we can live however we want. When we neglect God, forget about Him, and live without Him, we drift further from the absolute truth of God and anything that has been established by Him through design.

GOD'S RIGHTEOUSNESS IS ALL THAT MATTERS

Most believe that if a person lives a good life, they will be able to enter heaven. These same people can't understand how their own self-righteousness wouldn't be good enough for God.

The world believes that if you're good, you will go to heaven. Why would a loving God reject a person who has given of themselves for great causes? Why would He not accept one who has done everything right? Shouldn't all the good we have done outweigh the bad?

The Bible says that *"all have sinned and fall short of the glory of God"* (Romans 3:23), meaning that our sin makes us unrighteous before God. It all comes down to perspective. The world has defined righteousness from its own perspective. When we consider how righteousness looks from God's point of view, we better understand why self-righteousness doesn't work.

Only God can declare a person righteous. Because of our sin, we can never be righteous before Him. Our own good works can never take away our sin. This is why God sent His Son to die for us. He was the only one who could atone for our sin and make us righteous before God. When His righteousness becomes ours, we stand blameless before Him.

GOD IS PERSONAL

We read in 1 John 4:19, *"We love Him because He first loved us."* God has an infinite love that is beyond measure. It's a pursuing kind of love which can be, as Hebrew 12:29 says, *"a consuming fire."* It unveils the deepest desire of God's heart.

The most quoted verse in the Bible announces this amazing truth: *"For God so loved the world that He gave His only begotten Son, that whoever believes in Him should not perish but have everlasting life"* (John 3:16). Does this not indicate how personal God is, that He would send His very Son to die for us in order to reconcile us back to Himself? Would God take this action and then leave us alone without becoming involved in our lives?

God does everything for a reason because His purposes are always focused on us. He wants to be personally involved in our lives. Even though He has revealed Himself and His truth to us, He has left the decision up to us. We decide whether to believe in Him. As James 4:8 says, *"Draw near to God and He will draw near to you."* When we commit ourselves to God and accept what He has done for us, we end up in a personal relationship with Him. Accepting Jesus as our Savior, Lord, and King becomes personal.

God has proven that He is a personal God. He has given ample evidence, and it comes, for the most part, through how He reveals Himself to us.

There are nine witnesses to God's revelations and we encounter them at every stage of life. We therefore have no excuse to miss them. They prove His existence.

They can be divided into three sets of three. The first set is known as the general or extrinsic revelations of God, meaning those that we can directly observe. The second set, the major or Immanuel revelations of God, speak of His coming. The third set, the minor or life revelations of God, are shown in how God personally affects us.

CHAPTER FOUR
THE GENERAL REVELATIONS OF GOD

HAVE YOU EVER tried to get someone's attention? You may be going about your business, walking down the sidewalk, only to recognize someone from your past coming the other way. You shout out their name, wave your hands, and even jump up and down, but all to no avail. You then decide to approach and reacquaint yourself with them.

"Don't you remember me?" you say. "We went to school together."

At last, this person responds by recognizing you. You reminisce and talk about the good old days.

In a way, God is trying to get our attention like this. He is continually trying to make us aware of His existence, and we are continually asking God, "If You truly exist, reveal Yourself."

Revelation comes to fruition when both parties meet and acknowledge one another. God is purposeful in this regard, in that everything that happens to us has been planned so that we can become more aware of Him. Whether we know it or not, God wants us to know that He is there for us, guiding us along in our lives so we can have a personal connection with Him.

When He first created Adam and Eve, they were perfect in every way. They didn't have a sinful nature and didn't understand evil. Their relationship with God was perfect because their spirit-natures were connected to Him at all times. Their spirits controlled their beings and this meant that God was their priority. This epitomized the perfect relationship between God and our first parents.

Suddenly, in one moment, everything changed. When sin entered the picture, God wasn't the focus anymore. The self became our priority, because the flesh took over. We became selfish and our spirit-natures were suppressed.

As the years passed, those who came after Adam and Eve began to forget about God and focused on themselves. God became unimportant and the Bible reveals what happened to Noah's generation when they lived their lives without God. They didn't believe the one person who took God seriously. Noah presented the real God through the building of the ark and his outspoken declaration of God's judgment toward them. Why they couldn't see the reality of God, even in the general sense, is a mystery.

The general revelations of God are found in nature, the conscience, and history. These can also be understood as extrinsic revelations, because we can view them both directly and indirectly. We learn quite a bit from what we can see with our eyes, from what we perceive within ourselves, and from those things which have happened in the past. These insights can determine our truth and our view of God.

It's important that we interpret these revelations correctly because they will reveal who God is and His purposes for us.

NATURE (THE EXTERNAL WITNESS)

As was described in the first chapter, nature is God's handiwork. It reveals how creative, powerful, and glorious God is. Nature incites emotion within us because it can be so majestic in its beauty. Consider those moments when we look at mountains, fields of flowers, trees in the forests, pristine lakes and rivers, and colorful sunrises and sunsets. They all make us wonder about who God is that He would create such magnificent panoramas. Nature draws us close to God because it displays how amazing He is.

Paul wrote about nature's ability to reveal God's invisible attributes, and he warned the Romans about how they interpreted what they saw because God would judge them in the end by what they saw in nature:

> For the wrath of God is revealed from heaven against all ungodliness and unrighteousness of men, who suppress the truth in unrighteousness, because what may be known of God is manifest in them, for God has shown it to them. For since the creation of the world His invisible attributes are clearly seen, being understood by the things that are made, even His eternal power and Godhead, so that they are without excuse, because, although they knew God, they did not glorify Him as God, nor were thankful, but became futile in their thoughts, and their foolish hearts were darkened. Professing to be wise, they became fools, and changed the glory of the incorruptible God into an image made like corruptible man—and birds and four-footed animals and creeping things. (Romans 1:18–23)

Nature is quite impressive and everyone looks at it with awe and amazement. One can see why there are so many different ways to interpret it. We are curious to understand how it all came about. Why is it there? Why it is so majestic, so beautiful, and so contemplative?

Not only does God want to show His creative skills and majestic power through nature, but He seems to be testing us to see if we can acknowledge His greatness. He wants us to know Him as the God who provides.

And what about the universe? How do we understand it and why is it so humongous and beyond our comprehension? The universe is indeed vast, so much so that it surpasses our imagination. Who is God that He would purposely give us this glorious masterpiece? He wants us to know that He does exist and is the only one who could have created it all.

A bit of research reveals some key facts concerning the universe.

- The universe is constantly expanding.[15]
- It is made up of sixty-eight percent dark energy, twenty-seven percent dark matter, and five percent normal matter.[16]
- Only five percent of the universe is visible.[17]
- There are a billion trillion stars in the universe, more than the grains of sand on beaches.[18]

It is quite astonishing, even mystifying, to grasp that God is bigger than the universe. Even though this is difficult to believe, it forces us to acknowledge that God, who transcends the universe, wants us to know that He can be discovered through His creation. He wills for us to know Him through the external witness. It's difficult to understand why anyone would deny this truth.

When we look at the amazing world we live in, we can see that it is a wonder to behold!

In his phenomenal book, *The Collapse of Evolution*, Scott M. Huse perfectly articulates how nature can only come from a creative designer:

> Creationists view with a sense of awe the marvelous fit of organisms to their environment and their incredible interrelationships. Such complex and refined "adaptations," they reason, could never result from an aimless, purposeless, step-by-step process such as naturalistic evolution. The widespread beauty, intricacy, and perfection of life-forms found throughout the earth eloquently testify of the reality of a superintelligent Creator and Designer.[19]

He also expresses some of the rare creatures that God has so marvelously created:

---

[15] "The Universe Is Expanding Faster than Scientists Thought," *Science in the News*. October 30, 2019 (https://sitn.hms.harvard.edu/flash/2019/universe-expanding-faster-scientists-thought).

[16] "Dark Energy, Dark Matter," *NASA*. Date of access: November 13, 2023 (https://science.nasa.gov/astrophysics/focus-areas/what-is-dark-energy).

[17] Sophie Evans, "How Mere Humans Manage to Comprehend the Vastness of the Universe," *Scientific American*. October 11, 2019 (https://blogs.scientificamerican.com/observations/how-mere-humans-manage-to-comprehend-the-vastness-of-the-universe/).

[18] "Universe Facts," *National Geographic Kids*. Date of access: November 13, 2023 (https://www.natgeokids.com/nz/discover/science/space/universe-facts).

[19] Scott M. Huse, *The Collapse of Evolution*, Third Edition (Grand Rapids, MI: Baker Books, 1997), 23–24.

- The cheetah can run at speeds of seventy miles per hour.
- Certain insects can sleep for seventeen years.
- Weddell seals can remain underwater for forty-five minutes and dive to depths of 1,500 feet.
- Eight-armed, ink-shooting octopuses can eat their own arms and grow new ones.
- Archerfish can shoot water fifteen feet into the air and hit a bug.
- Peregrine falcons can swoop down on their prey at 150 miles per hour.
- Iron-eating bacteria can live ten thousand feet beneath the earth's surface, enduring pressures of three thousand PSI and scalding temperatures of 185°F.[20]

Do these unique creations prove to you that God exists? Is this enough to prove that only an infinitely intelligent designer could bring into existence such peculiar creatures?

The challenge goes out to those who doubt the existence of God. Go out and experience the external witness of nature. For a moment, forget about what the world teaches; even set aside the thought of God. Just look at nature. Marvel at its complexity and beauty. Experience the harmony of how everything fits together, how perfectly time guides nature like a symphony.

Eventually, one must come to the realization that only intelligence could have brought nature into existence. It should cause us to consider the complexity of God's creative work. Nature definitely proves His existence.

THE CONSCIENCE (THE INTERNAL WITNESS)

Our inner self, the authentic person we are, the essence of our true selves, is an amazing feat of divine engineering. The realization that we have feelings, desires, and wants demonstrates that there must be a reason for our existence.

Life presents us with that question. What makes us aware and conscientious? Life should compel us to understand who we are through the challenges placed before us. We soon learn more about our inner qualities and how the invisible realm affects our outlook. Whoever designed us had a purpose, and He gave us the wisdom to build our lives from the inside-out.

The Message Bible provides a clear picture of this in Psalm 139:13–16:

> Oh yes, you shaped me first inside, then out; you formed me in my mother's womb. I thank you, High God—you're breathtaking!

---

[20] Ibid., 23.

> Body and soul, I am marvelously made! I worship in adoration—what a creation! You know me inside and out, you know every bone in my body; You know exactly how I was made, bit by bit, how I was sculpted from nothing into something. Like an open book, you watched me grow from conception to birth; all the stages of my life were spread out before you, the days of my life all prepared before I'd even lived one day. (MSG)

The way in which God connected our physical, mental, and spiritual aspects to form independent and rational individuals is astounding. Yet here we are, living our lives in a real world with a sense of purpose and ingenuity. Within us, we have a drive to survive and a need for fulfillment. And when we look inward, we find that our nature gives rise to our thoughts, intent, and actions.

Does this not prove that we were designed to be authentic, accepting, open, and moral? Does this not indicate divine qualities? If we look deep within ourselves, we will find that most of who we are resembles God. The conscience makes it clear that we have an internal witness of God within us.

Henry C. Thiessen explains this internal witness as "an intuitive knowledge of God." He goes on to say:

> It is the presence in us of this sense of right and wrong, of this discriminative and impulsive something, that constitutes the revelation of God... it is the reflection of God in the soul... The Conscience in us reveals both the existence of God and to some extent the nature of God... It reveals that there is an absolute law of right and wrong in the Universe and that there is a supreme lawgiver who embodies this law in His own person and conduct.[21]

Three important verses in the Bible provide insight into this internal witness.

First, there is the source of this witness by way of the image of God. Genesis 1:26-27 states that God is the source of this revelation because He designed it to be part of us for the purpose of knowing Him:

> Then God said, "Let Us make man in Our image, according to Our likeness; let them have dominion over the fish of the sea, over the birds of the air, and over the cattle, over all the earth and over every creeping thing that creeps on the earth." So God created man in His

---

[21] Henry C. Thiessen, *Lectures in Systematic Theology* (Grand Rapids, MI: Eerdmans, 1979), 10.

own image; in the image of God He created him; male and female
He created them.

Second, there's the gift of discerning what is good and evil. The conscience was designed to give us an awareness of the difference between right and wrong. God gave us a replica of His moral qualities so we may know His standards. Even though we have a fallen nature, the image of God still resides within us. It's part of our moral center.

There is a symbiotic relationship between our conscience and our morality. Each of us has a moral gifting; some have higher standards, and others lower, but all of us have a persistent conscience. Hebrews 5:13–14 says,

> For everyone who partakes only of milk is unskilled in the word of righteousness, for he is a babe. But solid food belongs to those who are of full age, that is, those who by reason of use have their senses exercised to discern both good and evil.

Third, we have to maintain our conscience to make sure it remains effective. Children have a more transparent and innocent relationship between their conscience and fragile moral center. They won't fully understand the consequences of their actions until they feel the guilt of knowing that they've done something wrong.

If we don't acknowledge our awareness of having done something wrong and deal with it, the conscience will soon become desensitized. Our conscience could become immune to certain offences. Will we cross the line to commit sin? Will we just let our guilt ride the waves until it disappears?

Paul explained to Timothy that next to his faith, a clear conscience was his most essential weapon:

> This charge I commit to you, son Timothy, according to the prophecies previously made concerning you, that by them you may wage the good warfare, having faith and a good conscience, which some having rejected… (1 Tim 1:18–19)

The conscience allows us to know how to conduct ourselves, morally. It gives us a purpose and the will to do what is right, making us responsible for ourselves. It is therefore our responsibility to keep our consciences pure. Otherwise they can become defective and cause us to stray from God's standards.

In essence, we are somewhat of a copy of God. The conscience didn't just evolve; it was given to us. We can conclude that because we possess a conscience, there are absolute standards which we need to follow. The conscience, along with the image of God within us, reveals that God exists.

HISTORY (THE HISTORICAL WITNESS)

Throughout history, we have been guided by the will of God in order to become aware of His truth. History reveals that He is a personal and caring God. He has been our advocate when we've sought out truth.

This history is based on the Judeo-Christian story of how God guided His people in their faith. Deuteronomy 28 explains this promise of God:

> Now it shall come to pass, if you diligently obey the voice of the Lord your God, to observe carefully all His commandments which I command you today, that the Lord your God will set you high above all nations of the earth…
>
> The Lord will establish you as a holy people to Himself, just as He has sworn to you, if you keep the commandments of the Lord your God and walk in His ways. Then all peoples of the earth shall see that you are called by the name of the Lord, and they shall be afraid of you. (Deuteronomy 28:1, 9–10)

Our earliest history is written in the Book of Genesis, which begins with God creating the heavens and the earth (Genesis 1–2). The text showcases Adam and Eve's innocence, only for them to fall into sin, devastating the perfect world God had just created (Genesis 3).

Despite this failure, God kept to His plan of redemption and restored our relationship with Him by faithfully keeping His truth alive and revealing it to us. This historical path of truth has been paved through the stories of significant individuals and events which make us aware that God will always be the one to guide us.

When the entire world was involved in complete and violent sinfulness, God decided to pass judgment (Genesis 6:5–7). Only Noah, his family, and certain chosen animals were saved from a world-destroying flood through God's ark of mercy (Genesis 6–9). There is ample evidence of the historicity of this flood, from ancient traditions and writings to the recent sightings of Noah's ark at Mount Ararat and the physical features of the earth.

After the flood, God became more selective with humanity. The Tower of Babel became a symbol of diversity, by which God separated humanity into different nations (Genesis 10:1–11:9). He then chose Abraham and his descendants to become the nation of Israel so they could carry His torch in representing Him (Genesis 11:10–50:26).

Henry C. Thiessen explains this personal relationship between God and His people:

> God has revealed himself in the history of Israel… It is surely remarkable that at a time when the whole world had sunk into

the despondency of polytheism and pantheism, Abraham, Isaac, and Jacob, and their descendants should come to know God as a personal, infinite, holy, and self-revealing God, as the creator, preserver, and governor of the universe... God is represented as personally appearing to the patriarchs; as making himself and his will known in dreams, visions, and ecstasies; as communicating his message directly to them; and as revealing his holy character in the Mosaic legislation, the sacrificial system, and the service of the tabernacle and the temple.[22]

Moses, who was called into service by God from a burning bush (Exodus 3:1–12), became God's agent to deliver the Israelites from Egyptian slavery into the promised land (Exodus 3:16–17). Once there, the Israelites became accustomed to a way of life in which they were first disobedient toward God, and then repentant. This cycle of constant lapsing was a concern for God, so He selected judges, guided by His wisdom and power, to restore the people into right relationship with Him.

Samson, for instance, was just an ordinary looking man. Once the Spirit of God came upon him, however, he delivered the Israelites through phenomenal strength and abilities (Judges 13–16).

Afterward the Israelites decided that they wanted their own king, like other nations (1 Samuel 8:4–5). They chose Saul, who eventually failed God. Then God chose David, a shepherd boy who began his service to God by slaying Goliath, a giant who was almost twice his size (1 Samuel 16:1).

David became God's righteous king in heart, establishing the royal lineage of the coming Messiah. He kept God's truth alive by upholding His values and virtues, even when he himself fell into sin. David realized that God's grace and forgiveness was included in this truth of God (Psalm 51). The saving truth is essential in maintaining our fellowship with Him.

The major and minor prophets of old spoke God's truth through prophecies. Their words firmly revealed what was going to happen so the people could become aware of God's infinite sovereignty, reminding them of God's timing and plan, even when there came a period of four hundred years of silence during which God didn't speak to anyone.

The people had to demonstrate patient faith, waiting for God to fulfill His plan of redemption. Jesus became the incarnate Savior, the pinnacle of history. He became *"the way and the truth and the life"* (John 14:6). He fulfilled and restored everything that God held true. Even after His death and resurrection, He committed God's truth

---

[22] Ibid., 9.

to those who were willing to receive it—and this truth became implanted in their new natures.

This process was aided by the coming of the Holy Spirit, who became the vicar of Christ when He filled the upper room with His presence. The apostles Jesus chose, along with the others present on that occasion, became His ambassadors of truth (Matthew 10:1-4, Mark 3:13-19, Acts 1:12-2:1-4).

This led the church, which was initiated by Jesus Christ and inspired by the Holy Spirit, to bring together the people of God so they could present His truth to the world. Even Paul, who was converted supernaturally and called into service, worked tirelessly to present God's truth to those who had never heard of it (Acts 9:1-22).

After Jesus and the apostles, Christianity gave rise to the Catholic church, which was tested through persecution and martyrdom. At first this was due to Roman emperors who believed that they themselves were deities; they executed anyone who denied this doctrine. Despite these emperors trying their best to eliminate the Christian movement, it grew substantially among the common people and reached the heart of the emperor Constantine I, who became the first ruler to lead both state and church.

From then on, the establishment of Christendom became the focus of the Western Roman church (from the city of Rome) and the Eastern Greek Orthodox church (from the city of Constantinople), both of which governed the ways of Christianity throughout the Middle Ages, from approximately 590 A.D. to 1517 A.D.

The Roman church began to establish God's truth and doctrines. As well, isolated monasteries trained men as church planters and evangelists to reach new communities for God. Soon the churches of the European empires flourished, led by prominent bishops who freely shared the truth about God and the Christian way of life.

The Christian religion became part of everyone's life, though it was mostly controlled by the Pope. According to Catholic doctrine, the Pope was divinely appointed; whatever the church declared as truth came from God Himself though the papacy. If anyone went against this belief, it was considered heresy. Many valued men and women who presented different doctrines were excommunicated, forced to flee, or executed to prevent others from following in their footsteps. Tens of thousands of people were burned at the stake because of differences in belief.

Toward the end of the Middle Ages, frustrated with the control of the Papacy, various groups and individuals throughout Europe began to declare what Jesus and the early Christians had really believed. They brought the essential doctrines of Christianity back to its roots and declared that Jesus was the head of the church and that salvation came by faith alone (grace). Thus began the Age of Reformation, from approximately 1517 to 1648.

This movement was mostly influenced by Martin Luther. On October 31, 1517, Luther hammered his famous ninety-five theses to the front door of the Wittenberg castle church. This movement divided the Christian faith into three main groups: Catholic, Greek Orthodox, and Protestant. Each had different views regarding the essential truth of Christianity.

Many Christians began to distance themselves from Catholic authority to follow their own beliefs. New denominations cropped up and instituted their own doctrines. The race was on to advance the gospel to new mission fields like North and South America, Africa, Asia, and the remotest parts of the world.

Today, the church continues to be the keepers of God's truth. Even through persecution, the church continues to thrive because God is faithful to maintain and build it (Matthew 16:18). One can only imagine what this world would be like without it. Who would then become the conscience of God?

We, as the body of Christ, must continue to present the truth of God to everyone around us. It should not be hidden but rather revealed so that all may come to know how this truth came about.[23]

This path of truth, which has been paved throughout history, continues before us. Now we await the return of our Savior and Lord so that humanity's history can finally become complete. When this happens, all will finally know who God really is (Philippians 2:9–11).

As we look back through history, and look forward as it continues to develop, we will see that through the course of time history proves the existence of God:

> And He has made from one blood every nation of men to dwell on all the face of the earth, and has determined their preappointed times and the boundaries of their dwellings, so that they should seek the Lord, in the hope that they might grope for Him and find Him... (Acts 17:26–27)

---

[23] Recommended reading: Bruce L. Shelley, *Church History in Plain Language* (Nashville, TN: Thomas Nelson, 1982).

CHAPTER FIVE
THE REVELATION OF GOD'S WORD
(THE WRITTEN WITNESS)

IT HAS BEEN said that the pen is mightier than the sword. Paul, however, equates the sword of the Spirit with the Word of God, because the inspired written Word has the ability to penetrate our hearts with God's truth. It can precisely divide the essence of any truth (Ephesians 6:17, 2 Timothy 3:16, Hebrews 4:12).

Words speak right to the heart, from the sentimental greeting card or personal letter of affection to the note of thanks. They affect us all. Even the words of a judge can condemn or vindicate. Everyone anticipates what the judge is going to say.

So it is with the revealing Word of God. When we read its pages, we anticipate what it will say about God, about us, and what we should expect to happen in the future. This is why God gave us the Bible, so we could read about His truth and way of life. It is a life manual, a guide to everything.

The revelation of God's Word is the first of the major revelations of God. The second is Jesus, God's only Son, and the third is the Holy Spirit. These are the Immanuel revelations of God. Each have impacted humanity tremendously because they reveal the God who has come, revealing Himself and His absolute truth in person. Even today, they impact our lives because God's Word, through His Son and Holy Spirit, remains active and alive within us once we receive and believe in its truth.

The Holy Bible is a historical collection of God's inspired words through those individuals He chose, through His Son and Holy Spirit. The Bible is the written Word, Jesus the living Word, and the Holy Spirit the transforming Word.

THE BIBLE

The Bible contains sixty-six books that were written from the time of Moses to just after Jesus. The Old Testament is comprised of thirty-nine books, and the New Testament contains twenty-seven.

The Old Testament can be more appropriately called the Old Covenant because it is primarily a covenant between God and the nation of Israel. The New Testament can be more appropriately called the New Covenant because it is primarily a covenant between God and His Son. Both covenants are open to anyone who accepts their truth. With the Old, you had to live and believe like a Jew. With the New, you had to become a follower of Christ.

These covenants of truth are connected by Jesus Christ, who fulfilled the Old with the New. Their truth is so valuable because it comes from the Father, and Jesus brought to light the truth of God by becoming one of us. The truth becomes so authentic when it comes from the original source. In the Old Testament, Jehovah God became the source of truth. In the New Testament, it was Christ Jesus.

The Old Testament consists of the five books of Moses, the twelve historical books, the five books of poetry and wisdom, and the seventeen prophetic books, five being major and twelve being minor. This was the Bible Jesus and the disciples were able to access. They followed the more traditional divisions that the scribes and rabbis developed: the books of the Law, the Prophets, and the Writings.

The New Testament begins with the sayings of Jesus and what the disciples wrote about Him. These simple autographs encouraged others to start writing, including Paul, Luke, Jude, and the apostles John, Peter, and James. They were all inspired by Jesus and wrote about how He wanted people to live and conduct themselves. Jesus continually spoke about His Father in heaven and how important it was to honor and please Him.

The New Testament consists of the four gospels, the book of Acts, the thirteen epistles of Paul, the eight general epistles, and the book of Revelation.

THE OLD TESTAMENT BOOKS

The Pentateuch (The five books of Moses, the Torah)
- Genesis: The book of beginnings, from creation to the establishment of the nation of Israel.
- Exodus: The exodus of the Israelites to the promised land, going from slavery to freedom and being set apart to live holy lives.
- Leviticus: The establishment of holy laws, from the sacrificial to sanctification system.
- Numbers: The transitional period from the wanderings of the old generation to the new generation.
- Deuteronomy: Moses reminding Israel of the old covenant as the Israelites move from Mount Sinai to their renewal at Moab.

The Historical Books (The twelve history books)
- Joshua: Joshua becomes leader of Israel and trusts in God to take possession of Canaan.
- Judges: The judges convince Israel to trust in God again instead of believing in the gods of Canaan.
- Ruth: Ruth's faithfulness to God is revealed by her devotion and trust in Naomi and Boaz.
- 1 Samuel: Israel desires to trust in a king rather than God. King Saul is the first, after whom comes David.

- 2 Samuel: David trusts in God with his whole life, through his victories, sinfulness, and hardships.
- 1 Kings: Solomon unites Israel by trusting God but then falters, resulting in Israel's division.
- 2 Kings: The kings of Israel and Judah rule according to their trust in God. Elijah gives over the reins to Elisha.
- 1 Chronicles: The genealogies from Adam to David, followed by an examination of David's life and preparation of Israel for the temple.
- 2 Chronicles: The glory of Solomon's reign and the rule of the kings of Judah and whether they trusted God.
- Ezra: Israel's first return with Zerubbabel, and his second return with Ezra to restore Israel and the temple.
- Nehemiah: Nehemiah trusts in God to rebuild the wall and restore Israel with the renewal of the covenant.
- Esther: Esther is chosen as queen and trusts in God to help Mordecai defeat the evil Haman.

Poetry and Wisdom Books (The five books of stories, songs, proverbs, and poetry)
- Job: An example of God allowing pain and suffering to help us trust Him.
- Psalms: A book of worship songs and poems which celebrate God as the center of life. He is worthy to be praised.
- Proverbs: A book of wisdom that is not to be taken lightly or forgotten.
- Ecclesiastes: An examination of life, concluding that God is all that matters.
- Song of Songs: An encouragement to find love and to build upon it.

Prophetic Books (The seventeen writings of the prophets, major and minor)
Major Prophets
- Isaiah: Including prophecies against nations, of the Messiah, and about the comfort and deliverance of Israel.
- Jeremiah: Including prophecies to Judah, about the fall and restoration of Jerusalem, and to Gentile nations.
- Lamentations: Written in acrostic, Jeremiah laments over Jerusalem's destruction and siege.

- Ezekiel: Including prophecies about the judgment against Judah, the Gentiles, and the restoration of Israel.
- Daniel: Through six stories and four visions, Daniel prophesies what will happen in the future.

Minor Prophets
- Hosea: Hosea marries a harlot to embody God's faithfulness to Israel and the nation's adulterous life.
- Joel: Joel becomes the voice of the imminent Day of the Lord in judging and restoring Judah.
- Amos: Including eight Gentile judgments, Israel's sermon and vision judgments, and Israel's restoration.
- Obadiah: Obadiah prophesies judgment on the house of Esau and how Israel shall possess them.
- Jonah: Jonah disobeys his call to Nineveh. After being devoured by a big fish, he finally obeys.
- Micah: Micah travels to Jerusalem to prophesy about their judgment of sin, restoration, and repentance.
- Nahum: One hundred years after Jonah, Nahum speaks of Nineveh's destruction and Judah's deliverance.
- Habakkuk: Burdened by Judah's sin and hardheartedness, Habakkuk prays mercy and trusts God.
- Zephaniah: Zephaniah prophesies about the judgment to come for all nations, including Judah. There is a call to repentance and promise of salvation.
- Haggai: After the exile, Zerubbabel and the remnant are called to rebuild the latter temple.
- Zechariah: After eight visions and four messages, Zechariah prophesies that Jerusalem must repent and accept the Messiah.
- Malachi: Malachi exposes Israel's polluted ways and promises the comings of Elijah and the Messiah.

THE NEW TESTAMENT

The Gospels (The four books of the words and works of Jesus Christ)
- Matthew: Presenting Jesus as the King of the Jews, the long-awaited Messiah.
- Mark: Presenting Jesus as the obedient and willing Servant, the wonder worker.

- Luke: Presenting Jesus as the Son of Man, the righteous and risen Savior.
- John: Presenting Jesus as the Son of God, the eternal and holy Redeemer.

Book of Acts (The second book of Luke)
- Acts: Including Christ's ascension and the coming of the Holy Spirit to help the early church to continue His work.

The Epistles of Paul (The thirteen books written by Paul primarily to the early church)
- Romans: Paul writes that justification comes through faith because Jesus Christ is the salvation of God.
- 1 Corinthians: Paul's advice on the divine order for the church by addressing its divisions and immorality.
- 2 Corinthians: With the help of Titus, Paul explains his ministry and answers his accusers and critics.
- Galatians: Paul establishes that there is a contrast between grace and the law, of faith and works.
- Ephesians: Paul writes that we have been given every spiritual gift and must utilize them in conduct and service.
- Philippians: Paul encourages his readers to focus on the mind of Christ, humility, and service to have unity and joy.
- Colossians: Paul writes of the importance of placing Christ as our priority in church and life.
- 1 Thessalonians: Paul exemplifies true Christianity and exhorts the church to continue to grow until Jesus's return.
- 2 Thessalonians: Paul encourages his readers to endure persecution and disorder until the day of the Lord.
- 1 Timothy: Paul encourages Timothy to lead and instruct his church to become orderly and faithful.
- 2 Timothy: Paul exhorts Timothy to remain strong, oppose apostasy, and diligently preach the Word.
- Titus: Paul exhorts Titus to establish his church with qualified elders, sound doctrine, and works.
- Philemon: Paul extends kind counsel for Philemon to forgive a runaway slave and receive him with love.

The General Epistles (The eight books written by church leaders to believers)
- Hebrews: The author provides reasons for Christ's superiority over Judaism in life, faith, and the law.
- James: James writes of expressing one's inward faith outwardly through trials, words, and actions.
- 1 Peter: Peter exhorts his readers to be true followers of Christ in what they endure.
- 2 Peter: Peter encourages readers to grow in their faith, not waver, and be aware of false teachers, enduring until Jesus's return.
- 1 John: John writes of fellowship being key to understanding God.
- 2 John: John exhorts a woman and her children to walk in God's truth.
- 3 John: John encourages his readers to walk in the truth and not be proud.
- Jude: Jude makes us aware that apostasy and false teaching will increase in the last days.

Book of Revelation (The apocalyptic message of dreams, signs, symbols, and visions)
- Revelation: A consummation of all that God established from redemption and judgment to the ultimate restoration.

ORAL TRADITION

From Adam to Moses. There is the source of truth and then there is the transmission of it from one person to another. This process began through an oral tradition. Once writing became available, these spoken words were written so that not only could they be heard but read.

Before the advent of writing, oral tradition was the means by which God's truth was passed from generation to generation. The patriarchal families before Moses put to use their gift of memory, teaching their children all the stories and precepts that were given to them. They were able to recite everything from memory.

There is an exercise to prove the authenticity of the oral tradition. Have a group of people form a circle until the first and last person meet; there could be anywhere from ten to twenty people. The first person will tell the second person a short but detailed story about some incident. This story is then repeated from the second person to the third person and so on, from one to the next, until the very last person hears it from the second last person. He or she then dictates the story as they remember hearing it, exposing any alterations from the original.

This is akin to the line of truth that extends from the original source through time. The closer you are to the original source, the more authentic the truth is. The further away you get, the greater the possibility of the truth becoming distorted.

The Book of Genesis can be tested in this way to determine how reliable it is in telling the stories from Adam to Moses.

It is certain that Moses was the first writer of the Old Testament. He authored the majority and most pertinent parts of the first five books of the Bible. Since he doesn't appear until the book of Exodus, though, we must conclude that the content of Genesis somehow came into his possession from another source. When we look at the historical lineage between Adam and Moses, we find that there are only six links, or generations, separating them.

Adam would have passed on God's truth to Eve and their children, as well as their children's children, who eventually gave it to Methusaleh, who gave it to Shem, who gave it to Isaac, and Levi, and Amram (with Kohath), and finally Moses.[24] Each would have added to this knowledge and passed it along to the next person.

From Jesus to the Gospels. The oral tradition was established because people were hungry to take hold of what Jesus said. His words of truth were profound. It was as if God was there Himself. Jesus was aware that His words had to be simple, for His audience had to rely on their memories. This is why He spoke in parables and parallelisms. Even His disciples had to listen intently.

As soon as they took hold of the sayings of Jesus, his audience would go home and teach them to their children and friends. Since it was far too expensive to produce any type of scroll to take notes, people remembered these words through the process of application, recitation, and memorization.[25] The more they kept to this process, the more accurate the transmission of these stories became.

The first writings of the gospels weren't written down until about thirty to fifty years after the ascension of Jesus. Individuals began writing the sayings and works of Jesus through the course of hearing about them. No one knows for sure which sources were used, but it is clear that four separate accounts were copied down of Jesus's three-year ministry, including His teachings and accomplishments. These are credited to Matthew, Mark, Luke, and John. The first three became known as the synoptic gospels, because of their similar content. John's gospel came later as a unique supplement.

Mark's writings may have been initiated with the help of Peter, who encouraged Mark to write down what Jesus had said and done.[26] This is most likely why Mark

---

[24] *The Timechart History of the World* (London, UK: Parkgate Books, 1997), 4.
[25] Arthur G. Patzia, *The Making of the New Testament* (Downers Grove, IL: InterVarsity Press, 1995), 40.
[26] Ibid.

was the first gospel to be written, between A.D. 55 to 65. The gospels of Matthew and Luke were written a few years later, from A.D. 58 to 68. John's gospel followed around A.D. 66 to 98.

Prior to the writing of Mark, a literary source known as "Q"—from the German word *quelle*, meaning "source"—became available. It contained roughly 230 sayings of Jesus. The writings of Mark and Q account for the "two-source theory," which helps explain the content of the later books by Matthew and Luke.

B.H. Streeter came up with the "four-source theory," which includes Q, Mark, and the materials unique to Matthew and Luke.[27] From compiling these source materials into books, the translators recorded the gospels' titles as being told "according to" Matthew, Mark, Luke, and John. This signifies that these books came from either the oral traditions or writings available at the time.

THE PURPOSE OF THE BIBLE

Ever since Hammurabi, a well-known Babylonian king, pounded his two hundred fifty legal and religious laws into an upright stone monument around 1750 B.C., people have recognized the importance of writing things down in order to bring unity and understanding into daily life. They helped establish a standard for how one should conduct oneself before leaders, fellow citizens, and God.

This is why nations have been built and founded upon constitutions. These legal documents act like binding contracts, establishing the principles that the nation has agreed upon. Constitutions bring people together—to unify, unveil honesty, and give purpose.

The Bible did the same. It revealed who God is, what His standards are, and how we can have a personal relationship with Him.

The Word of God begins by unifying us as believers to become, as Paul puts it, one body: *"For as the body is one and has many members, but all the members of that one body, being many, are one body, so also is Christ"* (1 Corinthians 12:12). We are united together as God's people, a body of believers which forms the bride of Christ, His church. The Bible is our constitution. It unites us as one.

The Word of God is also personally reflective. It causes us to honestly look at ourselves to see where we stand with God. It reveals the lives of many people, exposing their successes and failures before God. He wants us to see ourselves honestly because He provided the means to forgive us, save us, and restore us. The Bible completely changes us in every aspect, and it is so beneficial for us to see this in writing. The Word of God also cleanses us by reminding us that God so faithfully removes our filth (Psalm 119).

---

[27] Ibid., 53.

Lastly, the Word of God is a permanent record of God's standard, which can be seen through the law. Only one law was given to Adam and Eve (Genesis 2:16–17). All they had to do was not eat from the Tree of the Knowledge of Good and Evil. This was the entire Bible for them. God set before them one law and they agreed to it. They were aware of the consequences of breaking it.

God wanted their obedience. In fact, obedience was so important to God that He personally wrote down the Ten Commandments on two tablets of stone and gave them to Moses at Mount Sinai (Exodus 20:1–17, 31:18, 34:1–4). These laws were written by the finger of God Himself.

In truth, the Bible can be summed up by the Ten Commandments. The first four commandments relate to how we should conduct ourselves before God. The remaining six relate to how we should conduct ourselves before others.

Jesus simplified the Ten Commandments even further by condensing them into two: the Shema and the golden rule: "Love God with all" and "Love your neighbor as yourself" (Deuteronomy 6:4–5, Mark 12:29–31). When we obey these two rules, we fulfill all that God requires of us.

Every book in the Bible repeats these rules in its own unique way. This gives us purpose and fulfillment, allowing us to witness how we should live before God and others.

THE WRITTEN WITNESS OF THE OLD TESTAMENT

God wanted us to understand His truths and His laws. Writing down the important things about life brought people together so they could be united by the truth. The law became a witness, a standard of conscience, that dictated how one should live before a holy God.

God instructed Moses in Deuteronomy 31:24–26 to write down all the laws in a book so He could give them to Israel:

> So it was, when Moses had completed writing the words of this law in a book, when they were finished, that Moses commanded the Levites, who bore the ark of the covenant of the Lord, saying: "Take this Book of the Law, and put it beside the ark of the covenant of the Lord your God, that it may be there as a witness against you…"

After the Israelites' victory at Ai, Joshua wrote upon stones a copy of the law of Moses at Mount Ebal (Joshua 8:32–35). He was instructed by God to remember the importance of always taking to heart this written witness:

> This Book of the Law shall not depart from your mouth, but you shall meditate in it day and night, that you may observe to do according to all that is written in it. For then you will make your way prosperous, and then you will have good success. (Joshua 1:8)

When Josiah became king of Judah, he was given the book of the law, which was found by Hilkiah the high priest while workers repaired the house of the Lord. This book was read before King Josiah by Shaphan the scribe. Once he heard the words, he tore his clothes because the laws written in it were not being kept by the people. Josiah made a commitment to this written witness:

> Then the king stood by a pillar and made a covenant before the Lord, to follow the Lord and to keep His commandments and His testimonies and His statutes, with all his heart and all his soul, to perform the words of this covenant that were written in this book. And all the people took a stand for the covenant. (2 Kings 23:3)

Jeremiah brought forth a prophecy in which this written witness became an internal testimony of the heart. God wanted to keep His words of truth alive in the heart of individuals. This would be accomplished with the coming of Jesus and the Holy Spirit, by renewing believers' spiritual nature to be able to receive the living Word of God:

> Behold, the days are coming, says the Lord, when I will make a new covenant with the house of Israel and with the house of Judah—not according to the covenant that I made with their fathers in the day that I took them by the hand to lead them out of the land of Egypt, My covenant which they broke, though I was a husband to them, says the Lord. But this is the covenant that I will make with the house of Israel after those days, says the Lord: I will put My law in their minds, and write it on their hearts; and I will be their God, and they shall be My people. No more shall every man teach his neighbor, and every man his brother, saying, "Know the Lord," for they all shall know Me, from the least of them to the greatest of them, says the Lord. For I will forgive their iniquity, and their sin I will remember no more. (Jeremiah 31:31–34)

THE WRITTEN WITNESS OF THE NEW TESTAMENT
When Jesus was tempted by Satan in the wilderness after His baptism, He set the example by showing us the importance of declaring God's truth in the face of

deception. Three times He was tempted to believe in another truth, and each time he expressed a truth from the Word of God (Matthew 4:1–11, Luke 4:1–13).

Jesus frequently declared that His source of truth came from the Father, and if a person was to understand this they only had to believe in His words:

> Most assuredly, I say to you, he who hears My word and believes in Him who sent Me has everlasting life, and shall not come into judgment, but has passed from death into life. (John 5:24)

> It is written in the prophets, "And they shall all be taught by God." Therefore everyone who has heard and learned from the Father comes to Me. (John 6:45)

> He who has My commandments and keeps them, it is he who loves Me. And he who loves Me will be loved by My Father, and I will love him and manifest Myself to him. (John 14:21)

> For I have given to them the words which You have given Me; and they have received them, and have known surely that I came forth from You; and they have believed that You sent Me. (John 17:8)

God's written Word causes us to grow in our relationship with Him.

> But whoever keeps His word, truly the love of God is perfected in him. By this we know that we are in Him. (1 John 2:5)

This relationship becomes a witness. It is confirmed again by 1 John 5:1–3:

> Whoever believes that Jesus is the Christ is born of God, and everyone who loves Him who begot also loves him who is begotten of Him. By this we know that we love the children of God, when we love God and keep His commandments. For this is the love of God, that we keep His commandments. And His commandments are not burdensome.

God's written Word is authentic because the Holy Spirit began inspiring men to write about God's word of truth through the experiences He gave them:

> All Scripture is given by inspiration of God, and is profitable for doctrine, for reproof, for correction, for instruction in righteousness, that the man of God may be complete, thoroughly equipped for every good work. (2 Timothy 3:16–17)

The written Word of God is truly a major revelation of God. Every word reveals that God has come. His revealed truth has been declared by so many people, under His supervision and inspiration, that there can be no doubt that He is real. The Bible proves the existence of God.

CHAPTER SIX
THE REVELATION OF JESUS CHRIST
(THE LIVING WITNESS)

AS WE DISCUSSED earlier, God cannot be infinite unless He exists within an infinite relationship, and He does—in the form of the perfect composite that is the Father, Son, and Holy Spirit. Since God is infinite in every respect, there must exist a perfect kind of infinite relationship within His Being. He is still One God, but He is represented by three distinct persons existing together as a whole. This is the Trinity, three together as one. It's also why a man can be a father, husband, and son at the same time. He is still the same person, but he has different components or identities. The same is true of God.

We have the Father, who is the first person of the Trinity. He represents the sovereign authority of God. Nothing happens without His approval. The will of the Father takes precedence because He will always know what is best.

Jesus is the second person of the Trinity. He represents the unconditional servanthood and submissiveness of God. He will personally accomplish the will of the Father to bring glory to God.

The Holy Spirit is the third person of the Trinity. He is the executor of God, the activating personal agent of the Godhead. He will fulfill God's purposes through His transforming influence and convicting power.

The focus of this chapter is on the second person of the Trinity, Jesus Christ, the unique Son of God. Without Him, we would have no personal revelation of God, no fulfillment of His Word, and no restoration of what God established.

The incarnation, the God-made-flesh revelation of Jesus Christ, was necessary in order to restore our position and relationship with God. Jesus, being God's Son, was the only one who could accomplish this. He had to become human in order to save, redeem, and restore.

The revelation of Jesus Christ is highly personal, especially to those who witnessed His birth, life, death, and resurrection. It wouldn't have seemed reasonable to anyone to even consider the notion of God becoming human. How could He allow Himself to be sentenced to death, through no fault of His own, while He Himself resided as Judge?

This is why there must be a Triune God with three separate persons. Only that way could God's plan of redemption come to fruition. The Father sent His Son to become human, Jesus became this perfect human by humbling Himself willingly, and the Holy Spirit initiated the process by performing the miracle of conceiving Jesus through the chosen human vessel, Mary.

It all came down to the payment of sin, which required a final judgment. A flawless human being had to shed blood in order for this payment to be made in full. Sinless Jesus, who became sin, was thus judged by God and sentenced to death. Once this payment was made, atoning for humanity's sin, all people throughout time were set free by God. Jesus then resurrected as the risen Savior.

God was able to distinguish between His humanity and His Godhood. Jesus represented the human side. The Father represented the deity side. This was the only way to bridge the gap between God and humanity.

JESUS, THE WORD OF GOD (JOHN 1:1–2)

By looking at John 1:1–18, we discover the purpose for the revelation of Jesus Christ. The revelation of God becoming human was witnessed by John, one of Jesus's closest friends and disciples. He revealed Jesus's most intimate words and their importance in establishing who He really was, thus establishing Jesus as the true Son of God. From His relationship with the Father He also became the Word of God:

> In the beginning was the Word, and the Word was with God, and the Word was God. He was in the beginning with God (John 1:1–2)

The Greek term for "Word" here is *Logos*, which refers to a speech, word, or reason. If we were to interchange these words, the phrases could variously be translated to refer to the speech of God, the Word of God, or the reason of God. This brings out a distinctive meaning revealed by Jesus, the living Word of God or the living witness of God. He is the reason for our existence and very life with God.

Since Jesus came from the Father, He is the personal messenger of God. It was as if God mailed Himself to us, saying, "Here I am. Believe in Me and you will have eternal life." This is why John presented Him as the *Logos*.

Jesus revealed the authentic truth of the Father, and this was only possible because Jesus and the Father were together in the beginning. Their relationship existed on equal terms; they worked hand in hand, their authoritative and submissive divine natures joining together to accomplish what needed to be done. The incarnation brought the Logos to humanity as God's vessel of truth to be received and accepted.

The question we must ask ourselves is this: will we accept this living witness of God as the life-giving Word of God? This is why Jesus was so persistent in His message to those who sought God's truth. See how Jesus, the *Logos*, presented the truth in the form of parallelisms:

- Jesus is the Lamb of God (John 1:29), taking away the sins of the world.
- Jesus is the Light of Understanding (John 3:19-21), causing us to become aware of God's truth.
- Jesus is the Living Water (John 4:10–14), permanently renewing our inner natures to never thirst again.
- Jesus is the Bread of Life (John 6:32–35, 48–58), continually sustaining and satisfying us.
- Jesus is the Good Shepherd (John 10:1–18), the One who gives His life for His sheep.
- Jesus is the Resurrection and the Life (John 11:25–26), causing us to never die and live forever.
- Jesus is the Way, the Truth, and the Life (John 14:6), the reason that we live.
- Jesus is the True Vine (John 15:1–8), obtaining an everlasting relationship with God.

Jesus's clear message of truth can be summed up by the text of John 10:10: *"I have come that they may have life, and that they may have it more abundantly."* This abundant life with Jesus leads to a more fulfilled relationship. He personally changes us to become more intimate with God and His truth, more aware of Him, and more fulfilled in our lives. The Living Word of God, Jesus, becomes our life of truth.

JESUS, THE CREATOR OF EVERYTHING (JOHN 1:3–5)

Before becoming human, Jesus was eternally co-existent with the Father and the Holy Spirit. This Being, at some point in eternity past, became intimately personal in the creation of both the invisible and visible worlds. At what point did God decide to begin His creation? This is a big, ponderous question. No matter how long God waited to begin, He always knew that His creation would be part of a plan that included us.

God faithfully continues His perfect and purposeful work of fulfilling His will. Everything must fulfill itself to the end. God will therefore guide His plans until they are accomplished.

John 1:3–5 reveals that Jesus was involved in fulfilling this sovereign plan of God:

> All things were made through Him, and without Him nothing was made that was made. In Him was life, and the life was the light of men. And the light shines in the darkness, and the darkness did not comprehend it.

CHAPTER SIX: THE REVELATION OF JESUS CHRIST

Whether we realize it or not, God is personally involved in each of our lives, and Jesus has always been a part of this plan. His role was not only to become human but to personally guide God's plan, His truth, by being the living witness of God in every moment of humanity's existence from beginning to end.

It began with creation. The God of Genesis 1 is translated as *Elohim*. Though this is a plural form of God, it can be treated as singular, in which case it would refer to the one supreme deity.[28] In Genesis 1:26, we read that God said, *"Let Us make [humanity] in Our image…"*

According to author Paul E. Little, some believe that when God created, "Elohim was to be understood as a revelation of the Trinity of God to man, and that man's awareness of this truth was later lost through the Fall."[29]

Here we have the Trinity involved in the creation of the universe and everything within it. Elohim created by means of the Word and the Spirit (Genesis 1:1–3).[30] Jesus is the active Word of Creation; indeed, He is the reason *why* all life was created.

In Revelation 4:11, John saw Jesus as the One who was worthy to be praised and glorified, because He created all things and it was by His will that everything exists and was created. The apostle Paul also describes the preeminence of Christ in creation:

> He is the image of the invisible God, the firstborn over all creation. For by Him all things were created that are in heaven and that are on earth, visible and invisible, whether thrones or dominions or principalities or powers. All things were created through Him and for Him. And He is before all things, and in Him all things consist. (Colossians 1:15–17)

Paul's declaration signifies that Jesus truly is deity. He describes the image of God not just as an image but the real and authentic person of God becoming visible. Jesus is firstborn over all creation not as a created being but by His status and position as the One who opens the gates to everything beneficial to humanity.

Jesus is also the first human to have been permanently resurrected. This secures our eternal life with God. Jesus, being one hundred percent God, became one hundred percent human in order to be the first to provide the way for our salvation and new life with God.

---

[28] J.D. Douglas, *The New Bible Dictionary* (Grand Rapids, MI: Eerdmans, 1962), 478.
[29] Little, *Know What You Believe*, 29
[30] Ibid., 28.

JESUS, THE ANGEL OF THE LORD (THE OLD TESTAMENT)

After creation, Jesus began His involvement as God's witness in the lives of the people of the Old Testament through His work as the Angel of the Lord. They were well aware that God occasionally revealed Himself to them personally. They called Him God's Angel and felt that if they glimpsed the face of God, they would die on account of God's holiness. God mentioned this to Moses: *"You cannot see My face; for no man shall see Me, and live"* (Exodus 33:20). However, people felt safe looking upon the Angel of the Lord.

The Angel of the Lord became God's representative. In specific incidences, He demonstrated divine acts of God. He first appeared visibly when He presented Himself to Hagar when she and Ishmael fled from the presence of Sarah (Genesis 16:7-13). After He assured her that they would be taken care of, they were encouraged to go back to Sarah, who named Him "the God who sees."

Later, in Genesis 21:17-21, when Hagar fled from Sarah and Abraham for the last time, she heard the voice of the Angel of the Lord from heaven. He provided her with the water she and her son needed. This began her life of trust in Him.

The Angel of the Lord also appeared before Moses in the burning bush (Exodus 3:1-6), and most likely in disguise when He blessed Jacob upon wrestling with him (Genesis 32:22-30).

Abraham heard the voice of the Angel of the Lord just before he prepared to slay Isaac, his son, as a sacrifice to God. The Angel of the Lord stopped him, saying, *"Abraham, Abraham! ...Do not lay your hand on the lad, or do anything to him; for now I know that you fear God, since you have not withheld your son, your only son, from Me"* (Genesis 22:11-12).

The Angel of the Lord later spoke to people through dreams, as He did with Jacob (Genesis 31:11-13).

It became common to remark upon how similar the Angel of the Lord was to God. People called His acts and words comforting, discerning, and full of wisdom (2 Samuel 14:17, 20). He had divine authority.

In Judges 2:1-5, the Angel of the Lord had the authority to pass divine judgment. Because of Israel's disobedience to God's command against making any kind of covenant with the inhabitants of the promised land, the Angel of the Lord passed judgment on them. The Canaanites became a continual thorn in their side.

Other references to this divine judgment can be found in 2 Kings 19:35, where the Angel of the Lord destroyed 185,000 Assyrians, and in 1 Chronicles 21:9-30, where He gave the order to slay seventy thousand men of Israel because of David's disobedience.

The Angel of the Lord had the authority to call people into service and direct them. In Judges 6:12, while speaking to Gideon under the terebinth tree, the Angel said, *"The Lord is with you, you mighty man of valor!"* The Angel of the Lord called Gideon into service by having him deliver Israel from the hands of the Midianites.

He also gave Elijah direction in 2 Kings 1:3 and 15.

The Angel of the Lord had the authority and power to perform miracles. In regards to one such miracle, we read:

> The Angel of God said to him, "Take the meat and the unleavened bread and lay them on this rock, and pour out the broth." And he did so.
>
> Then the Angel of the Lord put out the end of the staff that was in His hand, and touched the meat and the unleavened bread; and fire rose out of the rock and consumed the meat and the unleavened bread. And the Angel of the Lord departed out of his sight. (Judges 6:20–21)

Other miracles can be found in Exodus 14:19–31, where the Angel of the Lord divided the Red Sea, and in Numbers 22:21–35, where He spoke through Balaam's donkey.

In Judges 13:1–25, the Angel of the Lord had the authority to bless and predict the future. In Genesis 48:15–16, He had the authority to become a redeemer. This was expressed by Israel when he blessed Joseph. He acknowledged the Angel of the Lord as his Savior:

> God, before whom my fathers Abraham and Isaac walked, the God who has fed me all my life long to this day, the Angel who has redeemed me from all evil, bless the lads; let my name be named upon them, and the name of my fathers Abraham and Isaac; and let them grow into a multitude in the midst of the earth.

The last reference to the Angel of the Lord comes to us in Zechariah 3, where we read that Zechariah received a prophetic vision from the Lord. Joshua, the high priest, stood before the Angel of the Lord, with Satan accusing him. Joshua was clothed in filthy garments and the Angel of the Lord asked those who stood before him to take them away. The Angel of the Lord had the authority to remove iniquity and cleanse. He gave Joshua new and clean garments, demonstrating that He had the ability not only to remove iniquity and cleanse but to endow one with righteousness.

JESUS, THE LIGHT OF THE WORLD (JOHN 1:6–11)

After the work of the Angel of the Lord was completed, there came four hundred years of silence during which God didn't speak to anyone. As He kept silent, generations passed with believers reading and trusting in the Old Testament books that the scribes kept current and true.

They held on to the prophecies of the coming Messiah. Malachi 3:1 mentions one such prophecy, which states that God would send a messenger to prepare the way of the Lord:

> Behold, I send My messenger, and he will prepare the way before Me. And the Lord, whom you seek, will suddenly come to His temple, even the Messenger of the covenant, in whom you delight. Behold, He is coming…

When Jesus spoke to His disciples, He confirmed that this messenger was like the prophet Elijah (Matthew 11:7–15), the forerunner of the Christ sent by God. Luke 1:17 declares that this messenger was John the Baptist:

> He will also go before Him in the spirit and power of Elijah, "to turn the hearts of the fathers to the children," and the disobedient to the wisdom of the just, to make ready a people prepared for the Lord.

John 1:6–11 states that this was what the people of God were waiting for. It was a real test of faith to wonder where God was and if He would really send a Savior. But God is always faithful to His Word and He did send John the Baptist as a witness to prepare the way for Jesus's arrival as the Light of the World:

> There was a man sent from God, whose name was John. This man came for a witness, to bear witness of the Light, that all through him might believe. He was not that Light, but was sent to bear witness of that Light. That was the true Light which gives light to every man coming into the world.
>
> He was in the world, and the world was made through Him, and the world did not know Him. He came to His own, and His own did not receive Him.

John the Baptist had the power of the Holy Spirit on his life and demonstrated this authority of God by telling people about the coming of Christ. People believed him to the point that he attracted followers who became his disciples.

Once John saw Jesus, he declared Him as the *"Lamb of God who takes away the sin of the world!"* (John 1:29) How could those who saw John's life of ministry, full of power and authority, deny the words of truth he spoke? Even the prophecy about him in Isaiah is profound:

> The voice of one crying in the wilderness: "Prepare the way of the Lord; make straight in the desert a highway for our God. Every valley shall be exalted and every mountain and hill brought low; the crooked places shall be made straight and the rough places smooth; the glory of the Lord shall be revealed, and all flesh shall see it together; for the mouth of the Lord has spoken." (Isaiah 40:3–5)

Jesus is the light of the world, a shining beacon that points to God and His truth. One only has to read in the gospels about this light, which is proved authentic through His teachings and supernatural miracles of healing and deliverance.

Despite these amazing signs, some people would not believe and rejected Him as God's light. They just couldn't understand Him as God's Savior and deliverer; in their view, He was a contradiction. They wanted outward victories and Jesus wanted inward victories. God wanted to change the individual on the inside rather than change them on the outside. God's new life begins internally.

JESUS, THE GIVER OF NEW LIFE (JOHN 1:12–13)

Jesus came to the earth as a human so He could become our Savior. He could have lived a normal life, like everyone else, and eventually died—but in order for this to happen, He would have had to have a sinful nature, which He did not. Because He was sinless, He would have lived forever as a human.

He also could have chosen not to talk to anyone, to mind His own business. But He did not. His purpose was to die for us, to reveal God to us, to teach us about God's way of life and help us understand how to obtain eternal life. He did all this as God's living witness in order to give new life to anyone who wants it.

John 1:12–13 states that this new life is a regenerated spiritual life:

> But as many as received Him, to them He gave the right to become children of God, to those who believe in His name: who were born, not of blood, nor of the will of the flesh, nor of the will of man, but of God.

Jesus lived on the earth for thirty-three years, died as the sacrificial lamb for our sins, and then rose from the grave glorified so we could rise with Him in the end. This was the finale of Jesus's purpose and role as God's living witness for humanity. He is our Savior, Lord, and King forever. Without Him becoming human, our new life with God would never have become reality.

JESUS, THE GIVER OF GRACE AND TRUTH (JOHN 1:14–18)

There are some who believe that we must be good enough to save ourselves by our own righteousness. In reality, God decided to save us. Just before dying on the cross, Jesus said, *"It is finished!"* (John 19:30), meaning that His work was completed and He had fulfilled all of God's requirements.

As a result, God's grace (unmerited favor) and truth (righteousness) could be offered to us as free gifts.

Ephesians 2:8 says, *"For by grace you have been saved through faith, and that not of yourselves; it is the gift of God…"* We must realize that our own good works can never be good enough to save us. God's gift of grace and righteousness is the only way to be saved. This gift must be accepted by faith.

John 1:14–18 gives us the revelation of Jesus as God's gift of grace and truth:

> And the Word became flesh and dwelt among us, and we beheld His glory, the glory as of the only begotten of the Father, full of grace and truth.
>
> John bore witness of Him and cried out, saying, "This was He of whom I said, 'He who comes after me is preferred before me, for He was before me.'"
>
> And of His fullness we have all received, and grace for grace. For the law was given through Moses, but grace and truth came through Jesus Christ. No one has seen God at any time. The only begotten Son, who is in the bosom of the Father, He has declared Him.

Our new life with God is centered around Jesus. He guided God's truth from creation and throughout the Old Testament period as the Angel of the Lord, continuing on through His life, death, and resurrection on the earth. He now sits at the right hand of God in heaven and continually intercedes for us (Romans 8:34). One day He will return to bring us home with Him forever.

This living witness of God, Jesus Christ, is proof that God exists, because He has personally revealed to us all that God is, and all of His truth, each step of the way.

CHAPTER SEVEN
THE REVELATION OF THE HOLY SPIRIT
(THE TRANSFORMING WITNESS)

THERE ARE SOME who say that the Holy Spirit is a kind of energy, or force, who mysteriously influences our decisions through intuition. They claim He is not really a person but rather an impulse which helps us to make decisions. According to this view, He is just another name, another power, another form of the Father. Because of this uncertainty, He is the most misunderstood and neglected person of the Trinity.

The Bible states that the Holy Spirit is really a person and that He is an aspect of God. Those who have been affected by Him know Him as the One who walks alongside a person in their relationship with God.

Jesus explained to His disciples that the Holy Spirit would become their Helper (from the Greek, *parakletos*) once Jesus was resurrected and returned to His Father in heaven:

> But when the Helper comes, whom I shall send to you from the Father, the Spirit of truth who proceeds from the Father, He will testify of Me. And you also will bear witness, because you have been with Me from the beginning. (John 15:26–27)

The Holy Spirit, who proceeds from the Father, was sent to us by Jesus to help us in our walk with God. His ministry draws us closer to God so we can have a more authentic relationship with Him. He is also called the Spirit of Truth, and this truth always points us toward Jesus and what He has done for us. He becomes our life with God.

It is difficult to explain the Holy Spirit to anyone who doesn't understand Him. He works invisibly, mostly behind the scenes, and sometimes in the forefront where everyone can see. Acts 1:8 tells us that we *"shall receive power when the Holy Spirit has come upon [us]"* and that we will witness him everywhere. This power is a witness of transformation.

THE TRANSFORMING INFLUENCE OF THE HOLY SPIRIT
Transforming the lives of people, which is most important to God, is the purpose for the revelation of the Holy Spirit. He becomes the life-changer, the One who transforms the inner natures of believers so God can dwell in them.

Nicodemus, a Pharisee who came to Jesus by night, had trouble understanding this transformation. He couldn't figure out how it could happen. Jesus told him, *"I say to you, unless one is born again, he cannot see the kingdom of God"* (John 3:3). In other words, unless we undergo this inner change, we cannot understand God's way of life.

Nicodemus responded with a question: *"How can [one] be born when he is old? Can he enter a second time into his mother's womb and be born?"* (John 3:4).

Jesus answered him this way:

> Most assuredly, I say to you, unless one is born of water and the Spirit, he cannot enter the kingdom of God. That which is born of the flesh is flesh, and that which is born of the Spirit is spirit. Do not marvel that I said to you, "You must be born again." The wind blows where it wishes, and you hear the sound of it, but cannot tell where it comes from and where it goes. So is everyone who is born of the Spirit. (John 3:5–8)

In this passage, Jesus explains to Nicodemus that there are two births we can experience. The first is obvious to everyone, since we are all born into this world from the womb. The second is the rebirth of our spirit-nature.

Jesus wanted Nicodemus to be aware that there is a distinction between the two. Because we have been born with a sinful nature, and are controlled by this nature, we can also experience an inner transformation, being reborn with God's infallible nature.

When we allow God to come into our lives, He gives us a new nature which gives us free access to Him. We then enjoy a connection to God like we've never felt before, and this transformation is enhanced by the Holy Spirit. He is the transforming influence in our lives. Once this transformation happens, the sinful nature with which we were born no longer controls us. We don't have to cater to its needs. The new nature God gives us, which is a regenerated or converted nature, becomes alive, carrying the characteristics of divine righteousness. Change happens when we allow this new nature to influence us.

THE OLD VS. THE NEW

The physical aspect of life can be easily understood. Every day we are influenced by the visible things we see and deal with. We aren't confused because we're familiar with the laws of the physical world. Physicists will tell you that there is a logical reason for everything we observe.

When it comes to the spiritual aspect of life, the situation becomes more perplexing. How can we begin to explain it, and why is there so much confusion about whether our inner lives can really be transformed?

Yet we know that we do change through the years. We learn about ourselves and change who we are through the trials and ordeals we face. We have the capacity to change ourselves through these experiences that make us who we are and influence who we will become. These changes occur while we live with our selfish natures in the sinful world. This sinful nature brings out the worst of us, and also the best of us.

But the inner transformation we're talking about in this chapter goes beyond simple maturation. This change is undertaken by God. It is God-inspired, God-initiated, and God-given. We may refer to it as being "born again," or "conversion." It's an instantaneous transformation from the old to the new and it happens when we accept Jesus into our lives as Savior and Lord, entering into a relationship with Him. It is a spiritual gift of renewal.

The Bible compares these two natures, which are opposites. There is the old man versus the new man (Colossians 3:5–11), the old creation versus the new creation (2 Corinthians 5:17), walking in the flesh versus walking in the spirit (Galatians 5:16–17).

Eventually we realize that we have truly changed from doing things the old way, the sinful way; instead we do things the new way, the godly and righteous way. This is the transformation God has always wanted for us and He implements this change as part of His redemptive plan, which began right after the Fall. This transformation is available to everyone, because the Fall resulted in both the gradual death of our physical bodies and the instant death of our spirit-natures.

God wanted to restore us to the state in which Adam and Eve lived in the garden of Eden before the Fall. They were in right standing with Him in every respect. But when they sinned, death entered the picture and they became separated from God.

We too inherited this death, both of our bodies and our spirit-natures, and became separated from God. This is why it's so important to undergo the spiritual rebirth that restores us to our original state of right standing with God. We rejoin God's family as His adopted sons and daughters.

This is why the Holy Spirit is so important. He is our spiritual advisor, always pointing us in the right direction. He wants us to be transformed so we can become more intimate with God, more aware of His truth, and better able to live before Him.

THE UPPER ROOM

The upper room was a gathering place in Jerusalem where people ate, met, and fellowshipped. It had the capacity to hold about one hundred twenty people. We can read about the first time the disciples were introduced to this space:

> Now on the first day of Unleavened Bread, when they killed the Passover lamb, His disciples said to Him, "Where do You want us to go and prepare, that You may eat the Passover?"

> And He sent out two of His disciples and said to them, "Go into the city, and a man will meet you carrying a pitcher of water; follow him. Wherever he goes in, say to the master of the house, 'The Teacher says, "Where is the guest room in which I may eat the Passover with My disciples?"' Then he will show you a large upper room, furnished and prepared; there make ready for us."
>
> So His disciples went out, and came into the city, and found it just as He had said to them; and they prepared the Passover. (Mark 14:12–16)

It became a very important place for the disciples and followers of Christ, because this is where the Day of Pentecost began. Jesus commanded them not to depart from Jerusalem but to wait for the promise of the Father, which was the baptism of the Holy Spirit.

The word pentecost means fifty, which is why it happened fifty days after the ascension of Christ. At Pentecost, the Holy Spirit filled the upper room with His presence and filled every person within. They were all baptized with the Holy Spirit, which was manifested through the speaking of tongues:

> When the Day of Pentecost had fully come, they were all with one accord in one place. And suddenly there came a sound from heaven, as of a rushing mighty wind, and it filled the whole house where they were sitting. Then there appeared to them divided tongues, as of fire, and one sat upon each of them. And they were all filled with the Holy Spirit and began to speak with other tongues, as the Spirit gave them utterance. (Acts 2:1–4)

This phenomenon, this mysterious and unexplained act, went against what was natural. It was spiritual by nature, something unseen, and would have caused outsiders to question the validity of what had just happened.

Picture a group of people praying and waiting for something to happen. Suddenly, a magical presence of some sort begins to fall on them, causing them to speak without inhibition in a language they had never heard. Were you to look in, you would have thought this was some kind of play, a rehearsal of actors playing out a scene.

But this was a special work of the Holy Spirit. It was something brand new, something never seen before. What a way to introduce the first spiritual gift! The invisible workings of the Holy Spirit were becoming visible as a sign of God's reality.

This was a special moment for God and the first Christians, who were suddenly transformed from within. They experienced the presence of the Holy Spirit and what

He could do. They weren't alone anymore and realized the truth of what Jesus had said to them earlier about the Holy Spirit being their Helper. God was still with them, still guiding and working through them, building a body of believers to continue what Jesus had established.

The Holy Spirit is the One who united and equipped the followers of Christ to become the bride of Christ, His church, and that spark was initiated in the upper room. This event birthed the New Testament church and introduced the moving of the Holy Spirit.

THE PRESENCE OF THE HOLY SPIRIT

As the moving influence of creation, the Holy Spirit is the guardian of God's creation. Each person of the Trinity took part in maintaining all that they created. Afterward the role of the Holy Spirit became significant because His specialty was establishing the presence of God in people's lives. This was evident in the Old Testament, and especially so in the New Testament.

The Holy Spirit directed everything pertaining to God from a heart of genuine love. This became more apparent as we learned more about God and His desire to change us for the better. He was in the people business and focused on us. The Bible contains many examples of this. It's amazing how many lives were changed once they encountered the presence of the Holy Spirit.

Encountering the Holy Spirit is a wonderful experience. Through Him, we are able to fellowship freely with God and feel complete joy, for there is nothing like being in the presence of God (Psalm 16:11). The Bible presents to us a complete history of God's presence in the lives of people.

This history began with the building of altars. In the Old Testament, God revealed the importance of these altars. They were built as places to make covenants with God and other humans, to present offerings and sacrifices, to worship and call upon the name of the Lord, and to witness agreements.

Cain and Abel practiced their fellowship with God by offering Him sacrifices (Genesis 4:1–7). God accepted Abel's sacrifice but not Cain's. After the birth of Enosh, Seth and his fellow countrymen called upon the name of the Lord (Genesis 4:25–26); so did Abraham (Genesis 12:8; 13:4). And the first thing Noah did after being saved from the flood was build an altar and offer a sacrifice to God (Genesis 8:20–22).

This became a rule: a special place committed to God equals His presence. Jesus mentioned this in Matthew 18:20: *"For where two or three are gathered together in My name, I am there in the midst of them."* It becomes so simple when we realize that this formula—place equals presence—can be employed to have an amazing encounter with God.

Many people choose to run away from God, and this is why they don't experience His presence. You can run away from God, like Jonah did, but eventually God will get your attention. All He wants from you is for you to stop and listen.

These days, we're too busy to spend time with God. It's important that we make an effort to spend time with Him so we can experience His presence. This becomes our spiritual foundation. From there, when we experience life with God in the world, we grow and mature as Christians to become more like Jesus every day.

The Tabernacle. Along with altars came the introduction of the Tabernacle. As the Israelites grew in number while wandering in the wilderness, it became important for them to remain the people of God. God Himself wanted to establish the building of the Tabernacle so He could dwell within it amongst His people.

Exodus 25:8–9 describes God's desire for Israel to make Him a sanctuary:

> And let them make Me a sanctuary, that I may dwell among them. According to all that I show you, that is, the pattern of the tabernacle and the pattern of all its furnishings, just so you shall make it.

This is why God created us in the first place, so we could have fellowship with Him. Even though sin separated us from God, He provided a way to take away our sin through the death and resurrection of His Son, Jesus.

However, before the atoning work of Christ, the Tabernacle became the first tent to house the presence of God. It became a holy place, allowing the Israelites to enter His presence despite their sin; they knew God would make them righteous by faith through Christ's future atonement. This is where they were filled with the Spirit of God and transformed.

God needed a place where the people could meet and worship Him, and the Tabernacle met that need. Most of the latter chapters of Exodus describe how the Tabernacle and its furnishings were built. Once it was finished, the glory of the Lord filled the Tabernacle so that even Moses couldn't enter it (Exodus 40:34–35). Joshua didn't want to depart from the Tabernacle because there he experienced total freedom with God (Exodus 33:11).

The Tabernacle became so important to God that one tribe, the Levites, were made responsible not only to be His ministers but to take care of it, including erecting and taking it down so it would be ready for transport whenever the Israelites had to move.

Entering the Tabernacle meant that you belonged to God, that He accepted you, loved you, and forgave you. It meant salvation and life with God.

The temples of the Old Testament. Once the Israelites were established in their own land, the next step was to find a permanent residence for God's presence. David had the desire to do this for God, but God told him that he wasn't to build the temple; he was too badly stained with the blood of his enemies (1 Chronicles 22:8). Instead God would allow Solomon, his son, to build the temple.

So David collected all the necessary materials and treasures that would be required in building the temple (1 Chronicles 22:1–16). It then took Solomon seven years to complete the project, finishing around 975 B.C. (1 Kings 6:37–38).

In 587 B.C., Nebuchadrezzar looted and destroyed Solomon's temple during the Babylonian siege. It wasn't until the reign of Cyrus that a second temple was authorized to be built by the exiles who returned to Jerusalem (c. 537 B.C.). They returned with the vessels which had been looted by Nebuchadrezzar and started to rebuild the temple under Cyrus's decree (Ezra 1–3).

Despite some opposition, the exiles completed rebuilding the temple during the sixth year of the reign of King Darius around 519 B.C. (Ezra 6:15). It was almost destroyed in various conflicts with other nations through the centuries, but it stood for five hundred years through rebuildings and refittings—until King Herod came along.

Under Herod, the reconstruction of this temple became very extravagant. The work began in 19 B.C., with the main sanctuary being finished ten years later. The rest of the structure continued its work until A.D. 64.

The temple was destroyed by the Romans in A.D. 70.

We realize that God's presence can only manifest on holy ground—or, in this case, a holy place. This is why altars, the Tabernacle, and the temples of the Old Testament were important. They were sanctified, set apart by God as holy places where the people could meet with Him.

The Holy Spirit, likewise, could only come upon people in the same way. When the Holy Spirit came upon people during the Old Testament era, they were aware of Him. After all, David wrote, *"Do not cast me away from Your presence, and do not take Your Holy Spirit from me"* (Psalm 51:11). Even though the Holy Spirit's work was limited during this period, He still enhanced the lives of Old Testament believers by occasionally coming upon them to do the work of God in their lives.

The temple of the Holy Spirit. The holy of holies was located at the innermost part of the Old Testament temple. The high priest was allowed to enter once a year on the Day of Atonement (*Yom Kippur*). This was important because the priest was able to make atonement for the sins of Israel and the world.

This atonement was a representation of the permanent blood sacrifice Jesus would later come to give for all humanity, including those who lived in the past, those who currently lived, and those who would live in the future. Jesus's atoning work served as an eternal payment for the consequences of sin. Because of His righteous sacrifice, we can become righteous to the point that our physical bodies, along with our renewed spirit-natures, can be holy enough to receive God's presence within us.

Once Jesus died and rose again, the veil of the temple, which separated the holy of holies from the holy place, was torn in two from top to bottom. Not only this, but graves were opened and the bodies of many saints were raised out of their graves. They were able to go into Jerusalem and appear to many (Matthew 27:51–53).

After His sacrifice, no longer did humans have to go to a specific place to experience the presence of God. His presence is now able to dwell within us. Our bodies can become temples of the Holy Spirit. Paul tells us, *"Or do you not know that your body is the temple of the Holy Spirit who is in you, whom you have from God, and you are not your own?"* (1 Corinthians 6:19)

How amazing it is for God to live within us! This is what makes Christianity so unique. We don't have to rely on ourselves to be transformed; we can allow God to transform us from within. The Holy Spirit makes Jesus real to us. He causes us to worship God in every respect and gives us the spiritual tools we need to grow and mature in our relationship with God.

Jesus states in Matthew 16:18, *"I also say to you that you are Peter, and on this rock I will build My church, and the gates of Hades shall not prevail against it."* Through the Holy Spirit, Jesus is building His church. The Holy Spirit enhances our relationships within the church, equips us with the tools we need to build the church, and edifies us so we can bear fruit inside and outside the church.

THE FRUIT OF THE SPIRIT

The transforming influence of the Holy Spirit can be seen by the fruit we reveal in our lives. We have the capacity to walk in the Spirit, displaying His characteristics. Galatians 5:22–23 describes the ninefold fruit of the Spirit:

> But the fruit of the Spirit is love, joy, peace, longsuffering, kindness, goodness, faithfulness, gentleness, self-control.

We won't display only one of these qualities; we will display them all at once. You're either filled with the Spirit or you're not. When you are, you have these characteristics of the Spirit within you. Whatever is deep within your heart will come to fruition through your actions.

We can also choose to walk in the flesh. Galatians 5:19–21 describes these fleshly characteristics:

> Now the works of the flesh are evident, which are: adultery, fornication, uncleanness, lewdness, idolatry, sorcery, hatred, contentions,

jealousies, outbursts of wrath, selfish ambitions, dissensions, heresies, envy, murders, drunkenness, revelries, and the like…

The fruit we bear in our lives is determined by which part of us we want to display, the Spirit or the flesh. It's a matter of attitude, like putting on a cloak. When we allow the fruit of the Spirit to display itself, we allow our spirit-natures to shine. But if we allow the sinful nature to take prominence, we display selfish qualities.

Spending time in the presence of God helps us to bring out the qualities of the Spirit. People will notice us by our actions. Displaying the fruit of the Spirit transforms us.

THE GIFTS OF THE SPIRIT

The Holy Spirit has the authority to give special spiritual gifts so the church can be edified to bring unity and joy into the lives of its people. These gifts can be used as ministering tools to reveal who God is, or they can be used to encourage and cause people to believe in God. The church is a symphony and the Holy Spirit is the conductor who leads it in carrying out the exploits of God. Without the Spirit, the church is dead.

The gifts of the Spirit help us in our conduct and service of God. There are three groups of spiritual giftings: manifestation, ministry, and motivational.

The manifestation gifts (1 Corinthians 12:4–11). These are used by all of the people some of the time. There are three gifts of utterance: prophecy, speaking in various tongues, and the interpretation of tongues. There are also three gifts of power: faith, working miracles, and healing. Finally, there are three gifts of revelation: the word of wisdom, the word of knowledge, and discerning of spirits.

The ministry gifts (Ephesians 4:11–12). These are used by some of the people all of the time. These special gifts are extended to apostles, prophets, evangelists, pastors, and teachers. They are usually used in leadership roles for the equipping of the saints for the work of ministry and the edification of the body of Christ.

The motivational gifts (Romans 12:4–8). These are used by all of the people all of the time. The gifts can be observed in seven different types of people: the perceiver, the server, the teacher, the exhorter, the giver, the administrator, and the compassionate person.

Do you see yourself in any of these types? If not, pray and ask the Holy Spirit to give you a gift with which you can be used of God to edify and encourage those around you. If you're a follower of Christ, you have a new nature and the presence of the Holy Spirit within you. You belong to God and His church. God will give you a special spiritual gift through the Holy Spirit.

Who would have thought that a bunch of nobodies, like the disciples Jesus chose, would end up becoming apostles and leaders of churches who led God's people through the workings of the Holy Spirit, who were purposely changed and transformed? If He did it for the disciples, He definitely can do it for you.

The transforming witness of the Holy Spirit is proof that God wants you to be part of His plan. He exists and is there for you.

CHAPTER EIGHT
THE GOD OF THE MOMENT
(THE SPECIAL WITNESS)

THERE ARE MOMENTS in life when you experience something profound. Perhaps a vehicle has lost control and is heading toward you; it looks like it's going to smash right into you, but for some reason it misses and your life is spared. Or perhaps you're late to arrive at the airport and miss your flight; later you hear on the news that the plane crashed. Something small like a chat with someone could cause you to change your mind and do something differently than planned, allowing you to come home safe and sound.

It's amazing how many chance happenings we face on a daily basis. It can seem impossible that somehow they've been designed or allowed by God to change our minds or deliver us from a bad outcome. Who is God that He would be so intentional with us, so sovereign?

In Psalm 37:23–24, David wrote,

> The steps of a good man are ordered [established] by the Lord, and He delights in his way. Though he fall, he shall not be utterly cast down; for the Lord upholds him with His hand.

Yet Jesus says in Luke 13:4–5,

> Or those eighteen on whom the tower in Siloam fell and killed them, do you think that they were worse sinners than all other men who dwelt in Jerusalem? I tell you, no; but unless you repent you will all likewise perish.

In those days, people thought that if a person was a bad sinner, they would experience some kind of injurious judgment from God. Something bad would happen to them. And those who were good would have God's blessing and not suffer.

But life isn't like this at all. Both good and bad happen to everyone. The best we can do with the time we have on this earth is to live before God with reverence and integrity, always doing our best to glorify Him with who we are, what we have, and what we do and say.

God gave us the gift of life, which implies that He has a plan for each of us. Therefore He knows everything about us and what will happen. He wouldn't leave us on our own, because He loves us each beyond measure.

The Bible states that God wishes for all to come to a saving knowledge of Christ, that none would perish (2 Peter 3:9). But life throws us many curves and every decision we make has a tremendous effect on us. Our free will produces unpredictability, and God knows this. That's why He gives us personal and timely revelations, to let us know that He is with us no matter the circumstance we face.

We call these the minor revelations of God, and they specifically focus on the individual. Even though they are considered minor, they can have major impacts on our lives. They are intended for specific people for a specific purpose.

There are three types of life revelations: the God of the moment, the God of the person, and the God of the future. In this chapter, we will explore the first type.

GOD REVEALS HIMSELF TO US SPONTANEOUSLY

At a certain point in time, God reveals Himself to us in a spontaneous way, either directly or indirectly, naturally or supernaturally. Perhaps God uses an individual to help us in a situation, intervening through an act of deliverance or encouragement. Or perhaps He circumvents an occurrence on our behalf without us even being aware of it. Sometimes He provides for us in a way we didn't see coming, or gives us a special revelation when the timing is right.

Many of the natural occurrences we experience, whether planned or otherwise, can be acts of God. Our lives can be ninety-five percent normal, with nothing serious or unusual happening, but the remaining five percent can really affect us. Maybe you lose a loved one, face a challenging event, or take a step of faith outside your comfort zone.

These life-altering experiences can test one's faith in God. We wonder what He's trying to say or do. From our point of view, we have our own plans and desires. But when something changes, we can feel overwhelmed, discouraged, or sidetracked. The result is a life lesson that's hard to understand and accept. However, when you have time to think about it, you will realize that He was with you through it all. He wants to let us know that He personally comes alongside us, and sometimes He even reveals Himself in a special way.

God uses these experiences for a number of reasons: to get our attention, to cause us to change direction, to refocus on what's important, and to let us know what is going to happen. He is the God of the moment, aware of every second of our lives. When the time is right, He will specifically reveal Himself to you to fulfill His purpose in your life.

THE THREE MOST POWERFUL GOD-OF-THE-MOMENT EXAMPLES

Moses. Consider how God gained Moses's attention. Moses grew up amongst royalty, had a great education and upbringing, and most likely was headed toward absolute success. But when he murdered an Egyptian for beating one of his own, he ran away from his affluent life and became a fugitive.

Most likely, he thought his life was over, that he had destroyed everything he'd worked for. Perhaps he thought God was done with him. So he fled Egypt, fearing for his life, and ended up in the land of Midian, where he met his wife and started a family.

Despite what happened, God had something special for Moses. He obtained Moses's attention by way of a burning bush:

> And the Angel of the Lord appeared to him in a flame of fire from the midst of a bush. So he looked, and behold, the bush was burning with fire, but the bush was not consumed. Then Moses said, "I will now turn aside and see this great sight, why the bush does not burn."
>
> So when the Lord saw that he turned aside to look, God called to him from the midst of the bush and said, "Moses, Moses!"
>
> And he said, "Here I am." (Exodus 3:2–4)

This became a special witness for Moses. It was a supernatural revelation of God. This was both a God-moment and the turning point of his life. At the burning bush, God revealed to Moses who He was, the role Moses would play to deliver Israel, and the purpose he should focus on. Who else but Moses could have experienced God through a burning bush?

Paul. Consider how God gained Paul's attention. After the stoning death of Stephen, the witnesses placed their clothes at the feet of Saul, the persecutor of the early church. He relentlessly wreaked havoc and took believers of Christ into custody to be judged, not caring what happened to them. Saul thought he was doing God's work.

He had grown up well-educated, part of the Pharisee community, and was a stalwart in the Jewish tradition. But when the time was right, he experienced a dramatic revelation from God. It was definitely a wake-up call, like being hit by a two-by-four:

> Then Saul, still breathing threats and murder against the disciples of the Lord, went to the high priest and asked letters from him to the synagogues of Damascus, so that if he found any who were of the Way, whether men or women, he might bring them bound to Jerusalem.
>
> As he journeyed he came near Damascus, and suddenly a light shone around him from heaven. Then he fell to the ground, and heard a voice saying to him, "Saul, Saul, why are you persecuting Me?"

> And he said, "Who are You, Lord?"
>
> Then the Lord said, "I am Jesus, whom you are persecuting. It is hard for you to kick against the goads."
>
> So he, trembling and astonished, said, "Lord, what do You want me to do?"
>
> Then the Lord said to him, "Arise and go into the city, and you will be told what you must do." (Acts 9:1–6).

God can be unique in how He gets our attention. Sometimes He gives it a personal flavor to make it more memorable. For example, only Saul could have been thrown off his horse by a blinding light. This definitely got his attention!

This became his God-moment, and it changed his life. It even resulted in the changing of his name from Saul to Paul.

Not only did Paul experience this special, supernatural revelation of God, he also experienced his conversion. That conversion became complete when he received his sight back three days later (Acts 9:9, 17).

Elisha. Consider how God obtained Elisha's attention. Even though Elisha knew, like everyone, that God was going to take Elijah away into heaven by a whirlwind, he waited for confirmation that God would remain with him once Elijah was gone.

Elisha wouldn't let Elijah out of his sight. Three times when Elijah asked him to stay and wait, Elisha said to him, *"As the Lord lives, and as your soul lives, I will not leave you!"* (2 Kings 2:2, 4, 6). He was waiting for his God-moment:

> And so it was, when they had crossed over, that Elijah said to Elisha, "Ask! What may I do for you, before I am taken away from you?"
>
> Elisha said, "Please let a double portion of your spirit be upon me."
>
> So he said, "You have asked a hard thing. Nevertheless, if you see me when I am taken from you, it shall be so for you; but if not, it shall not be so." Then it happened, as they continued on and talked, that suddenly a chariot of fire appeared with horses of fire, and separated the two of them; and Elijah went up by a whirlwind into heaven. (2 Kings 2:9–11)

Not only did Elisha receive a double portion of Elijah's spirit, but he performed twice as many miracles. Who else but Elisha would be the one to witness God take Elijah home into heaven by way of a whirlwind? This was his God-moment and it definitely confirmed what he had already known: God would be with him.

THE CONVERSION EXPERIENCE

We experience life in so many different ways. We especially like to experience the good moments, the ones which make us happy. This is because we want to capture joy and then replay that feeling over and over again, like watching a scene from a movie. These positive feelings give us a sense of satisfaction and fulfillment.

Conversion is like this. It's an experience we don't want to let go. We experience the mystery of God revealing Himself to us and the joy of having that personal encounter with Him.

Every believer in God and follower of Christ will have a conversion experience. These are God-moments. It can seem like nothing happened after such a moment, but we will eventually notice an inner change; something will feel different. Perhaps it will be a difference in our character, in that we suddenly want to do things the way God wants us to do things. Perhaps we gain an understanding of how important it is to please Him in whatever we do.

The conversion experience is the beginning of our newfound relationship with God. He becomes so real to us that we can't help but notice how much He has impacted our lives. Nothing is greater than when God becomes personal. Having an actual relationship with God is the most amazing feeling in the world.

Because it is best to remember your conversion experience, you should write down the details. How did it happen? Once it's written, you can share your conversion story with others. It will become one of the most important experiences of your life.

THE SUPERNATURAL REVELATION EXPERIENCE

Another type of God-moment is the supernatural revelation experience. Just like Moses, Paul, and Elisha, every believer in God and follower of Christ will have at least one moment in their lives when God delivers a personal and unique supernatural revelation of Himself.

When we commit ourselves to God and get serious about our relationship with Him, we'll face a moment when He reveals Himself and His purpose for us—when the time is right.

For me, God revealed Himself in a very unique way.

In 1989, on the Saturday before Victoria Day, I said a confessional prayer and asked God to reveal Himself to me in a real way—invisibly. After contemplating this request, I said out loud, "It's easy for You to reveal Yourself to me invisibly, but how about visibly? Would You reveal Yourself to me visibly? That way I'll know You are with me and that my prayers will be answered."

I put out this fleece, like Gideon, as a sign between me and God, as a way to strengthen my relationship and faith in Him.

Just moments later, while I was still praying, I heard a series of knocking noises. Someone was approaching my room, knocking along the wall of the hallway until He came a stop at my door. It was the perfect volume, not too loud and not too startling.

My dad opened the door gently, which made me turn and look toward him.

"Hello, Thomas," he said.

"Oh. Hi, Dad. What can I do for you?"

He then asked me an interesting question: "Do you think I could survive a head-on collision?"

"Dad, you're a good driver. You're also pretty strong. I think you should be okay."

He paused for a moment. "Do you think there is anything that could change what's going to happen?"

I couldn't understand what my dad was trying to get at. Perplexed, I didn't know how to answer, so I didn't say anything.

"Goodbye," he said.

"Bye, Dad."

He left.

After a few seconds, I was still contemplating what had just happened. Wanting to talk to my dad a bit more, I then got up from my knees, opened the door, and ran after him.

But he was gone. How could he have disappeared so fast? Where had he gone?

Thinking back on this incident made me realize that it had happened a bit too perfectly. Only God could have masterminded a scene like this. My dad never knocked on the walls to get my attention and he never spoke my name, Thomas, in full; he always called me Tom.

And when I think back on how my dad appeared that day, the image I recall also seems too perfect. He had no gray hair. His eyes were sharp. He spoke with perfect diction. I can't even remember whether he wore any glasses. I don't remember noticing his crippled left hand. Everything about him that day was absolutely perfect, no flaws at all.

It is said that we all have an angel who looks like us, to protect and guide us. The Bible mentions an example of this in Acts 12. Peter was freed from prison by an angel and then walked to the home of one of his fellow disciples. Once there, he announced himself at the closed door. A girl inside, Rhoda, recognized Peter's voice but didn't open the door; she was too excited.

When she told the other disciples that Peter was standing outside, they scoffed at her.

"It must be his angel," they said.

Well, this is what I experienced firsthand. I either saw my dad's angel or it was Jesus Himself disguised as my dad. I honestly believe the latter. After all, God doesn't have any flaws. He has to be perfect in every way, free of defect.

Not too long after that, my parents left on a holiday with some friends to Radium Hot Springs. Before driving away, my dad approached me to let me know when they would be coming back.

"What about the head-on collision you talked to me about?" I asked.

He didn't know what I was talking about. He was just as surprised as I was and made it known that he had never talked to me about a head-on collision.

"Then don't go, Dad. Stay here."

"But the plans are already in motion," he replied. "We're going."

That was the last conversation I had with my dad. And it's also when I realized that I'd possibly had my very own God-moment a few weeks earlier.

Still, I wasn't quite sure.

After spending a few days in Radium, my parents parted ways with their friends, who lived in Vancouver, and began traveling back to Calgary along the Trans-Canada Highway. It was just like any other day. The skies were clear, without a cloud to be seen. The temperature was about thirty degrees Celsius and one could see for miles. It was the perfect day.

Back in Calgary, I was scheduled to work until 6:30 p.m. An hour before then, though, I received a frantic phone call from my sister. She was mumbling her words through tears and I could barely understand her.

I eventually found out that the Banff Springs Hospital wanted us to come to Banff to see our parents. They had been involved in a serious car accident.

At that moment, I knew my dad was gone. I'd had a premonition earlier, around 4:00 p.m., and remembered calling out, "Oh Dad!" I later found out that the accident had happened right around 4:00 p.m.

My sister and I drove speedily to Banff. The trip was fairly quiet and we didn't talk much.

When we finally arrived, we were ushered into our mom's room.

"Your dad passed away," the staff told us.

We broke down as a family and comforted each other.

Afterward, my sister and I walked the streets of Banff. We were grieving and going through the motions, walking senselessly like zombies. At last we sat on a bench and just watched other people living out their lives, wondering if they too knew that our dad was gone.

We later learned from the police investigation that witnesses reported a vehicle driving across the highway and smashing head-on into my parents' car. The police believed the other driver may have been looking at a map, or possibly just admiring the scenery at the time of the accident.

The front left portion of my parents' forward bumper was hit at a forty-five-degree angle, causing them to spin. My dad was killed instantly, but the force of the impact somehow spared my mom. After looking at the wreck of their car, I was amazed to see the pocket around her seat where there was hardly any damage. She walked away with only bruises and lacerations.

What would my sister and I have done if our mom had gone too?

The other driver, we discovered, was a visitor from Israel, touring Canada with his thirteen-year-old son. He ended up with a broken leg and spent some time at a different hospital.

I realized months afterward, piecing together what happened that day, that I'd definitely experienced a supernatural God-moment.

While trying to grasp the essential purpose of why this had happened, though, it dawned on me that my dad's passing could have been my own fault. During my prayer time with God, for some reason I had asked Him to take my dad home. Why? Because my dad had once told me that he didn't belong in this world. He couldn't seem to fit in.

Guilt began to consume me. I couldn't understand why God had answered that specific part of my prayer. Why had I said that? Had I really asked God to take my own dad from me? It was a tough pill to swallow! It took a very long time for me to accept my dad's passing without blaming myself.

This God-moment changed my life when I accepted what had happened and stopped blaming myself. Maybe it had just been my dad's time to go. Maybe some disease would have eventually taken him. Who knows? All I know is that God is sovereign and has everything under His control.

He gives us these supernatural revelations because He wants us to trust Him and be aware of His presence alongside us. These special moments help us later in life when we look back for reassurance that we're in a good place with God.

How about you? Have you experienced a supernatural revelation? If not, ask God to give you one. Then wait patiently, even if it seems like you're waiting a long time. If you're serious about God and your relationship with Him, expect Him to reveal Himself to you in a very unique and special way. It will become your God-moment.

UNDERSTANDING THE GOD-MOMENT

It will change you. Our lives are grounded by our relationship with God, which begins with prayer. When you're spending time with God in prayer, you're at your most vulnerable and transparent. God sees your heart. And when you're honest with

CHAPTER EIGHT: THE GOD OF THE MOMENT

Him, you see where you stand with Him. The Holy Spirit will also point out aspects of your life that need to change.

When I began my quest to become serious in my relationship with God, I had no idea how much it would change me. Change begins by having a repentant heart, and I wanted to repent of my ways. This began by confessing my sins before God. That's what triggered my God-moment.

When I felt God's forgiveness and grace, I asked Him to reveal Himself to me in a visible way. Even when He did answer my prayer, I didn't fully understand it until much later. Though it took me a while, my supernatural experience with God raised me to a whole new level.

It will define your purpose. We all want a life of purpose. There has to be a reason for us being here. We know that God is purposeful in all His ways, so it makes sense that He would have a purpose for us.

When God reveals Himself to you, you will know that He would have a good reason for doing it. Once God revealed Himself to Moses at the burning bush, Moses knew his purpose for the rest of his life. Paul knew his purpose after the blinding light incident; it revealed to him that he had been going about life the wrong way, and God pointed him in the right direction. Elisha didn't know if God would make him into a prophet while he was working on his father's farm, and most likely he thought that was his purpose in life; after his God-moment, he became one of the most powerful prophets of all time.

Having a God-moment is like being commissioned for a purpose. Take note of what God is saying to you, what He's revealing. When I look back at my life, before my supernatural revelation I was just doing what everyone else was doing. I worked, pursued my personal interests, and enjoyed life. I really didn't have an authentic purpose. I just lived day to day, not planning for the future.

But after my God-moment, I decided to go to Bible school—and that's where I grew in my relationship with God and came to understand where this special revelation of God was taking me.

If you want to find your purpose in life, ask God for your own supernatural revelation experience. It will give your life meaning and purpose.

It will enhance your life. Once you've experienced your supernatural revelation of God, your life will never be the same. You won't be able to help but trust God in whatever you face. You will be enabled to stay on track with Him.

But be careful! Many forget about their experience with God. Remember that He gave you that experience for a reason and you must have the courage to continue with it. When you keep it at the forefront of your heart and mind, it will enhance your life.

CHAPTER NINE
THE GOD OF THE PERSON AND GOD OF THE FUTURE
(THE PERSONAL AND PROPHETIC WITNESS)

ONE OF THE greatest feelings in the world comes right after we accomplish something. When we pursue dreams, goals, and personal pursuits, they give us a sense of fulfillment. They can consume us!

Everyone is so unique and special. When we begin to find ourselves, we shine and let the world know who we really are by pursuing our passion.

However, we can be deterred from what is important. We spend most of our time being distracted from our purpose. We go about the business of life, meeting our obligations and checking items off our to-do lists. We have errands to run, tasks to perform, deadlines to meet, meals to prepare, children to look after, etc. When do we have time for ourselves? Even more important, when do we spend time with God?

In order for us to take notice of what's happening to us, we need to allow for quiet moments of reflection. Paul tells us in 2 Corinthians 13:5–9 that we need to examine ourselves to prove our faith in God, knowing that we are made strong through Jesus's humanity. We need to see who we are in Christ, appreciating what God has done for us. We need to believe He is going to do something special in our lives, and that those tribulations we face on a regular basis will produce perseverance, character, and hope because God loves us and wants the best for us (Romans 5:3-5).

This is why God reveals Himself to us and why we should trust Him with our future. This trust is enhanced by reading His Word and relying on the guidance of the Holy Spirit in our daily affairs. Ultimately, God enriches our lives. He knows us best, even the number of hairs on our head (Matthew 10:30). How can we neglect the One who gives us such profound insight into ourselves? How can we neglect the One who invests Himself in us and gives so much?

Whatever happens to us, we should try seeing from God's point of view. Because He is eternal, He sees the complete history of time in one glance. This is why He can see the end from the beginning. This is why He wants to be personally involved in our lives—because He knows what's going to happen to us.

Imagine how God sees you, where you are right now and where you're going to be in the future. Once you realize that God has everything under control and has planned it, He becomes both the God of the person and the God of the future.

In other words, God becomes personal to us when we find Him. Because of this, His plans for us are specific and unique. This causes us to become more attuned to Him as He becomes our greatest personal influence.

CHAPTER NINE: THE GOD OF THE PERSON AND THE GOD OF THE FUTURE

THE GOD OF THE PERSON (THE PERSONAL WITNESS)

There is nothing greater than watching your children grow day to day. You intimately know everything about them, what they like and what they hate. You know their strengths and weaknesses and do your best to help them deal with both. You want them to become amazing individuals, to reach their full potential in every area.

It's a great responsibility to be personally involved with your children, watching them grow and seeing what they're capable of. And this is why our relationship with God is so personal. He is our Father, watching over us and seeing how we grow and mature.

When God implemented His decrees, He set out about to fulfill everything He wanted to accomplish according to His will. This included bringing into the world every single person who was to be born, knowing their purpose and predetermining every situation they would face. This is a difficult concept to grasp because we can't fathom how God would know how everything turns out, how He knows what decisions we will make.

This predetermination is part of God's established truth, which introduces us to three preordained aspects of His personal witness to us: his foreknowledge, election, and predestination.

God's foreknowledge. It's hard to imagine how God can know in advance what the future holds. Nothing is hidden from Him. He knows everything about us and what will happen, including our needs before we ask about them (Matthew 6:8).

As Herbert Lockyer writes, "there is no contradiction between God's foreknowledge and our freedom of choice."[31] We can therefore live our lives the way we want and make decisions freely. With this comes the understanding that, despite our independence, God decides what is best for us because His purposes are higher than ours.

Paul offers this insight from the Holy Spirit:

> And we know that all things work together for good to those who love God, to those who are the called according to His purpose. For whom He foreknew [foreknowledge], He also predestined to be conformed to the image of His Son, that He might be the firstborn among many brethren. Moreover whom He predestined, these He also called [election]; whom He called, these He also justified; and whom He justified, these He also glorified [predestination]. (Romans 8:28–30)

---

[31] Herbert Lockyer, *All the Doctrines of the Bible* (Grand Rapids, MI: Zondervan, 1964), 152.

We can conclude that God's foreknowledge determines everything, including our election, which is God choosing us, and our predestination, which is our destiny. This means that God has an absolute foreknowledge of everyone, everything, and every event that is going to happen. Realizing this should give us a new perspective, from which we can better understand how personally God can act toward us. He becomes our Abba, our most intimate Father who oversees all to guide us along.

God's election. God's election is similar to finding the love of your life, that one special person whom you want to meet, get to know, and hopefully spend the rest of your life with. Choosing this person is very personal.

God already knew about those believers who would be His. He knew who would accept Him and who would reject Him. Those who wanted God to be part of their lives are chosen of God. The fact that this was done even before creation, before time began, demonstrates that He knew who would find Him, want to be saved, and want to become a Christ-follower.

> ...just as He chose us in Him before the foundation of the world, that we should be holy and without blame before Him in love, having predestined us to adoption as sons by Jesus Christ to Himself, according to the good pleasure of His will, to the praise of the glory of His grace, by which He made us accepted in the Beloved. (Ephesians 1:4–6)

God knew in advance who would believe in Him and His truth. He chose them as His own, electing them to become part of His family and enjoy the commensurate benefits. It isn't that we choose God, but that He first chooses us (1 John 4:19). God chose to save us and accomplished this by His grace, which He provided through His Son, Jesus Christ.

Election is based not on human merit but on God's grace. Romans 11:5–6 explains it this way:

> Even so then, at this present time there is a remnant according to the election of grace. And if by grace, then it is no longer of works; otherwise grace is no longer grace. But if it is of works, it is no longer grace; otherwise work is no longer work.

Since God's sovereign will has been established since eternity past, His election has likewise been established. Romans 9:11 says, *"for the children not yet being born, nor having done any good or evil, that the purpose of God according to election might stand, not of works but of Him who calls."* God is personally involved in our lives as a result of election, and because of this we become His servants to be used by Him for His purposes (Luke 6:13, Acts 9:15, 1 Corinthians 1:17–18).

God's predestination. Predestination is the doctrine regarding what the future holds for believers. Each believer has been predestined to become an adopted son or daughter of God (Ephesians 1:5). From God's infinite wisdom and love, He established plans according to His sovereign will to redeem those who would become His and give them eternal life.

Everything we've learned thus far points to the fact that predestination can be seen in God's provision; He has bestowed His personal revelations to us. This is why His witness is personal, because the main objective of our predestination is not for us only to be included in Christ's inheritance (Ephesians 1:11) but to be conformed into the image of Jesus, presentable to God for His glory.

> But we all, with unveiled face, beholding as in a mirror the glory of the Lord, are being transformed into the same image from glory to glory, just as by the Spirit of the Lord. (2 Corinthians 3:18)

We all have a unique and personal story that explains how we found God, how we were transformed to live our lives for Him, and how Jesus became personal to us as our Savior, Lord, and King. These stories are the basis of our personal relationship with God.

Even when life can be uncertain, we can know that eventually we will all be made perfect and glorious before God. This is why God can be known as the God of the future.

THE GOD OF THE FUTURE (THE PROPHETIC WITNESS)

The future can only be accurately predicted if one knows what's going to happen. We can be good prognosticators through weighing probability. There are those who are gifted at this and even turn it into a profession.

God, having the foreknowledge of what is going to happen, imparts this knowledge to us as a way for us to trust Him and comfort us in knowing that He has everything under His control.

He primarily guides our lives in three ways: by the Word of God, by the burden that is within us, and by the circumstances we face. These are prophetic tools.

By the Word of God. The Bible is a life manual. God has inspired it in order to reveal who He is and impart principles for us to live by as Christians. It distinguishes between what is good and what is evil. There is God's way of doing things and then there is the opposite. We must decide whether to obey God or not, whether to do things His way or someone else's.

God also speaks to us through His Word. It has recorded, through foreknowledge, what is going to happen in the future. When we read and meditate upon it, He gives us insight into what to do.

By the burden that is within us. This can be thought of as intuition, or a prompting. There are times when we yearn to do something and wonder whether we should act on it. So we look to the Holy Spirit as the One who executes the will of God in our lives. His leading can be confirmed by a prophetic word—but it's done mostly, if not always, by the Word of God.

When you feel such a burden within you, make sure that it lines up with the principles of God, His way of doing things.

By the circumstances we face. Sometimes God uses the circumstances in our lives to direct us in a certain way. When a door closes, usually God opens another.

Use the situations you're facing as an opportunity to look to God for answers and determine which direction you should go. When you face difficulty, unbearable pressures, a unique situation, or even sickness or death, God, in His quiet way, without you even realizing it, is looking out for your best interest. He is guiding you through thick and thin, through good and bad. Trust Him in all your circumstances; He is trying to not only get your attention but lead you in the right direction.

THE PROPHETIC WORD OF GOD

The Word of God is a prophetic book containing many prophecies which have come to fruition. In fact, Jesus fulfilled thirty-three of them in one day.[32]

Prophecy is history written in advance, the foretelling of future events.[33] This prophetic witness of God can be both corporate and individual.

Corporately, it's the means by which God brings forth His plans, predictions, and judgments. For example, God spoke to the nation of Israel through prophets who declared His messages to the people. Most times, these prophets received words of God directly to be given at a future date, but they also sometimes came through visions and dreams. Interpreting them was a gift from God to confirm that He alone gives prophecy.

Individually, God spoke specific messages to those who were about to experience important events. The Bible contains many examples of this.

Joseph had numerous dreams which predicted what was going to happen to him (Genesis 37:5–7, 9–10). He became known to his family as a dreamer (Genesis 37:19).

---

[32] Rex Humbard, *The Prophecy Bible* (Akron, OH: Rex Humbard Ministries, 1985), 38.
[33] Ibid., 31.

Abraham received a vision in which God spoke to him about finally becoming a father (Genesis 15:1–4). This was later confirmed when the Lord personally appeared before Abraham and Sarah (Genesis 18:1–10).

Both Cornelius and Peter received separate visions from the Lord about what was going to happen to the Gentiles concerning salvation. Afterward, when they finally met, it became apparent that the Gentiles were able to receive the gospel just like the Jews (Acts 10:1–48).

Even today, God speaks to us through His Word. When we read certain passages, the Holy Spirit reveals to us new insights about God or ourselves. Or perhaps He points out something we need to change or focuses our attention on a certain sin we need to confess and deal with. This is why the Bible is so prophetic; it causes us to change our ways and focus on what's important.

God's prophetic witness can also be corporate and individual at the same time. This was seen in how God helped Joseph interpret the dreams of the butler and baker (Genesis 40), as well as the dreams of Pharaoh (Genesis 41:1–36). It was seen, too, when God helped Daniel interpret King Nebuchadnezzar's concealed dream of the *"great image"* (Daniel 2:31). This was God's way of imparting to the people knowledge of the coming eras and how they would be divided until the end of time.

This brings us to the prophetic law of double reference, which refers to the phenomenon of certain prophecies being fulfilled twice, once very soon after the giving of the prophecy, and again in the distant future.[34] Nebuchadnezzar realized that he was represented at the beginning of the great image prophecy; he was the golden head of the statue. This fulfilled his part of the prophecy, but the other parts were a prophetic witness of what the future was to bring forth.

Jesus also provided an example of this by first predicting the destruction of the temple, which occurred in A.D. 70. This event also symbolized *"the beginning of sorrows"* (Matthew 24:8), leading to the distant future when humanity would have to prepare to face the last days. Jesus gave these signs of what was to come well before His second coming (Matthew 24).

The Book of Revelation is the ultimate prophecy, the complete endgame consummation of all things. John wrote this prophetic book from the island of Patmos under the influence of the Spirit's power. God gave him the prophecy so we could know what is going to happen in the future.

The beginning chapters concern the church and what is to happen to her. This is followed by a description of the opening of the seals which begin the tribulation period, followed by the trumpets and bowls, establishment of the nation of Israel as

---

[34] Ibid.

God's chosen witness, and the revealing of the Antichrist, the Beast, and Satan. Next follows the pouring out of God's wrath and judgments and the final Armageddon, at which Jesus will be victorious and establish His domain on the earth, defeating Satan and his regime. We then read about the bema seat of Christ and the great white throne judgment.

After this comes the renewal of everything and a description of the eternal bliss we will experience while spending eternity with God. This most assuredly should cause us to know that God absolutely holds the future in His hands.

THE BURDEN OF GOD

When God gave prophets words to speak, or write, they were given a burden, or unction, to deliver the message, thus freeing themselves of it. They would experience no release from this burden until it was fulfilled or accomplished through declaration.

Habakkuk felt a burden for his people (Habakkuk 1:1) because he saw their stubbornness and hardheartedness and wondered why they didn't turn to God and change from their sinful ways. God ended up using Habakkuk as His voice of judgment. Even when it didn't seem like his words were heard, the prophet soon realized that only the just would live by faith but God's ways would always prevail (Habakkuk 2:4). Eventually God would become the joy and strength of our salvation (Habakkuk 3:17–19).

This is why God gives us these burdens. They become prophetically personal. He wants us to turn back to Him, to see that He holds our lives and future in His hands.

Jonah learned about this prophetic burden the hard way. He ran away from his burden to declare God's judgment on Nineveh. He thought that he could release himself of the burden by having the men aboard his ship throw him into the sea.

But God didn't accept this fate for him. Instead God decided to have a big fish swallow him, giving him three days to contemplate what to do. Jonah only became free from his burden when he released the words of God's judgment to Nineveh.

God does the same for us today. He has given us the gift of prophecy through the Holy Spirit. After Pentecost, people began to feel the urge to speak prophetic words of God through His Spirit, which came about either in a known language or in tongues. This gift is mostly used for edification, but it comes with the same burden felt by the Old Testament prophets. Paul explains how it works:

> Pursue love, and desire spiritual gifts, but especially that you may prophesy. For he who speaks in a tongue does not speak to men but to God, for no one understands him; however, in the spirit he speaks mysteries. But he who prophesies speaks edification

and exhortation and comfort to men. He who speaks in a tongue edifies himself, but he who prophesies edifies the church. (1 Corinthians 14:1–4)

Paul had the problem of sometimes hearing too many people speak prophecies on the same occasion. He limited the number of prophecies to no more than three (1 Corinthians 14:27–29).

Prophecy was also used as a sign to unbelievers that God was the one who had given the prophetic words to indicate that He was in their midst (1 Corinthians 14:23–25).

The burden of God through prophecy is a reminder that God truly is personal, because He wants us to know how the future will affect us.

God also gives us personal burdens, or promptings, which we must obey. He will guide us to fulfill special missions, projects, or ministries. If you feel an inner burden, you must be certain that it comes from God. You can test this by confirming that its purpose is God-focused and not self-focused. It will always be confirmed by the Scriptures (2 Timothy 3:16) and by the peace of God which passes all understanding (Philippians 4:7).

THE DETERMINING CIRCUMSTANCES OF GOD

The most dramatic question we can ask is, "Why, God? Why have You allowed this to happen to me?" We feel especially confused when we face a circumstance that seems to be more than we can bear. We want our lives to be perfect. When we view God as a personal and loving Father, how can He then allow such bad things to happen to us, devastating us to the point that we want to turn our backs on Him?

There are close to eight billion people living on the earth and each has a personal story. Some are rich, but most are poor. Some face death, whether through starvation, sickness, disease, war, or natural causes. Some face hardships, whether psychological or physical. Others have it easy. Then there are those who live with disabilities—the blind, deaf, mute, the handicapped, and the scared.

Do we blame God for allowing these things to happen?

The fact is that God created everything perfectly good in the beginning. There was no sin or flaw in creation. The course of human history was designed by God to proceed according to His plan. Every person would have lived out their lives in a perfect state.

But when sin entered the scheme of things, it affected every aspect of creation. Yet God knew this, too, and allowed the effects of sin to take hold. As a result, pain and suffering became part of our reality. Humans would have to deal with death as a natural consequence of life.

It isn't that God made this happen. We did. But God had to allow the effects of sin to run their course. For how long? Only God knows. Humanity's free will and act of disobedience caused the perfect world to become the one we have now.

In fact, it was inevitable that sin would enter the world. If God had stepped in to stop Adam and Eve from sinning, someone else would have corrupted the world in their place.

The fact is that God only had one perfect plan of restoration. Jesus, the son of man, could only die once, and it had to happen according to God's timing.

Even after His victory over sin and death, our world remains imperfect. There are still challenges. Our glorified transformation cannot take place until the history of humanity runs its course. We must therefore live faithfully as best we can despite our circumstances. Jesus gave us hope in our position with God, and the faith to believe in Him to overcome our circumstances.

Since circumstances are a part of life, God uses them in two ways: to cause us to trust Him and to lead us in a certain direction. They also vary in length, from a momentary mishap to a lifelong addiction. We must realize that God knows everything that will happen to us and walk alongside us through it.

This should cause us to look within to see what motivates us. How do we understand ourselves in the midst of our circumstances? What is God trying to say to us? Since we live our lives by faith in God, we must trust in His process. Persevering through our circumstances while trusting that God is with us brings out our best. This is how we change. This is how we inspire hope. This is how we let others see who God is.

God allows us to go through these situations in order to change us for the better. From our human perspective, it can be tough. It may seem like things are getting worse instead of better. But when we look at it from God's point of view, we see the big picture. It's hard to appreciate the big picture when we have to deal with what's right in front of us, but it can be summarized by the message God gave to the church at Pergamos:

> He who has an ear, let him hear what the Spirit says to the churches. To him who overcomes I will give some of the hidden manna to eat. And I will give him a white stone, and on the stone a new name written which no one knows except him who receives it. (Revelation 2:17)

The hidden manna is the spiritual food God gives us to help us deal with our circumstances. The white stone mentioned in this passage is the not-guilty ticket Jesus gave us after His victory on the cross. The new name is the name God gives to us because of what we've gone through.

Each person will go through something unique. Sure, we may experience similar challenges and understand each other to some extent, but in the end our circumstances are special and help us better understand ourselves and develop a deeper faith in God. We overcome what is before us for God's purposes and glory.

We overcome because Jesus overcame. We overcome so that we can become more like Him. God wants to present us as His own, worthy of belonging to Him because He died for us and paid for us.

Circumstances can be specific and personal. How we deal with them will lead us to a greater understanding of ourselves and what our lives will mean in the end—all for the glory of God.

CHAPTER TEN
THE GOD CONNECTION

THERE ARE THOSE who wonder if there is more to life than we perceive. When life is difficult to deal with, when it feels like we're just going through the motions without purpose, we question whether it's all worth it. When this happens, we search for a truth to provide some kind of meaning. Once we've found a reasonable answer, we become vibrant and functional again, living with all the vim and vigor we can muster.

The answers we come up with generally deal with how much wealth can we obtain, what kind of influence we can possess, what kind of relationship we can build, and what kind of personal fulfillment we can achieve. These are our most common priorities.

The most sought-after question relating to the meaning of life relates to God. Is He the answer we're looking for? And when He doesn't respond, do we give up on Him?

It all comes down to how we connect to God. This brings us to a deeper understanding of who He is. If we don't understand this connection, we won't understand the reality of God. We'll interpret His revelations incorrectly.

Sometimes when we connect with someone, we feel a spark of chemistry. If we get married, it's usually because of this kind of connection, this can't-live-without-you feeling that unites the two as one (Genesis 2:24).

As a married couple, we connect on three levels: the physical, emotional, and spiritual.

First, we express ourselves through intimate physical relations. The second connection is emotional, in which we express ourselves through our intelligence, will, and emotions. The third way is spiritual. We can express ourselves through a language that doesn't have to be spoken. We sense and feel the essence of who we are through an inner awareness.

When we think about God, we must consider not only who He is but what He is. This is how we connect with Him.

God is a spirit being with no material body. This requires us to utilize our spirit-natures to give us a better understanding of Him. Since we can't associate with Him in the physical sense, most of us use our mental facilities to try and connect. We can succeed, to an extent, because we express our thoughts and feelings to God and He can do the same with us. We enjoy free access to each other.

But how else are we going to pray to Him unless we express ourselves through our own souls? Even if we utilize our intelligence, will, and emotions, this still doesn't

CHAPTER TEN: THE GOD CONNECTION

fully connect us to God because our minds cannot comprehend or understand God. If we try to connect with Him mentally, it won't fully succeed.

Those who don't believe in God find it difficult to understand how one can connect with Him. They can't figure it out. Since they can't connect with Him, they don't believe in Him. This is because they've neglected the only way by which a human can completely and fully connect to God. It can only be done through spiritual means. Only our spirit-natures can fully comprehend and understand God. Spirit to spirit, this is a straight line to God. He designed us this way, in order for us to fellowship with Him.

If you want to connect with God, you must use your spirit. The Bible explains this by giving us three different connections that are based on a type of person: the spiritual person, the natural person, and the carnal person.

THE SPIRITUAL PERSON	THE NATURAL PERSON	THE CARNAL PERSON	
God's Spirit ↓	The World's Spirit ↓	God's Spirit ↓	The World's Spirit ↓
Our Spirit (Regenerated Spirit) ↓	Our Spirit (Unregenerated Spirit) ↓	Our Spirit (Regenerated Spirit) ↓	
Our Soul ↓	Our Soul ↓	Our Soul ↓	
Our Flesh	Our Flesh	Our Flesh	
A God-Centered Life	*A Self-Centered Life*	*A World-Centered Life*	

Before anything else, we need to be motivated. Where does our motivation come from? Our spirit-natures. From there, our connection type affects our soul. At that point, we use our understanding of truth to make decisions. This then results in the type of action we want to physically accomplish.

GOD'S SPIRIT

God's Spirit is who He is. He is absolutely boundless. He sees everything, knows everything, and directs everything to fulfill His purposes. Though God can speak to our minds and reveal Himself and His truth personally—such as how He reveals

Himself through the nine witnesses we've previously discussed—we really begin to understand the heart of God when the communication happens in our spirits.

He wants to communicate with us and desires for us to be aware of His infinite wisdom and perpetual truths. Whatever we face in life, whether it's with ourselves, others, or circumstances, God's Spirit is always ready to connect with us, thus ensuring that He is there to help when needed.

Paul writes about this connection with God:

> But God has revealed them to us through His Spirit. For the Spirit searches all things, yes, the deep things of God. For what man knows the things of a man except the spirit of the man which is in him? Even so no one knows the things of God except the Spirit of God. Now we have received, not the spirit of the world, but the Spirit who is from God, that we might know the things that have been freely given to us by God. (1 Corinthians 2:10–12)

This wisdom from God can be known by how it's presented. When we gain an insight, we sometimes wonder whether it came from God. His truth and wisdom will always be confirmed by His Word, and it will always come with a peace that passes all understanding. James 3:17 says, *"But the wisdom that is from above is first pure, then peaceable, gentle, willing to yield, full of mercy and good fruits, without partiality and without hypocrisy."* This is how we know, from within our spirit, that the wisdom being given to us comes from God.

THE WORLD'S SPIRIT

The Bible says that Satan is the prince of this world (John 14:30). Whether people believe this or not, we can see that the world's motives can be fairly selfish. Since Satan is one of the most selfish beings ever known, we can figure out that his influences have crept into our way of life. He has the ability to deceive us into doing things we shouldn't be doing. It also doesn't help that he takes advantage of us by tempting us into committing sin.

Since Satan is a spirit being, he and his cohorts can influence our minds through our spirits. We must choose whether to do something about it—and it's a choice between doing things God's way or Satan's way. And Satan's way is the world's way.

The world has accepted the truths that Satan has propagated. These truths tell us that we don't need God, that we don't need to live by His truth, we can live the way we want, and we can achieve our own happiness by doing whatever's necessary to obtain it. This is the kind of wisdom the world wants us to live by.

James 3:14–16 explains how this wisdom is expressed:

> But if you have bitter envy and self-seeking in your hearts, do not boast and lie against the truth. This wisdom does not descend from above, but is earthly, sensual, demonic. For where envy and self-seeking exist, confusion and every evil thing are there.

We must therefore be diligent in understanding how these connections work. We must be mindful of who is influencing us, God or the world. Which one do we want to follow? At any moment, we either obey the Spirit of God or the spirit of the world.

OUR SPIRIT

Our spirit-natures are God-conscious, because we are connected with God through our spirit. This is our spiritual conduit to the supernatural world.

Our spirit-natures can be either unregenerated or regenerated. When we have an unregenerated spirit, we are separated from God, less aware of Him and more aware of those invisible forces outside of God. When we have a regenerated spirit, bringing us closer to God, we are more aware of Him and less aware of those influential forces which try to persuade us to distance ourselves from Him.

When God created Adam and Eve, their spirits had total control of their being. It controlled their mental and physical realms. They obeyed God. Their spirits entrusted their being to focus on Him. He became their number one priority.

After they sinned, however, their spirits no longer had control over their being. Their flesh took over. Their desire to obey God and worship Him no longer took precedence. Their flesh prevailed and they focused their priorities on themselves.

This still hasn't changed today. Our spirit-natures are just as selfish as before. We pursue our fleshly desires and worldly fulfillments from a selfish fallen nature. This is why our spirits need to be transformed, so they can be used in the right way. Only God can enact this kind of change. Only He can renew our spirits so they can be used to connect with Him.

God has provided a way for us to be restored, for our spirits to once again take control of our being.[35]

OUR SOUL

Our souls are that part of us which is self-conscious. They contain the essence of who we are.

Watchman Nee tells us that we are made conscious of our existence by the work of our souls. The soul is the seat of our personality, and the elements which make us

---

[35] This was discussed in Chapter Seven. The spirit and the flesh forever strive against each other, trying to take control.

human belong to the soul. The intellect, thought, ideals, emotion, discernment, and decisions are but various experiences of the soul.[36]

When our flesh hurts, it affects the soul. When our spirits are troubled and we have doubts, it affects the soul. And when the flesh and spirit war against each other, it affects the soul.

The spirit and flesh are completely separate. In fact, they are opposites. They cannot connect or communicate with each other. Like oil and water, they never mix.

This is where the soul comes in. The soul is the mediator between the spirit and the flesh. It's the buffer zone, the caught-in-the-middle individual who can't decide what to do. Eventually the soul must decide whether to fulfill its fleshly desires or its spiritual yearnings.

The soul is who we are. It possesses our intellect, which includes a range of personal traits, such as our personality, our gifts and abilities, and the knowledge and experience we have accumulated throughout our lives. God has given us this ability to learn so we can make our own decisions in how to live. This is where our will and volition come in. They help us to fulfill our desires. They give us purpose and goals to pursue so our lives can have meaning.

Eventually our soul experiences, those rooted deep within us, express themselves through our emotions. From our influences and motivations, whether they come from God or the world, our soul must decide what to do.

OUR FLESH

Our flesh—in other words, the body—is that part of us which is world-conscious. It houses our spirit and soul and can become the most important part of who we are.

When we look our best, it's an expression of our true inner self. It says to others that we like ourselves—and if we look good on the outside, we feel good on the inside. This helps to demonstrate healthy self-esteem.

There are, however, times when we view others according to a certain standard. In other words, we end up judging them. This judgment is part of our culture and it's definitely a result of our fleshly nature. It makes us worldly. We judge others by how they look, what they possess, and what they do. We surrender to this vain mentality because our flesh wants control. It wants to rule. It wants us to be better than everyone else.

When it has preeminence, the flesh can become very needy. We become slaves to it by taking care of it, fulfilling its needs, and satisfying its desires. When this becomes our priority, the development of our spiritual and natural character becomes secondary.

---

[36] Watchman Nee, *The Spiritual Man* (New York, NY: Christian Fellowship Publishers, 1968), 35.

Are we going to allow the flesh to have control and focus our lives on the vain things in life? Which part of life is the most rewarding and fulfilling? Which is the most important to focus on—the spiritual, the natural, or the carnal?

THE SPIRITUAL PERSON

The truly spiritual person has a regenerated spirit. This comes about at the moment we accept Jesus into our lives. God gives those who are His a new spirit, a transformed spirit. This spirit is born from above and is given to us so we can understand God and His truth. Once we undergo this rebirth of our spirit-nature, we have a sense of being continually connected to God. When we're in right standing with Him, it's a spiritual connection we feel in our daily lives.

This spiritual connection begins with God, our primary influence and the source of our motivation. We experience God and discover His truth in our renewed spirit, enhancing our relationship with Him. These experiences are then absorbed into our soul and memories. They infiltrate our intellect, will, and emotions, establishing the foundation of our identity with God.

The result is that we live for God. We develop a God-centered life in which He is our highest priority. His purposes become ours, and He becomes our reason for living. Our attitudes and actions reveal this spiritual life because we focus everything we say and do on worshiping God.

The Bible contains many references to the spiritual person:

> But the hour is coming, and now is, when the true worshipers will worship the Father in spirit and truth; for the Father is seeking such to worship Him. God is Spirit, and those who worship Him must worship in spirit and truth. (John 4:23–24)

> And those who are Christ's have crucified the flesh with its passions and desires. If we live in the Spirit, let us also walk in the Spirit. (Galatians 5:24–25)

> Coming to Him as to a living stone, rejected indeed by men, but chosen by God and precious, you also, as living stones, are being built up a spiritual house, a holy priesthood, to offer up spiritual sacrifices acceptable to God through Jesus Christ. (1 Peter 2:4–5)

THE NATURAL PERSON

The truly natural person has an unregenerated spirit. This comes about at the moment of conception. We are born into this world with a spirit-nature that has been corrupted by sin, meaning that it's natural for us to be sinful and selfish. We spontaneously sin against everyone, including ourselves, and especially God. This is the way we are. We can't help it; we're human.

We also can't help the fact that we're all in the same boat, trying to survive in a world that brings so many challenges upon us.

Sometimes the world can be cruel. At other times, it can be wonderful. For the most part, if we're sincere and honest, we do our best to help each other out. But we also tend to seek out our own interests. We pursue our dreams and hope the world can help us achieve them. This actually does bring us together as a species; we function well this way, with the world motivating us.

We are naturally connected by the influences of the world. Experiencing the world and its truths, however, points us away from God. The world doesn't acknowledge Him, which results in us living only for ourselves. We develop a self-centered life with our highest priority being our own purposes. We are our own reason for living.

The Bible also has much to say about the natural person:

> So I perceived that nothing is better than that a man should rejoice in his own works, for that is his heritage. For who can bring him to see what will happen after him? (Ecclesiastes 3:22)

> It is sown a natural body, it is raised a spiritual body. There is a natural body, and there is a spiritual body. (1 Corinthians 15:44)

> But the natural man does not receive the things of the Spirit of God, for they are foolishness to him; nor can he know them, because they are spiritually discerned. (1 Corinthians 2:14)

THE CARNAL PERSON

The truly carnal person has a regenerated spirit, but it has become stagnate due to neglect. He stands on the fence of both worlds. Even though he has a regenerated spirit, he would rather follow the fleshly side of his nature. He knows that God is there, but he would rather set Him aside. Pleasing his own selfish desires is more important.

Because of this, his fellowship with God is torn. God waits patiently for him, allowing him to follow his reprobate ways, so that perhaps he will come to his senses and return to the God whom he earlier found and accepted.

This desire for the world has such a person living a life for himself. He develops a world-centered life, making himself his own priority and living for his own purposes. His life revolves around his own pleasures and fulfilling his fleshly desires. His attitudes and actions reveal a worldly life.

Here's what the Bible says about the carnal person:

> O wretched man that I am! Who will deliver me from this body of death? (Romans 7:24)

> For those who live according to the flesh set their minds on the things of the flesh, but those who live according to the Spirit, the things of the Spirit. For to be carnally minded is death, but to be spiritually minded is life and peace. Because the carnal mind is enmity against God; for it is not subject to the law of God, nor indeed can be. So then, those who are in the flesh cannot please God. (Romans 8:5–8)

> And I, brethren, could not speak to you as to spiritual people but as to carnal, as to babes in Christ. I fed you with milk and not with solid food; for until now you were not able to receive it, and even now you are still not able; for you are still carnal. For where there are envy, strife, and divisions among you, are you not carnal and behaving like mere men? (1 Corinthians 3:1–3)

What kind of person will you become? Which are you right now? Which do you want to become? It begins with what influences you and ends with worship.

Hopefully you choose to focus on developing your spiritual life, because it's more than worth it. When God becomes part of your life, nothing is more fulfilling than Him. He loves us and desires to save, sanctify, and stamp us as one of His own so we can spend eternity with Him. This can only happen when we fully connect ourselves to God.

CONNECTING WITH GOD THROUGH SALVATION

Salvation is a three-step process which God established and provided through His Son, Jesus Christ. He made it available to everyone as a free gift, which is accepted by faith, so we can have a personal relationship with Him now and forever.

Justification. This is the first step, and it brings freedom from the penalty of sin. When we accept Jesus as our Savior, the one who took our place in judgment, we stand blameless before God because we belong to Him. The Bible calls this being *"in Christ"* (2 Corinthians 5:17). He took upon Himself our sins and atoned for them through His death and resurrection, meaning that His righteousness can now be ours. We are therefore justified because of our connection with Him.

Sanctification. This is the second step, and it brings us freedom from the power of sin. Now that we belong to God, we are set apart to live holy lives for His glory. Jesus becomes our Lord, because He works to change us from within, sanctifying us so we can become more like Him. We are therefore sanctified, because connecting with Him causes us to become joint-heirs with Him, both in life and in death.

Glorification. This is the third step, and it brings us freedom from the presence of sin. When the last trumpet sounds, when Jesus returns to the earth in His second coming to receive those who are His, we will all be changed in the twinkling of an eye. We will be transformed from our corruptible selves to incorruptible, from mortal to immortal. This will be our final victory and glory. Jesus will then become our King for all eternity, because of what He has done for us.

We are connected to God because of Him. Would you accept Jesus Christ into your hearts right now to become your Savior, Lord, and King? This is the only way to have a relationship with God and discover His way of life.

PRIORITIZING OUR SPIRITUAL LIFE

Since connecting with God is done through our spirit-natures, we must give priority to the spiritual life in order to enhance our relationship with God. If we want to know more about Him and His way of life, we need to live and think differently. We're so inclined to view our world from the physical and mental realms that we rarely consider it from a spiritual lens. It's normal for our fleshly natures to take control of our thoughts, desires, and actions.

We easily relate to the world from a physical and mental perspective. Spiritually, it's an unreliable guessing game. This is why we need to take the time to develop the spiritual part inside us. The more we practice utilizing it, the more we'll be able to understand how it works.

This is why Enoch was such an interesting person. Genesis 5:24 says, *"And Enoch walked with God; and he was not, for God took him."* What does this verse mean? It doesn't mean that God physically walked beside Enoch, but rather that Enoch devoted his life to God. He was a highly spiritual person with his priority set toward God at all times. He was connected to God in all his daily activities. He related with God first through his spirit, which then influenced the rest of his being. His thinking and living flourished from the spiritual.

The final two verses in Jude explain that Enoch was also a prophet, prophesying about the things of God to those around him:

> Now Enoch, the seventh from Adam, prophesied about these men also, saying, "Behold, the Lord comes with ten thousands of His saints, to execute judgment on all, to convict all who are ungodly among them of all their ungodly deeds which they have committed in an ungodly way, and of all the harsh things which ungodly sinners have spoken against Him." (Jude 14–15)

During a time when people lived their lives predominately through their fleshly nature, it's amazing that Enoch managed to be different. The Spirit of God came upon him continuously, a testament to his dedication and understanding of the spiritual life. One can only imagine how others viewed him when they saw him approaching! "Look out! Here comes Enoch. How is he going to judge us this time?"

This is the kind of attitude from others we're afraid of. We're leery about those who live like Enoch. This is because we don't understand the spiritual life. We're afraid of where it may take us.

God wants us to know about the spiritual life because this is how we learn about Him and become most fulfilled. The physical and mental realms can only take us to a certain level, whereas the spiritual realm takes us to a higher level—a level of fulfilment. The spiritual will always enhance the mental and physical, but our personal growth and understanding of life mostly comes from the spiritual side.

Enoch was so used by God, and so fulfilled in his life, that God took him home to heaven without experiencing death. This story gives us a great way to understand the importance of the spiritual life!

Walking with God means that our worship, purpose, and priorities are focused on God, and this is achieved when we allow our regenerated spirits to exercise control.

We will feel more complete when we utilize every part of us, including the spiritual. When we don't use our spirit-natures, we feel empty and unfulfilled. Will you take the challenge of pursuing your spiritual nature and developing it? There is nothing more fulfilling. Lead by your spirit and balance everything else behind it.

CHAPTER ELEVEN
THE SPHERE OF TRUTH AND THE CIRCLE OF FAITH

TRUTH IS SO important because it's the foundation which determines who we are and what we will become. Truth is worth pursuing and building our lives upon.

This is what separates us from the animals. We're rational beings who use reason and intellect to distinguish what is important in order to help us make decisions and guide us into doing what needs to be done to maintain a life of happiness and purpose.

So how do we find this truth?

The truth related to our existence, for example, has been debated throughout history by intellectuals who have explained what has happened to us, why we're here, and how we can solidify our knowledge. We look for a personal truth we can reasonably believe in.

Even though truth seems subjective when it comes to personal belief, we tend to scrutinize what others say and measure their words carefully to see if they follow our beliefs. Yet we must understand that determining which truth suits us best must come from conviction based on a solid and reasonable foundation. When we realize that God is the only reasonable answer, we do our best to seek Him out. This is done by discovering the revelations of God.

If He exists, we can understand our purpose. If He does not exist, we must find our own truth. The problem is that God is many things to different people, and thus our understanding of truth is varied. This is why we must correctly discern the revelations of God, to understand Him and His truth.

And since we are real, we can understand who God is by looking at ourselves and seeing how these revelations affect us.

THE COMPLETE SPECTRUM

Many people only perceive the visible aspect of life because believing in something you can see makes sense. It has a logic based on science, giving us the proof we need to declare what is fact and what isn't. We like to believe that truth can be proven naturally through physical evidence.

Then there are those who only look to the invisible aspect of life. For example, gurus explain that life is more spiritual than physical because truth can only be revealed from within. All logic and reason must be removed, they say, because they block the path of understanding truth which only arises from the divine inner soul.

Can God be included in our understanding of the physical world? Is it absurd to think that the physical world can be influenced through spiritual means? Some say yes and others say no. Hinduism declares that everything is God; He is revealed and seen through the physical world. Naturalists declare that the physical world can only be influenced and controlled through natural processes.

What then is the truth? Is God part of everything or is He separate from everything? Is He involved in every aspect of life or is He not?

We are naturally curious about how something invisible, like an energy force, can influence the visible world. If we only look at ourselves and nothing else, how can we explain our sentient existence contained within a physical body? Why do we disregard the evidence that reveals both the visible and invisible aspects of life functioning together? Why can't we utilize every aspect of who we are to solidify our understanding of truth?

Our understanding of truth, therefore, must arise from the complete spectrum of who we are. We are more than just the visible, more than just the invisible.

This is where the sphere of truth comes in, with its different perspectives. It will help us to understand how to get to the truth using every area of understanding to discover answers.

THE SPHERE OF TRUTH

What defines us as human beings? How does this help us define our truth? Most of our important decisions are based upon the sphere of truth, which in turn will help us develop a personal truth that we can live with and stand upon.

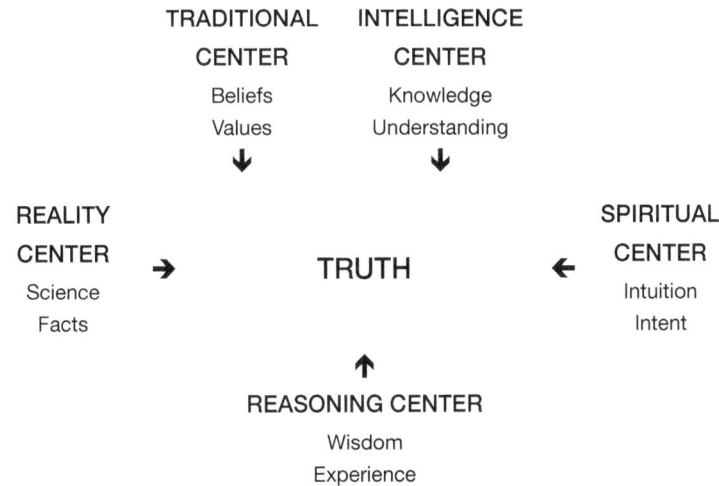

The sphere of truth consists of five areas which influence the decisions we make.

The first area is known as the reality center. This center looks at the physical evidence, the visible proofs of what we see with our eyes. This is the area where facts are confirmed by science. This approach to life is so automatic that we generally believe anything we can see. In this realm, results can be proven mathematically and scientifically.

The second area is the traditional center. This is what we believe in and trust. This area deals with the beliefs and values we were taught while growing up, whether religious or not, and which helped to influence the way we live. Some believe that we understand truth by believing in the traditional concepts we were taught. We believe that we can improve ourselves by standing on these traditions. They focus us on the most important part of life, which includes a belief and trust in God—or if not God, then something else.

The third area is the intelligence center. Our brains have the capacity to store a large amount of information. Throughout our years of living, we gain more and more knowledge and soon it becomes a repertoire of stored files which we can access when needed. With this comes understanding because in order to make sense out of something, we need to know the facts and how it affects the truth. We then can make an intelligent decision about what we are seeking.

The fourth area is the spiritual center. We operate in this realm by having a "gut feeling" that something unseen is going to happen. We can intuit when something isn't right. We may even sense a spiritual presence and perceive how it wants to influence us. Some people have more insight into this area than others because they're more sensitive to spiritual matters. They better understand people's intent—what they want and even how God wants us to live.

The fifth area is the reasoning center. This is the apex of the decision-making process and it determines where we stand on any particular point. In this realm, we collect all the facts, intelligence, and traditional and spiritual insights we have been exposed to. We then decide what the truth is and what we should do. Our reasoning is personal and based on our experiences and circumstances. Whatever we've reasoned out becomes the truth we live with. It becomes a part of us and influences who we become.

THE ELEPHANT SCENARIO

To explain how the sphere of truth works, let's walk through something I call the elephant scenario. When we encounter an elephant—at the zoo, for example—we automatically recognize it from the reality center. We have no reason to doubt that we've seen an elephant. We are sure.

CHAPTER ELEVEN: THE SPHERE OF TRUTH AND THE CIRCLE OF FAITH

When we go to our traditional center, we remember from what we've been taught what an elephant looks like and how it acts. We believe what we've been told about elephants.

From our intelligence center, we open our internal files on the subject of elephants and recall that they are huge and gray, having big ears, long tusks, and elongated trunks.

We don't even have to consult our spiritual center, although we can perceive that elephants are aware of the world around them, for they seem to be afraid of mice, for example. When they see a mouse, they usually run away, perhaps to prevent being tripped or to avoid stepping on it.

When we look to our reasoning center, we will have no doubts whatsoever, no reason to deny that what we have seen is the truth. The animal we see is one hundred percent an elephant.

But what if the elephant we see is purple in color? How would we deal with that?

We would begin to question the reality of what we're seeing. The reality center would look to the intelligence center for answers to see if there are any facts available on purple elephants.

We would then look to our traditional center to see if anyone actually believes that purple elephants exist, perhaps through secondhand or historical knowledge. We may hope that someone else can verify that they're seeing the same thing we are. More than anything, we want others to confirm that what we're seeing is real.

We then proceed to our spiritual center and wonder if we may sense anything unusual. Maybe the animal is a type of illusion, or a figment of our imagination. Perhaps it's a spiritual being that only appears in the guise of a purple elephant.

We finally end up at our reasoning center, which is where we contemplate whether purple elephants exist. We conclude that there is no such thing as a purple elephant. We keep repeating this in our minds, just to confirm that we're not going crazy.

When we consider how the sphere of truth is used, we begin to perceive that we need to be careful. The sphere of truth can lead us astray.

We will now test this by examining a story which contains no deceptions whatsoever.

A PARABLE OF NO DECEIT

Consider the true story of a man in his twenties who loved the arts and the classics. Stephen grew up admiring what his parents brought home with them. When he was old enough to receive his inheritance, he bought his own home and couldn't wait to furnish it with everything he loved, including: a three-seated couch with high back arches and floral patterns, a loveseat with the same design, robust maple chairs, a red kitchen table, white-marbled countertops, light-colored tapestries, and black cherry hardwood floors.

But the most important part of Stephen's collection was his paintings. He loved them because they were authentic and original. He had spent hundreds of thousands of dollars to obtain them.

One day, Stephen met a man with the same interests. In fact, Roger was an amazing painter and furniture-maker. They went on many adventures, looking to purchase items at auctions. They became close friends and did everything together.

Eventually Stephen achieved his goal of furnishing the perfect home. He beamed at this accomplishment. He had accumulated everything he wanted to the point that others wanted to tour his house to admire his incredible collection.

There came a day when Roger came for a visit to inform him of something: he had to leave for good, and most likely they would never see each other again. Stephen was heartbroken, since Roger was the only real friend he had.

Not long after, Stephen began to grow bored and unfulfilled. He had nothing to do anymore since his house was complete. All he could do now was look at what he had collected.

Soon he invited experts from nearby museums and auction houses to see what all his possessions might be worth. When they examined everything, they were astounded to discover that all the items were fakes.

What had happened? Roger had created replicas of everything Stephen owned, then stole the originals and left the counterfeits in their place.

While reading this story, were you, like Stephen, deceived? We experience such a languishing feeling when we realize that our lives could be founded on a lie.

The sphere of truth can be used to find any kind of truth, even a deceptive one. These counterfeits can appear to be genuine. They can make sense and seem logical. In a world where truth is relative, we may be persuaded that it doesn't matter how we live our lives, as long as we live with conviction.

THE CIRCLE OF FAITH

Of all the decisions that are most important, none is greater than your decision about God. Everything else is secondary. It's vital that we learn the proper concept of God so we can build our lives around Him.

How do we do this? By adding another component to the sphere of truth. This new component will help to build and strengthen the truth we believe in.

> Now faith is the substance of things hoped for, the evidence of things not seen...

CHAPTER ELEVEN: THE SPHERE OF TRUTH AND THE CIRCLE OF FAITH

> But without faith it is impossible to please Him, for he who comes to God must believe that He is, and that He is a rewarder of those who diligently seek Him. (Hebrews 11:1, 6)

This new component, faith, is what keeps our truth strong and alive. It keeps us going. Nothing is greater than having faith in yourself and in someone you can trust, especially God.

The Message Bible puts it this way:

> The fundamental fact of existence is that this trust in God, this faith, is the firm foundation under everything that makes life worth living. It's our handle on what we can't see. The act of faith is what distinguished our ancestors, set them above the crowd.
>
> By faith, we see the world called into existence by God's word, what we see created by what we don't see. (Hebrews 11:1–3, MSG)

With unwavering faith, we are able to believe in something that is unseen. Whether or not a person is religious, they deploy faith, often without being aware of it. Those who don't believe in God still believe in something; their faith is merely focused on something else. Even an evolutionist applies faith toward their belief in a chance happening, a scenario whereby the universe sprang up on its own.

This is why faith is necessary in finding a truth that's worth pursuing. The circle of faith is an important component of the sphere of truth. It enhances our lives and confirms to us that the truth we believe in is the truth that has been revealed. This becomes a revelation.

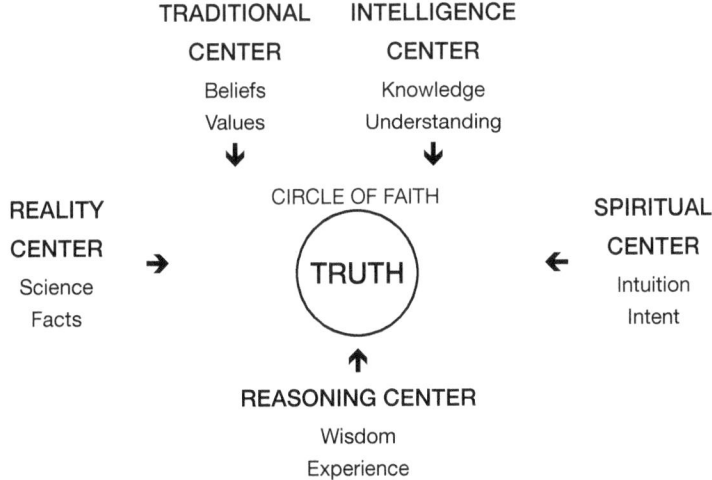

Faith that's rooted deep in our soul is that part of us which believes in who we are. It permeates every aspect of our being, uniting our various parts.

God has given each of us a measure of faith because we need it in order to survive. Without it, we would have no hope. We wouldn't be able to accomplish anything. Through the course of finding the truth, faith acts as a catalyst. It assists us in making decisions, which in turn helps us to believe in a personal truth.

There is a measure of faith in each of us. Some have a large portion; others have a small one. For example, Abraham displayed a great amount of faith throughout his life.

And then we encounter Gideon, who had a smaller portion. Gideon tested his lack of faith by asking God to perform certain impossible tasks. Once God answered these requests, he trusted in the faith he had, focused it on God, and rose to the occasion. He ended up accomplishing exploits beyond his imagination (Judges 6:11 to Judges 8:32).

No matter how small your faith is, you can still use it in a tremendous way. Jesus told His disciples, *"[I]f you have faith as a mustard seed [the smallest of all seeds], you will say to this mountain, 'Move from here to here,' and it will move; and nothing will be impossible for you"* (Matthew 17:20). When we step out in faith, we will be amazed at how greatly we benefit.

In 1 Corinthians 13:13, Paul wrote, *"And now abide faith, hope, love, these three; but the greatest of these is love."* These three qualities are the primary traits of influence. They fuse themselves to our will, emotion, and intellect. They contribute to our attitudes. They help in our need to accomplish things. They contribute to our relationships. They influence our decisions and direct us toward the truth. Let us use these qualities, especially our faith, to believe in a truth that's worth living for.

THE FOUR TYPES OF PEOPLE

We are all gifted differently from each other, with unique abilities and talents that identify us. Our most obvious gifts are the ones others can see and appreciate—our athleticism, singing, dancing, musical skill, artistry, entrepreneurialism, organization, leadership, speaking, teaching, writing, etc.

These gifts are meaningful because they augment our purpose and self-worth. They generally don't affect how we view God, but we can use them to glorify Him as the One who gave us these gifts in the first place.

The gifts that affect our truth are mostly invisible. These include our moral compass, beliefs, values, spiritual insight, intellect, will, emotions, and personality traits. They can lead us in a certain direction, either toward God or away from Him.

There are four basic types of people, each with a specific influence that affects their view of God: the intellectual, traditionalist, spiritualist, and moralist. Whether singlehandedly or in combination, these each determine the truth we believe.

The intellectual. The first type of person is the intellectual. Such an individual has a very logical mind and can understand difficult concepts. They are usually mathematical and scientific in their thinking, and they base most of their decisions on fact. They easily believe in evidence that can be seen with the eyes.

Science on its own has the merit of logically explaining how everything works and fits together. It understands that the natural way of the world can be explained through natural means. But embracing your intellectual mindset means believing only what you can see through evidence.

Charles Darwin is an example of an intellectual. Using logical reasoning, he came up with the theory of evolution. Stephen Hawking, as well, follows this cerebral pattern; he used his gifting to explain the cause of the universe through natural processes without divine intervention.

These highly gifted thinkers relied on faith as well, one strictly focused on science. It led them away from any other possibility.

An intellectual's truth is a belief in naturalism because they see how perfectly science proves its worth. God doesn't exist to them because He appears to be absent. Evidence can only come from what they see with their eyes.

Still, there are many intellectuals who believe in God and their cognitive minds do not steer them away from Him. Their faith leads them to a belief in God both through the physical realm and through their own spirit-natures. Their intellect confirms that God is the master designer of both the physical world and the spiritual world. Only His intelligence could explain how everything came to exist.

The traditionalist. The second type of person is the traditionalist. Because they grew up in a certain way, they decide that it must be the right way to live. The truth they were given comes from those who have the benefit of experience, thus it seems to make sense.

Parents or guardians pass on their beliefs and values to the next generation, for whom this truth becomes the only one worth living by. They have no doubt about this truth. How can they not follow the beliefs they were raised with?

Both the religious and non-religious follow tradition. It's a practical way to introduce truth into our thinking and way of life. No other truth is necessary, though, because this truth, taught from childhood, can become a person's identity. Whether such a person believes in God, upholding tradition is paramount.

Those traditionalists who find God realize that they have total freedom with Him. They aren't required to primarily keep the truth they were raised with; rather, they can check to see if they match up with God's way.

The spiritualist. The third type of person is the spiritualist. These are the ones who have a heightened awareness of the unseen. They are sensitive to the spiritual aspects of life and are usually open to anything that helps them understand their inner truth. New internal insights lead to moments of awakening.

Emotions play an important role for spiritualists. One day, they may follow a certain truth that brings them peace, and the next day they may be discouraged because it hasn't brought them to the answers they hoped to find. Their view of God can be unstable due to wavering.

They are driven by their searching desire to stabilize their spiritual self. They want to achieve the ultimate fulfillment; once they have achieved nirvana, their highest self, they will have found the truth. Most end up with an unreliable view of God because they are unsure of who He is. Only God can renew and stabilize our spirituality.

Those spiritualists who have found God find that their spirituality is strong and secure in Him. They achieve a deeper understanding of Him because He becomes personally involved within them. Inner fulfillment results from having a personal relationship with God, since He changes us from the inside. Most spiritualists try to change themselves on their own, but this will never work.

The moralist. The fourth type of person is the moralist. They live by a high ethical standard—and they expect others to live by the same standard. Their right-and-wrong approach to life causes them to develop a reward system; if they're good, life will be good, and if they're bad, life will punish them. This way of thinking limits them to a life of dos and don'ts, and their view of God is limited in the same manner. God becomes rather impersonal in this regard; they see Him as someone who can be used to gain favors.

God wants us to live good and righteous lives. He wants us to devoutly desire to be good people. This does bring us a sense of accomplishment and pride, knowing that we have lived well. The problem is that if we live this way without God, we end up living only for ourselves.

What good is it if we gain the whole world and lose our own soul? (Matthew 16:24–26) This pertains not only to wealth, but to that which we focus our lives on. Living for ourselves is a loss, but living for God is a gain.

The moralist who begins to understand that God is more than a judge and rewarder realizes that goodness can only come from Him. This is where our motivation should come from. God's righteousness is the most important factor to consider. We are good because God is good. This understanding comes when we realize that we don't have to be perfect; we can come before God the way we are. Through His forgiveness, we can be accepted by a personal God who loves us despite what we have done.

CHAPTER ELEVEN: THE SPHERE OF TRUTH AND THE CIRCLE OF FAITH

INCORPORATING HIS TRUTH

We establish and develop our own truths, and then we bring God into the picture. Sometimes we completely leave Him out or expect Him to fit into our beliefs, following the paths we have set out for ourselves. This is why our view of God can become distorted. We base everything on our own beliefs and perspectives. God's perspective doesn't appear to be important. Why? Our intellect can't comprehend Him, our traditions can't find Him, our spirituality can't reach Him, and our morality can't perceive Him. This is what happens when we live by our own truth.

It should be the other way around. Truth must be established and developed by God. We should fit ourselves into His truth, His standard. When we do this, we gain a better understanding of Him. We must incorporate His truth into our lives. This is why these nine revelations of God are so important. They reveal God's truth.

The sphere of truth and circle of faith allow us to find a truth that's worth living for. They give us the tools we need to find the truth behind everything.

This brings us to the most important question: who are we living for? It's the most important decision of all. Everything in our lives must either stem from God or something else. We can see this by utilizing the sphere of truth and circle of faith to understand the reality of God.

YOUR CHALLENGE

As an assignment, utilize the sphere of truth to prove the existence of God. Write down the knowledge and experience that have led you believe that God is involved in your life. How has He revealed Himself to you?

Perhaps you haven't used all of the five areas of influence—the reality center, traditional center, intelligence center, spiritual center, and reasoning center. Write a few paragraphs about each area. For example, will you choose to believe only in the reality center and forget about the others?

This exercise will challenge you to look deeper to discover the absolute truth about yourself and your belief in God. You will be able to determine your truth and live your life accordingly.

Consider God through these following statements, insights, and questions, each pertaining to one of the nine witnesses we've previously introduced.

THE REALITY CENTER

- The external witness: All of creation declares God's handiwork.
- The living witness: Jesus is God with us in person (Immanuel). The disciples saw Him with their own eyes.

THE TRADITIONAL CENTER

- The historical witness: We can see God's hand in providing a pathway of truth to guide humanity from the beginning of time to the end.
- The written witness: The Bible tells us how God revealed Himself to us and how His truths and values can be implemented in our lives.

THE INTELLIGENCE CENTER

- The external witness: Is it possible for God to exist from what we can see with our eyes?
- The internal witness: Does our conscience, knowing the difference between good and evil, come from God?
- The historical witness: Does history reveal God in any way?
- The written witness: Does the Bible come from God?
- The living witness: Is Jesus God's Son as well as God Himself?
- The transforming witness: Does God transform lives through the Holy Spirit?
- The special witness: Has God revealed Himself to you in a unique and special way?
- The personal witness: How has God personally affected you? Does this influence your belief in Him?
- The prophetic witness: Do the prophecies in the Bible, as well as the ones in your life, prove that God is real?

THE SPIRITUAL CENTER

- The internal witness: Do you sense God from within? Does your conscience tell you how to live?
- The transforming witness: Is the Holy Spirit real? How has He affected your life?
- The special witness: Have you experienced a God-moment in your life? Have you been converted?
- The personal witness: What are your spiritual giftings? How has God revealed Himself to you?

THE REASONING CENTER

- From your wisdom and experiences in life, are you aware of God?
- Will you believe in Him and His truth?
- Will you conform yourself to live life His way or follow your own way?

PART TWO

NOW THAT WE'VE undertaken a progressive understanding of who God is and how He has revealed Himself to us, we will examine each of the nine revelational witnesses again to see how we can glean an understanding of their truths and incorporate them into our lives. This will deepen our relationship with God, enhance how we live before Him, and endow us with a more fulfilled purpose in all areas of our lives.

We will divide this study of the nine witnesses into three sections:

1. Asking questions to see where we stand on these revelations.
2. Identifying the truths we can glean from these revelational witnesses of God.
3. Determining how we can incorporate these truths into our lives.

With the external witness, internal witness, written witness, and living witness, we will utilize the sphere of truth process to gain a better understanding of the truths we can learn at every level of reasoning. This will help us to develop practical ways to enhance our ability to live for God.

The remaining witnesses can be invitations for us to personally use the sphere of truth process to identify the truths we want to live by, confirming that they agree with the major revelations of God, which are His Word, His Son, and the Holy Spirit. These three revelations should also confirm our personal truth, which comes from the minor revelations of God.

CHAPTER TWELVE
THE EXTERNAL WITNESS

THE EXTERNAL WITNESS includes nature, all the physical features of the earth, our solar system, and the universe. Anything that is visible to the eye can be used as a witness to prove that these physical parts of our world and universe came into existence at some point in time.

We are also part of this visible evidence. The physical realm came into reality, revealing that only an eternal intelligence could have caused it all to happen.

SCRIPTURE REFERENCES

- Genesis 1:1–2:1–3
- Deuteronomy 4:39
- Psalm 8:3, 24:1
- Psalm 102:25–27, 147:4
- Nehemiah 9:6
- Isaiah 6:3, 40:25–26
- Isaiah 44:6–8, 45:18–19
- John 1:1–3, 10
- Romans 1:18–20
- Colossians 1:15–18
- Revelation 4:11

QUESTIONS

1. What is more believable—that someone, like God, could have always existed or that something or someone could only evolve from a beginning, from nothing? Whatever the causation, the birth of the physical universe resulted from an original source, which gave cause to everything.
2. How old is the earth and the universe?
3. Does Genesis 1 give us a reasonable answer as to how long it took for God to create everything?
4. How does this differ from what evolutionists say?
5. What part of nature impresses you the most?
6. What part of our earth and solar system impresses you the most?
7. What part of the universe impresses you the most?

8. Do the physical features of our world and universe prove that God exists?
9. Does experiencing nature bring you closer to God?
10. How does nature, the earth, and the universe reveal who God is in regards to His character and abilities?

ESTABLISHING TRUTH

Intellectually. The primary question concerning the external witness is the matter of understanding how the physical features of the earth and the universe came into existence. It points to a source of origin which gave cause to a physical reality.

There are only two views which could explain how everything came to be, and they are complete opposites: a cognitive awareness of the reality of God versus a cognitive understanding of whether something can come from nothing or only come from something, which establishes a belief in either evolution or creationism.

It all comes down to whether there is a God or no God. While speaking at my church, Greg Koukl explained, "These two views cannot be connected, such as through theistic evolution, because they conflict with each other. How could God use a chance process to produce something that was designed? It would be design by chance, which is an oxymoron."

To investigate how life occurred and why it continues to exist, we will take a progressive look at the primary developments of the physical world. The essentials include defining evolutionary terms, understanding DNA constructs, looking at the fossil record, and proving that life can only come from life (biogenesis).

Evolutionists believe in naturalism. They base everything upon this; the natural world and universe can only be explained by and through natural means.

Jonathan Sarfati, a devout Christian researcher, states what naturalism is: "It is assumed that things made themselves, that no divine intervention has happened, and that God has not revealed to us knowledge about the past."[37] He goes on to reveal some of its ideas:

> that nothing gave rise to something at an alleged "big bang," non-living matter gave rise to life, single-celled organisms gave rise to many-celled organisms, invertebrates gave rise to vertebrates, ape-like creatures gave rise to man, non-intelligent and amoral matter gave rise to intelligence and morality, man's yearnings gave rise to religions, etc.[38]

---

[37] Jonathan Sarfati, *Refuting Evolution* (Green Forest, AR: Master Books, 2000), 16.
[38] Ibid.

According to this view, everything evolved and developed through natural processes. Somehow everything managed to better itself without any influence or help.

Is it possible that everything pertaining to life can only improve upon itself and gain more knowledge and intelligence every time there is an evolutionary change? Can the ability to learn be an evolutionary development or can it only be an actual gift from an infinite source?

Creationists believe in God. They believe that only an infinite and eternal Being could have created and established everything. From the smallest creation to the largest, only God could have created life and all the physical laws and properties to fulfill their purpose and potential. Only He could have set the boundaries, and only He could have designed the perfect plan to keep everything sustainable. All available knowledge must be given in advance, like a computer program, to allow all these processes of life to function properly and continuously.

Traditionally. To understand the evolutionary processes, we will define some of the main ideas. That way, we will see how naturalists explain life and its developments.

There are three different types of definitions for evolution. The first relates to change with regards to time, the second relates to the special theory of evolution (microevolution), and the third relates to the general theory of evolution (macroevolution).

1. Change over time. There is no dispute with this definition, because we can see the changes that occur with passage of time. Examples include the growth and development of towns into cities, how storms and precipitation develop in size and strength, and how stars age in regards to the gravitational forces affecting them and the materials and objects surrounding them.

We can also see how technology has evolved through the years. What has been designed and developed in a year becomes obsolete the next because something better and faster comes along. The automobile and computer industries are continually evolving to give us the best, replacing the old with the new.

2. Microevolution. There is no dispute with this definition either, because we can observe the small changes that occur within a species or organism. Adaptations arise due to changing circumstances. Different environmental demands can favor the process of natural selection and genetic mutations can affect an organism from within, but these factors do not transform the organism or species into something else.

Microevolution is all about insignificant changes, like color, shape, and size, which don't alter a creature very much. Examples include Darwin's observation of the finches, which he viewed at the Galapagos Islands, and the mutations that occur when bacteria and viruses become resistant to medicine.

3. Macroevolution. There is some dispute with this definition, because it infers that everything from the past has evolved into something completely different from what it started as, that it began as a simple organism and then evolved into a more complex creature. The end result of this process is the evolution of the modern human being.

This is the theory of how things gradually develop from the simple to the complex. According to macroevolution, all living things evolved by stages into something higher than itself over time.

Despite not actually being able to observe macroevolution at work in our known history, it is assumed that this is what happened in the distant past. This theory is also known as Darwinism. Greg Koukl provided a great definition, again while speaking at my church:

> What has been observed as small changes over a period of time, making differences in the physical structure allowing for minor bits of adaptation in an organism from generation to generation, has now been taken as a rule of thumb such that the amount of variation is unlimited. And if the amount of variation is unlimited then one can imagine this process going on into the future and can also extrapolate backwards on it so that all of the development of life from the beginning until now, the molecules-to-man hypothesis, can be explained by the same process that we see in microevolution.

Darwinism has become the focal point for evolutionists. Every year, new theories crop up to replace old ones. The result is that the textbooks now being used to explain evolution are relatively out of date. This is because researchers are still trying to figure out three main evolutionary inceptions:

1. The basis on which to support the existence of the very dense singularity that would have caused the Big Bang to happen.
2. The hope of discovering new transitional connections from within the fossil record in association with the geological timetable.
3. The proof to establish the capability of life to evolve from non-living matter.

These are a continuing problem for evolutionists. For the last one hundred sixty years, Darwinism has been trying to connect the dots. But evolutionists still don't have any logical explanation to satisfy these three points which would explain the evolutionary processes.

Perhaps science can give us a better understanding.

Scientifically. When considering what science has to offer, we will see that it reveals everything to have been perfectly planned in advance. Everything is designed to work very precisely. How could everything have just fallen into place by chance? It seems impossible. Can chance plus unlimited time equal eventually getting it right?

How could science support such a theory? Yet this unscientific chance happening is used to explain how everything could come to exist. The macroevolutionary concepts of Darwinism are not based on science, but rather on illogical assumptions.

The more we delve into the facts of science, the more evident it becomes that only an eternal intelligence could have founded the universe. There is actually more scientific evidence to prove God's existence than evolution. For some reason, we seem to have separated God from science and placed Him in a completely different category, despite the fact that He was the one who established the physical sciences in the first place.

We will begin by questioning whether a chance happening is possible. If it is, then the Big Bang would be a viable fact. However, a few observations have been given to us by Walter T. Brown Jr.:

> ...all the physical processes of life can only utilize the available knowledge already given... the amount of information in any system is finite... and no separate or isolated system has ever been observed to increase its informational content.[39]

This can be known as the law of necessary intelligence. Only an outside intelligence can increase the content of information in a system.

Evolution indicates that informational knowledge can increase on its own without any influence, but science shows that this is not possible. It hasn't been scientifically proven that a chance happening could occur. Only a designed mechanism can be responsible for the universe, because in order for the physical processes of life to work they must be preprogrammed with the proper information. This can only be done if knowledge is supplied in advance by an outside intelligence.

This concept is demonstrated through the masterful programming of DNA, the building block of life. Every living cell possesses the genetic materials needed to control every aspect of life. Our DNA contains all the unique information that determines what we'll look like, how we'll behave, and how our bodies will function.[40] This demonstrates design.

When considering the transitions in the fossil record, it soon becomes apparent that the so-called missing links that evolutionists try so hard to find will never be

---

[39] Walter T. Brown Jr., *In the Beginning...* (Phoenix, AR: Center for Scientific Creation, 1986), 2.
[40] Ibid., iii.

discovered, because they are not there. Even if there were a small number of new transitional discoveries, they still would not prove Darwinism. The fossil record would need to record millions, or even billions, of transitional forms to support evolution. The fact is these transitions are extensively missing; the gaps are huge.

The fossil record reveals very little evidence of the development from one kind of organism to another. Fossils do, however, show the appearance of fully formed species that abruptly died off, then were replaced later by other forms of life. This is proof of a worldwide flood, not an evolutionary process.[41]

The fossils dating back to the Cambrian period reveal complex species and multicellular life. If Darwinism is true, we should have seen fossils of single-celled organisms, simple creatures, and invertebrates, not the fully developed plant and animal phyla that reveal both comprehensive internal design and complex bone structures. In fact, out of the seventy phyla that have been classified from the Cambrian period, only thirty come from the upper layers. The facts of the fossil record prove extinction, not evolution.[42]

There are also inconsistencies in the vertical sequencing of fossils, because they are not found in the assumed evolutionary order. Walter T. Brown Jr. states that paleontologists have found eighty-six hoofprints of horses from the rocks in Russia dating back to the time of the dinosaurs. He also mentions that both dinosaur and human-like footprints have been fossilized side by side in the same rock, and that the bones of modern-looking humans have been found deep in rock formations that were formed long before man supposedly began to evolve.[43]

The single most important factor in the question of the origin of life is one's belief in either biogenesis or abiogenesis. Life either came from life or non-life. However, when we look at how life reproduces itself, we can see that life can only come from life. Spontaneous generation (abiogenesis) has never been observed. Only biogenesis has been proven scientifically.

Evolutionists focus their attention on trying to prove that life can come from non-life. They base their hopes on this by hiding in the crevices of the past, believing that an alleged Big Bang caused life to occur by chance to the extent that all life evolved from a pool of sludge.

Instead of looking back and putting our faith in the past, isn't it more prudent and verifiable to look to the present for truth? This points to the existence of God, because only He can explain why life continues to exist and why we are here.

---

[41] Ibid., 3.
[42] Ibid.
[43] Ibid., 4.

CHAPTER TWELVE: THE EXTERNAL WITNESS

Why then don't we believe in Him? It seems that some just don't want to, so they would rather believe in something else, like Darwinism.

Spiritually. Adam was given the knowledge to not only understand language but make use of his reasoning skills to find a purpose for everything. God gave him the intelligence to name everything the eye could see. Adam assigned a name to all of God's creations (Genesis 2:15–25). We could therefore conclude that Adam may have been the most intelligent individual ever. He may not have been the wisest, but he was definitely the most knowledgeable.

The Genesis 1 account inspires two camps in regards to the length of time during which creation occurred: new earth creationism and old earth creationism.

New earth creationists believe that everything was created in a literal six-day period. This knowledge could have come directly from God and been given to Adam. If we rely on oral tradition, we may conclude that the creation account could have been memorized by Adam and passed on to successive generations to reach Moses, who then wrote it down onto scrolls. The timespan for this period could be calculated as 2,432 years.

Evolution, on the other hand, would require about fourteen billion years to complete, measured from the proposed start of the universe.

Old earth creationists believe that there is a gap between Genesis 1:1 and Genesis 1:2. First God created the earth with prehistoric animal life, not through the evolution process. This life existed long before humans. When He did eventually create Adam and Eve, He refashioned the earth and created all the living aspects of life as described by Genesis 1:2–31.

However long it took God to complete His creation, we still must deduce that only He could have done it. It all comes down to whether one believes He is real and is the cause of everything. This requires a spiritual belief in the supernatural, and such a belief can be proven naturally.

REASONABLE CONCLUSION

Back in 1972, a Grade Five social studies teacher gave a rousing speech on the subject of evolution. He was very adamant that it was the only viable truth capable of explaining why we are here.

"We all came from monkeys," he stated. "And if you don't believe this, I will become upset with you because it is the absolute truth."

Moments later, after some contemplation, a brave student approached the teacher and asked him this question: "Why are there still monkeys around?"

This raises an interesting thought. If life began from nothing with the ability to evolve into something higher than itself, and if the evolutionary process was unlimited in nature, then wouldn't evolution continue indefinitely? Why has macroevolution seemed to have stopped?

Let us consider the following.

Biogenesis. Evidence reveals that the cycle of life is happening everywhere. There is no reason to doubt this because results have proven that life can only come from life. This proves creationism, not evolution. There is absolutely no evidence at all showing that life can come from non-life. This is not seen anywhere. Biogenesis proves that God is the Creator and master designer.

DNA constructs. According to Walter T. Brown Jr.,

> Natural selection cannot produce new genes; it can only select from preexisting characteristics. Additionally, no natural process is capable of producing a program. Genetic material is coded information which allows every cell in our bodies to function.[44]

This can only be possible if a higher intelligence was involved in implementing the process. DNA constructs like transmission and duplication could only have been designed by God.

Irreducible complexity. When looking at a detailed view inside a cell, we can see that it contains highly sophisticated motors called dynamos which can only function if all the parts are present together at once. The distinguishing feature of irreducible complexity is that if one part is missing or dysfunctional, the cell won't function at all. This is why it's difficult for a cell to gradually develop piece by piece. Because of irreducible complexity, the evolutionary process doesn't work. Only design is possible.

The fossil record and the geological timetable. These two factors are dependent upon one another. The fossil record relies on the formation of rocks over time, and those formations are dependent on the fossil record. Since the fossil record has too many inconsistencies within itself, how reliably does the rock formation reveal the truth about the geological timetable?

Evolution cannot accurately explain the cause of the fossil record; it only assumes that this is what happened. Only a worldwide flood, which is reported to have happened during Noah's generation, can explain how the fossils happened to form in the fossil record. This event happened about 4,350 years ago, further proving that the earth is less than ten thousand years of age.

The anthropic principle. The logic and precision by which the physical aspects of life work in harmony with the non-living properties of the world is astounding. The

---

[44] Brown, *In the Beginning*, 1–2.

way in which everything works together demonstrates remarkable planning. What are the probabilities that this plan, which keeps us in a safe and sustainable environment, came about by chance? There are too many variables which determine whether or not we can survive here on this planet. Only an outside intelligence could provide the means to sustain everything.

APPLYING TRUTH
Everything that can be visibly seen, including us, reflects and reveals God. We mirror Him and the physical features of the earth display His glory.

God is a very powerful Being who has the ability to do anything. This should cause us to stand in awe of Him, to wonder who He is and pursue Him with deeper conviction. The external witness declares the existence of God and reveals a very personal God who wants us to realize that He can be known and discovered through His creation.

Take some time to experience nature. Go on trips and view the incredible sights the world has to offer. Experience the presence of God in these places and give Him thanks. Make sure you are well prepared in your travels and that you consider your own safety. Use common sense, especially if you're alone with nature.

Read books on astronomy to help you experience the universe like never before. Observe in awe the amazing wonders and incomprehensible distances of God's creation. Discover microbiology, which is just as wondrous and amazing and then share your experiences with others. Keep a journal.

Also realize that God is our only hope, because His purposes for creating us are eternal. Darwinism is finite and shows that eventually all life ceases to exist. It gives us neither hope nor purpose.

As a final thought, consider who struck the match to initiate life. Evolutionists can only speculate on the cause. They haven't proved anything viable because they don't realize that life is an infinite and eternal concept which can only be initiated by an eternal presence.

TWO TYPES OF THINKING
Why have most educational institutions taken God out of the equation when it comes to explaining the origin of the universe and the development of life? It comes down to two types of cognition: theistic thinking and non-theistic thinking. Which type of thinking describes you? Does this influence the way you think and make decisions about God?

Non-theistic thinkers. These people believe that naturalism is the only way to explain the origin of creation. They have a tough time understanding how the universe came to be. How did God come into existence?

This type of thinking is more cerebral than spiritual. They don't believe that the spiritual can ever be involved in the processes of natural development. The two must be separate.

Non-theistic thinkers struggle to understand spiritual concepts and tend to relate them to the physical realm. They use mental processes to try to understand God and connect with Him. They also believe that living things can evolve on their own, getting better and more complex over time and increasing in knowledge without any outside influence.

Theistic thinkers. This type of person understands the spiritual meaning of existence and grasps that a divine presence is necessary in order for life to work. All knowledge must be available at once and be used to create, develop, and continue the processes of life as we observe them.

Additionally, theistic thinkers utilize the cerebral aspects of thinking as well as engage their spiritual understanding. They accept that the processes of life must have been preprogrammed in order to function and that God is a Being who has always existed.

MORE ADVANCED QUESTIONS

1. Do you tend to think theistically or non-theistically?
    a) Theistic thinking is premised on the idea that all the knowledge and intelligence that can be known must be available from an eternal source. That knowledge was used to create, establish, and maintain the physical universe and everything within it. Whatever has been created reaches its full potential because of this intelligence and evidence of design governs all life, from infancy to full maturation.
    b) Non-theistic thinking is premised on the idea that all knowledge and intelligence can evolve from a point of nothingness, developing from simple adaptations to more complex ones. Life therefore evolved naturally, going from simple forms to more complex forms. The universe and everything within it began by chance from non-living materials.

2. Do you believe in young earth creationism (God created everything in a literal six-day period) or old earth creationism (God first created prehistoric animal life before refashioning the earth for Adam and Eve)?

3. Do you believe in natural evolution (everything gradually evolved and developed on its own without divine intervention)? Is theistic evolution possible (God initiated the evolutionary process by introducing it as a physical law)?

CHAPTER THIRTEEN
THE INTERNAL WITNESS

THE INTERNAL WITNESS includes our conscience, soul, and spirit-nature. Everything within us proves that we were made in the image of God. These inner qualities gift us with the ability to know right from wrong, think with reason and understanding, express ourselves freely, interact with others with compassion and discernment, utilize our abilities to enhance our lives, and connect ourselves with the spiritual realm, especially when relating to God.

Please note that we will focus on the conscience in this chapter because it provides the truest sense of the internal witness.

It's best to simplify the internal witness in this way because our conscience is a moral replica of who God is and what He stands for. God gifted us with a finite copy of His moral attributes so we could relate with Him and live our lives the way He intended.

SCRIPTURE REFERENCES
The Image of God

- Genesis 1:26–27
- Genesis 5:3
- Genesis 9:6
- 2 Corinthians 3:18
- Colossians 3:9–10

The Conscience

- Psalm 7:3–5, 8; 25:20–21
- Romans 2:11–18
- 1 Corinthians 10:23–33
- 1 Timothy 1:18–19
- Titus 1:15–16
- Hebrews 5:13–14, 13:13–18
- 1 Peter 3:14–17

QUESTIONS

1. Have you ever felt guilty when you did something wrong?
2. Did the conscience naturally evolve within us or did God give us this moral sense so we could become aware of His standards?

3. Does everyone have a conscience?
4. Do you judge others and yourself?
5. Do you have a high or low standard of morality?
6. Are your actions dependent on your own standards of truth, or someone else's?
7. Is it okay to break the law as long as it doesn't hurt anyone?
8. Does it go against your nature to see others sin or break the law?
9. Do you get upset when you sin or break the law?
10. Have you ever experienced repentance or remorse?
11. Do you take pride in your work, relationships, personal developments, and achievements?
12. Do you feel like you have integrity? Do you feel like you're worthwhile?

ESTABLISHING TRUTH

Intellectually. The primary question concerning the internal witness relates to why we have this ability to sense the difference between right and wrong. We notice it through the feelings of guilt we experience after we've done something wrong, or the anxiety that settles over us when we don't do something we should. Where did this discerning conscience come from?

Most believe that God has given us this sense of morality as a foundational gift to help influence our actions, attitude, and speech. It's a way for us to acknowledge that God is with us in every aspect of our lives, that every decision we make must first pass through our conscience, which acts like a filter to decipher the bad from the good. We must then decide which path to take.

From this chapter's questions, we can see that almost all the answers should be "yes." This is because we have a decent understanding of the conscience and how it works. It permeates every part of our lives from how we conduct ourselves to how we interact with others to how we make decisions. We tend to do well and be good, trying our best to help and please others. This is the effect of the conscience. It's a mechanism to help us discern right from wrong.

Problems arise, however, when we ignore the conscience or cross the line to selfishly fulfill our ambitions no matter the consequences.

There are three main reasons we have the conscience:

1. It makes us aware of God's existence by reminding us of who He is.
2. It helps us to judge rightly, both personally and relationally, in whatever situation we face.

3. It enhances our lives by helping us conform to a certain code of conduct so we can achieve healthy relations, order, and purpose.

The bottom line is that the conscience steers us in the right direction. If we didn't have a conscience, our lives would be chaotic. We would live with uncertainty and loneliness, enduring lawlessness and destruction. The conscience is part of who we are—and when we join with those around us, we can live and work together as a society to achieve cooperative unity for the common good.

Those who believe that our conscience comes from God will conclude that He gave it to us so we could understand Him and relate *with* Him. We know about God because the conscience reveals to us His moral standard. We use this code to live as God intended. We use it in the same respect when relating to each other and in our everyday activities.

Alternatively, we can believe that our conscience arose by chance, evolving within us into a form of self-judgment, allowing us to implement our own moral standards according to our own truths.

We must decide whether to follow the intent of our conscience through God's eyes or our own. Our actions will determine who we live for.

Traditionally. When we consider the conscience, we can perceive its purpose. And knowing its purpose, we can understand it. To explain what a thing is, we must look to the fruit it produces. In this case, the conscience can be understood through our behavior. There are consequences to our actions. When we do something we shouldn't, our conscience will let us know. When we do something good and pleasing, it will fill us with a sense of satisfaction.

Since we know what the conscience is, and why we have it, we can determine where it came from. Why would we develop a way to penalize ourselves with guilt when we do something wrong? Only an independent Judge knowledgeable in moral conduct could have designed and incorporated a mechanism like the conscience. Indeed, only an omniscient and holy God could have established it.

Therefore, the conscience cannot be individual, subjective, or relative, but rather universal, objective, and absolute. This can be seen through our virtues:

- Compassion
- Humility
- Perseverance
- Temperance
- Goodness
- Respectfulness
- Patience

- Meekness
- Helpfulness
- Fairness
- Honesty
- Loyalty
- Kindness
- Thoughtfulness
- Merciful
- Purposeful
- Trustworthy
- Generous
- Honorable
- Responsible
- Gratefulness
- Hospitable
- Sincerity
- Prudence

These characteristics emulate God. He designed us to have these virtues so we could use them in every situation we face and in every relationship we have.

We can see this in God's creation of Adam and Eve. They were an open book, absolutely good in every respect. Even their nakedness didn't bother them. Their consciences were innocent.

Once they fell into sin, however, their outer and inner nakedness became so self-revealing that they grew embarrassed to even look at each other. From then on, the conscience became a self-judging measure of behavior. Because of the conscience, we know what evil is.

We have abused the conscience in many ways. We use it to get what we want through interrogation, manipulation, condemnation, and persuasion. We've found ways to manipulate people's consciences into making them tell the truth or do something they don't want to do. Interrogators are good at this, asking all the right questions. Advertisers and marketers tug at our hearts to force us to buy their products or support their cause. Asking questions forces us to look at ourselves with accountability.

We abuse the conscience by not taking it seriously enough. We test the limits of our conscience to see what we can get away with. We also minimize it through neglect and ignorance.

After Cain murdered his brother Abel, his conscience made him feel turmoil, realizing that death was real. He couldn't undo what he had done. And when Noah's generation lived their lives without God, doing whatever they wanted according to their own rules, God ended up judging them. They were out of control and didn't want to change from their wicked ways. They didn't consider the consequences of their actions.

In order for us to be at peace with ourselves and society, we must conform to certain rules and conditions. The conscience is the means by which we achieve this. However, with conformity comes rebellion. We decide whether to conform.

After World War II, the hippie movement was a way for young people to rebel against the mores of society by dressing unconventionally and living counterculturally. The hippies used psychedelic drugs as a nonviolent means to set themselves apart from society.

Later, the so-called yuppie movement was a way for young people to passively rebel against their parents' demands. They were tired of doing things according to expectations and wanted to go their own way. They felt that their parents were far too controlling.

Generation X took this trend to another level. Wanting to establish their own mark, they focused on high achievement to attain personal security and fulfillment. To them, Christmas became Xmas, God became less important, and they demanded their needs be met instantly. They squeezed the world for all of it's worth. This turned into a competition to see who could come out number one.

Millennials, or Generation Y, grew up with advanced technology, meaning they had to keep up. Information on everything and everyone was at their fingertips and social media made them feel entitled. Along with the rise of the internet, cyberbullying became a growing concern. The web could be used to take advantage of people's good nature. Identity theft violated people's privacy and made people prioritize protecting themselves.

Scientifically. Can the conscience be studied scientifically? Is it part of the mind? The spirit? Or is it a separate component altogether? We all have a slightly different moral compass, which suggests that some are more prone to keep their morals in check whereas others are more prone to test their limits.

It's difficult to explain why we decide to do certain things and why we stand firm against others. We can study the effectiveness of the conscience by examining our behavior, identifying what we've learned from our upbringing, and figuring out how external events influence us. Why do some conform to certain standards and others don't? Why are some people more persistently deviant than others? There is such a range of behavior, from remorseless psychopaths to those who are hypersensitive and punish themselves whenever they do something wrong.

These questions intrigue behavioral scientists. The study of behavior, known as psychology, first became prevalent around the 1600s. Although philosophers initially took the reins, it became more of an exact science when people turned their attention to understanding why people behaved the way they did.

Empirical philosophers realized that behavior could be determined by experience and that human nature and conduct could best be understood through observation. John Locke, who lived from 1632 to 1704, suggested that there is no basic human nature, but rather that our minds at birth are a blank slate that will eventually be written upon by experience. If you knew an individual's experiences, you could understand them.[45]

At first, psychology was more fixed in its concepts. Wilhelm Wundt, who established the first laboratory for the scientific study of psychology in Leipzig, Germany, identified the concepts of introspection, whereby one could look within and describe one's own conscious experience, and structuralism, whereby one could analyze one's observations into its basic elements and derive one's own conclusion.[46]

Then there came the need to look beyond the conscious experience and delve into a more complete study of behavior. J.B. Watson initiated the redefinition of psychology into the "science of behavior."[47] He concluded that there couldn't be a science based on conscious experience but rather on observable events. This included behavioralism, studying only what was observable, and Gestalt psychology, studying behavior as an organized whole as opposed to discrete parts.[48]

This led Sigmund Freud to expand into the area of psychoanalysis, which studied abnormal human behavior. These concepts introduced us to the different types of personalities and unconscious determinants of behavior.

Behavior became predictable as psychology expanded to become a more reliable science. Its many facets were intriguing.

No aspect of psychology was more interesting than working to understand the criminal mind. Profilers were able to predict criminal behavior by studying ulterior motives, victimology, signatures, and patterns of behavior. Many serial killers were captured because of this predictability.

Our understanding of morality is mostly due to our knowledge of the conscience. What was once considered abnormal can be considered normal to others according to their own reality.

---

[45] Audrey Haber and Richard P. Runyon, *Fundamental of Psychology, Second Edition* (Manila, Philippines: Addison-Wesley, 1978), 8.
[46] Ibid., 9.
[47] Ibid., 9–10.
[48] Ibid., 10.

Whatever the reason behind our actions, we are still responsible for them. This can be challenging. According to our selfish and sinful nature, we are capable of doing anything—even the most heinous acts.

When we lose sight of why we behave as we do, we lose sight of our understanding of God. He gave us the conscience as a gift so we could understand ourselves. The conscience is one of the most important aspects of who we are. When we lose our conscience, we lose ourselves.

Spiritually. Noah's generation failed because they had a major flaw. That society had no law or order. They neglected governmental control over their collective affairs. They weren't accountable to anyone, not even God. They allowed their spiritually depraved natures to dictate how they lived. Everyone lived according to their own rules, which almost resulted in annihilation. Why didn't they institute some sort of law to govern themselves? Why didn't they adhere to their consciences? This remains a mystery.

The law is important. It's a means to control our behavior and keep us on the proper side of conduct. When we don't follow the law, we must accept the consequences that are laid out by the justice system. We pay a price when our actions are too destructive and unpredictable.

Paul tells us in Romans 7:14 that *"the law is spiritual."* This is because we wouldn't have known about sin were it not for the law (Romans 3:20). The conscience, therefore, serves as our moral guide. It's a spiritual law of conduct (Romans 2:15). Our conscience and the written law are both guides for how to lead organized and controlled lives.

This is why God tells us to be holy because He is holy (Leviticus 11:44–45). He declares to us the importance of keeping the law so we can live in the right way, with honor and integrity.

The law keeps us in check. It keeps us in line. When we obey our conscience and the written law, which the Word of God has revealed, we respect and honor God. Not only does the law become a spiritual necessity, it becomes a necessity of life.

REASONABLE CONCLUSION

On October 1, 2017, Stephen Paddock decided to do the unthinkable by checking into a room on the thirty-second floor of the Mandalay Bay in Las Vegas. While people enjoyed a concert at the Harvest Music Festival below, he fired into the crowd from two smashed windows. Within ten minutes, fifty-eight people had died and eight hundred fifty were injured. He willingly took people's lives before ultimately taking his own.

What was his frame of mind? Why did he do it? Where was his conscience?

CHAPTER THIRTEEN: THE INTERNAL WITNESS

This tragedy reminds us how fragile life is and how important our decisions are. The more we care about those around us, the more we will protect them. If we don't care what happens, the more destructive we become. Our conscience inspires us to care more deeply, which influences our decisions.

Why do we make the decisions we do? It comes down to three factors: our belief in God, our ability to judge ourselves, and our willingness to conform to external rules.

1. Our belief in God. God doesn't change. His standards don't change. What does change is our view of God and whether we want to keep His standard of conduct. God has established His truth and morality ever since the beginning. They represent who He is and He expects us to follow His standard. He knows how important it is to live a certain way, to keep us from harm and make sure we remain in right relationship with Him and those who are around us.

The conscience, as His moral representative, is a constant reminder of how we are to live before a holy God. Our actions are important because they are a sign that we want to please and honor Him. If we believe He doesn't exist, we can believe that our actions and behaviors don't matter in the end; since there is no God, there will be no consequences. If there's no eternal Judge, there's no eternal sentence.

But believing in God is the greatest purpose of all, because He is the reason for everything. If He is number one in your life, He will become your highest priority. Your decisions and actions will follow suit.

2. Our ability to judge ourselves. Our basic personalities don't change very much. What changes is how we are influenced and motivated. We are creatures of habit, and this pertains to everything about us, determining who we are and what we become.

In the same respect, we judge ourselves. In fact, this ability to judge is part of our conscience. When it's effective, it helps us to develop what's important to us and better learn to grow and mature so we can reach our full potential.

We also relate ourselves to our environment. This is seen in how we develop as we are brought up and in the external events which affect us. Judging ourselves allows us to behave accordingly. If we are free to change our behavior, we have the ability to be healthy and productive. If we don't, we become victims of living in a different reality, living as people we were never supposed to be. We can live this way for a number of reasons: substance abuse, tragedy, abusive parenting, developmental challenges, low self-esteem, addictive or antisocial behavior, lack of empathy, etc. These are signs that we don't know how to adapt and cope.

How well we judge ourselves corresponds to how well we relate to the conscience, which is continually being bombarded with questions about how we should do things. We can continue to practice bad behavior, or we can do good. This ability to judge the difference between good and evil keeps our consciences healthy. If we lose this ability, the conscience grows ineffective.

3. Our willingness to conform to external rules. The law doesn't change very much either. What changes is how society changes the law over time in order to satisfy or fulfill its needs and desires.

We require order and structure, especially when it comes to knowing how we are to conduct ourselves as a whole. God was the one to establish the law, which is revealed in the five books of Moses. For example, in the Ten Commandments (Exodus 20:1–17), a set of universal laws of human conduct written by the finger of God (Exodus 31:18), He declared them to be holy and sanctified. Like any other laws of conduct in the Bible, there is no room for us to do as we please.

The conscience, as our internal observer of the law, allows us to live properly through knowledge. The secular world has followed what God initiated. Nations establish laws for the common good; not conforming to them can be detrimental. History has shown how much these human laws have changed in regards to conduct and lifestyle.

The question then becomes one of acceptance and toleration, even in the presence of contradiction. On the one hand, God tells us to love our neighbor as ourselves; on the other hand, when it comes to conforming to His standards, He tells us to live a certain way, which is not how the world wants us to live (1 John 2:15–17). We may not like what our neighbors are doing, but we are to love them regardless because we have been commanded to do so (Matthew 22:39). We must decide whether to conform to God's standards or the world's.

APPLYING TRUTH

It has been said that confession is good for the soul. There would be no confession were it not for the conscience. We wouldn't be able to confess our sins unless we had this moral sense. Being able to confess is a sign of a healthy conscience. Maintaining the still, small voice within us is necessary in order for us to live dynamic, productive lives.

Paul tells us in Acts 24:16, *"This being so, I myself always strive to have a conscience without offense toward God and men."* This is a lifelong commitment.

Here are some other benefits of having a clear conscience:

1. It is a sign of a mature individual (Hebrews 5:13–14).
2. It is an effective weapon in our lives; next to our faith, a good conscience confirms who we are and what truth we live with (1 Timothy 1:18–19).

3. It allows us to love others and share our lives and faith with them (1 Peter 3:16).
4. It affects our health and physical appearance (Psalm 32:1–4).

The key to obtaining a clear and healthy conscience is to systematically look inwardly and reflect not only on our actions but on who we are. When we lose this self-knowledge and moral sense, we lose our ability to discern right from wrong. We can instead develop a different reality for ourselves.

This can be seen in those who seem to have no conscience at all. It's difficult to deal with them, for they are unable to change. In fact, they can be terrifying.

There are steps you can take to ensure that your conscience doesn't lose its effectiveness.

Understand proper moral conduct by reading the Word of God. This is why God gave us the Bible, which is a way for us to know how to properly conduct ourselves before God and those with whom we interact.

The Bible also gives us insight into ourselves. James 1:23–25 explains that the Word of God is like a mirror through which we see ourselves, not only to perceive what is wrong but most importantly to correct it. The recommendation is for us to regularly reflect on our behavior and attitude, especially when it comes to acknowledging sin.

The Word of God has much to say about being aware of sin in our lives.

The Memory of Personal Sin

- Stealing: taking something that is not yours (Exodus 20:15, Leviticus 19:11, Zechariah 5:3, Romans 2:21, Ephesians 4:28).
- Cheating: getting something unfairly, not deserving something, or embezzling (Deuteronomy 24:14–15, Job 31:13, Jeremiah 22:13, Malachi 3:5, James 5:1–4).
- Lying: any designed form of deception committed for selfish reasons (Revelation 21:7–8, Leviticus 19:11, Colossians 3:9, Ephesians 4:25, John 8:44).
- Slander: backbiting, speaking evil of another, or speaking gossip (Proverbs 6:16–19, 16:28).
- Immorality: moral impurity of any kind, especially sexual conduct and fornication (Matthew 5:28, Job 31:1, 2 Peter 2:14, 1 Corinthians 6:9–18).
- Censoriousness: harboring bitterness (John 7:24, 1 Corinthians 4:1–7, 6:1–8, Galatians 6:1, Matthew 7:1–5, 5:21–24, Colossians 3:8).

- Rebellion: disrespecting parents or guardians, or others in authority (Romans 13:1–7, Hebrews 13:17–18, Ephesians 6:1–8, Colossians 3:17–25).

The Memory of Attitudinal Sin

- Levity: needless frivolity, speaking or acting like a fool, and undermining good standards (Proverbs 15:14, 24:9, Ephesians 5:3–4).
- Envy: wishing to see others fall or fail, or feeling hurt when others are praised (Job 5:2, Proverbs 14:30, 27:4, Galatians 5:25).
- Pride: selfishness personified (Proverbs 16:5–18, 21:24, 29:23, Titus 3:9, 1 Corinthians 1:26–31, 1 Peter 5:1).
- Ingratitude: treating people like dirt (Romans 1:21, Malachi 3:8–11, 2 Timothy 3:2, Exodus 20:12, Ephesians 6:2, Colossians 3:15).
- Anger: being bad-tempered or losing self-control (Proverbs 15:18, 22:24, Ecclesiastes 7:9, Matthew 5:22, Colossians 3:8).
- Cursing: swearing, taking God's name in vain (Exodus 20:7, Deuteronomy 5:11, Matthew 5:33–37).

The Memory of Damaged Witness Sin

- Hypocrisy: living a lie (Matthew 6:5–6, 7:3–5, 23:28, Luke 12:1, 1 Timothy 4:2, 1 Peter 2:1).
- Hindrance: blocking others from doing God's will and stopping those who want God in their lives (Ephesians 5:16, John 9:4).
- Hardness: returning evil for evil, grumbling and fighting back (Exodus 16:8, Philippians 2:14, 1 Corinthians 10:10, 1 Thessalonians 5:15, 1 Peter 3:9).
- Half-heartedness: shirking responsibility and being lazy (Ezekiel 33:8, Proverbs 24:12).
- Holding back: hoarding your money, talent, time, and possessions (Matthew 5:40–42, 6:19–21, 2 Corinthians 9:6–7).
- Broken vows: not doing something that you promised to do (Ecclesiastes 5:1–2, 5:4–6, Acts 5:4).

Confess your sins. In the Old Testament, when the Israelites realized they had committed a sin they brought their animal sacrifice to the priest, then placed their hands on the animal and confessed. The priest sacrificed the animal as a covering-up atonement for their offence.

This was a requirement of God in order to be in right standing with Him. Now that Jesus has become our eternal and permanent sacrifice, God's only requirement is that we confess our sins before Him.

There are two basic categories of sin: sins of commission and sins of omission. Sins of commission are those acts which, deliberately done, are contrary to God's law, like the personal and attitudinal sins just described. Sins of omission are like those found in a damaged witness; they are things we know we should have done but didn't.

Set aside a time and a place to regularly confess your sins, whether it's daily, weekly, or monthly. Making this a regular practice will strengthen your conscience.

Acknowledge how you are going to stop sinning and pay. It's important to learn to become a better person, especially when it comes to behavior. We must develop a code of ethics in order to maintain genuine and healthy relationships.

When we cross the line of conduct to the point of committing sins, we offend others. We hurt them and soon stop caring about them. And when we stop feeling guilty about our actions, our consciences are seared; our bad behaviors become a normal way of life for us.

If you do sin against someone, and if you feel remorse, what are you going to do to make things right? How are you going to pay that person back? Making restitution helps to restore your moral sense, as well as the conscience of the one whom you offended. This is why it's important not to go to sleep with your spouse, or leave things unresolved with a friend, without dealing with the offence. The same principle can be applied in your relationship with God.

CHAPTER FOURTEEN
THE HISTORICAL WITNESS

THROUGHOUT HISTORY, GOD has guided His truth and plans, bringing them to fruition. It all began with the first humans, Adam and Eve, and continued through the godly line of Seth to Noah. Afterward came the choosing of Abraham to found the nation of Israel and establish God's law through Moses's leadership.

Later in the history of the nation, David was selected to be king. From David's bloodline came the incarnation of God's Son, Jesus, who declared the truth of God. Then the Holy Spirit established the church as the body of Christ, keepers of His truth and His way.

This historical path has continued into modern times, and it will continue onward until the history of humanity is complete. This will be experienced during the coming period of tribulation, followed by the millennial reign during which God will judge every single person who has ever lived since the beginning of time.

The Word of God is the best historical document available. However, two other thoughtful and effective publications can help us to understand the Christian timeline, including the declarations God has given us throughout history. These books are *The Reese Chronological Bible*[49] and the *Open Bible, Expanded Edition*.[50]

God has intervened in order to implement His plans and knowledge of the truth at designated moments. These declarations come to us by way of His covenants with us. The Bible describes these covenants for our benefit to understand His ways and sovereign will.

SCRIPTURE REFERENCES
Creation

- Creation (3976 B.C.), Genesis 1:1–31, 2:1–4.

The Universal Covenants

- The Edenic Covenant (3975 B.C.), Genesis 2:15–17.
- The Adamic Covenant (3975 B.C.), Genesis 3:14–21.
- The Noahic Covenant (2318 B.C.), Genesis 9:1–19.

---

[49] *The Reese Chronological Bible* (Bloomington, MN: Bethany House Publications, 1980).
[50] *Open Bible, Expanded Edition* (Nashville, TN: Thomas Nelson, 1980).

The Theocratic Covenants

- The Abrahamic Covenant (1907 B.C.), Genesis 12:1–3, 28:3–4.
- The Mosaic Covenant (1462 B.C.), Exodus 19:5–8.
- The Palestinian Covenant (1423 B.C.), Deuteronomy 29:10–15, 30:11–20.
- The Davidic Covenant (1016 B.C.), 2 Samuel 7:4–17.
- The New Covenant (597 B.C.), Jeremiah 31:31–34.

Note that the New Covenant is revealed by an inward process, or inner transformation, which is available to anyone and is implemented according to two promises:

- The coming of a Savior (5 B.C.–A.D. 29), who is the incarnation of Jesus Christ, including His life, ministry, death, and resurrection (Luke 1:26–38, 2:1–20, Hebrews 1:1–3).
- The coming of a Helper (A.D. 29–present) during the period known as the dispensational age of the Holy Spirit, or the age of grace, and affecting the New Testament church (Matthew 12:18–21, John 5:26–27, Matthew 16:18).

QUESTIONS

1. Has God breached into our history to declare His truth and His covenants?
2. Discuss the universal covenants. How have they affected humanity?
3. Discuss the theocratic covenants. Are they still relevant today?
4. Discuss the New Covenant. How has it changed your life?
5. How have each of the nine revelational witnesses helped you to understand these truths and the covenants of God? Write down your thoughts and personal experiences relating to each one.

THE COVENANTS OF GOD

If God exists, wouldn't He make known His existence to us? And wouldn't He give us His truth and plans so we would know how to live before Him?

The Bible, which reveals the permanent words and truth of God, not only tells us what happened in history but also conveys the knowledge of Him as a personal and revealing God. History delivers a step-by-step progression which we can follow to understand the personal truth of God and make it a way of life for us.

Whether universal or specific, these covenants were given to help us understand His gifts of fellowship, guidance, and provision. They are relational agreements, causing us to accept His sovereign ways.

There are numerous ways in which we come to agreements between ourselves as humans. For the most part, these agreements are based on the honor system. When there is a need, the need must be met. If the person responding to the need responds negatively, the agreement is broken; if the response is positive, the agreement remains in effect.

From time to time, this agreement is verbal. For example, a father may ask his son to take out the garbage, or a boss may ask his employee to fulfill a certain task.

Other times, the agreement is written. This is often known as a contract, usually written between two or more parties with established guidelines so each party can fulfill their obligations. A covenant is, indeed, a binding contract.

God operates through covenants. He has given us the opportunity to not only live with Him but get to know Him, and because of this He has the right to establish guidelines for how those relationships are to proceed.

There are two types of covenants: unconditional and conditional.

Unconditional covenant. This type of covenant is one-sided. The giver of the covenant does all the work; all the receiver has to do is freely accept it.

Conditional covenant. However, a conditional covenant comes with obligations that the receiver needs to fulfill. As long as the conditions are met, the covenant remains in effect. If that changes, the covenant can be broken, for which there will be consequences.

Remember that God gave us the gift of free will—the freedom to choose how to respond to what He has given us. This is related to our natures, having been created in the image of God! We have the chance to have a real personal relationship with God.

Throughout history, according to the Bible, the covenants of God were given at specific moments to help us understand how to relate with Him and His ways. God established the physical laws of the universe to govern the cosmos. He also established theocratic covenants with humanity to govern their way of life on the earth. These universal covenants are a reality for everyone. God intervened on our behalf and implemented His plans for us.

THE UNIVERSAL COVENANTS

There are three universal covenants of God: the Edenic covenant, the Adamic covenant, and the Noahic covenant.

The Edenic covenant. This covenant is found in Genesis 1:28–29 and Genesis 2:15–17. Adam and Eve were charged with:

- populating the earth.
- subduing the earth.
- exercising dominion over the animals.
- caring for the garden of Eden and eating of its fruits.
- refraining from eating from the tree of the knowledge of good and evil, under the penalty of death.[51]

This covenant was established by God in perfection. Everything God had just finished creating was perfect and good. There were no flaws, no imperfections. Adam and Eve were sinless and knew only good. They had no idea what evil was or what it felt like to do anything wrong.

It is interesting that God would create the tree of the knowledge of good and evil and place it in the middle of the garden where, noticeably, Adam and Eve would cross its path on a daily basis. It was a certainty that they would be tempted to disobey God's command.

However, they didn't even know what temptation was. They probably had no desire whatsoever to eat from that tree. If they did, they likely would have built a fence around it to prevent them from doing so. But they were caught off-guard and innocently influenced by an outside source they didn't even know about.

Who else could influence their decision to eat from that forbidden tree but Satan, a fallen angel powerful and intelligent enough to cause one to succumb to temptation. The consequences of breaking this covenant resulted in the physical and spiritual deaths of not only Adam and Eve but every human being born after them.

Because of their disobedience, God needed to establish a second covenant with Adam, Eve, and the rest of humanity.

The Adamic covenant. This covenant is found in Genesis 3:14–24. It sets forth the conditions for the consequences of sin, at least until sin could be done away with. According to this covenant:

- The serpent and Satan were cursed and judged.
- Women would increase their duration of conception and endure pain when giving birth.
- Women would be made subject to their husbands.
- Men would have to work hard their whole lives to provide for their needs.
- All flesh would eventually die and decay back to the ground.

---

[51] Humbard, *The Prophecy Bible*, 5.

- Since everyone was to die spiritually, God provided hope in restoring what had been lost in the fall by implementing His plan of redemption.[52]

As a result of breaking the Edenic covenant, humanity now has to live with sin in their lives. Each human is a sinner and must face death.

From reviewing the six consequences above, we can see that the serpent was used as a tool by Satan to deceive Adam and Eve. The serpent, an animal Satan was particularly fond of, had the ability back then to stand upright. Because of the serpent's use by Satan, however, it was cursed to later move on its belly.

Instead of walking alongside the men of their lives, women are now subject to them, because of the curse, concerned with their needs and wants. In regards to bearing children, women can only imagine what it would have been like to give birth without pain.

Men, on the other hand, have to deal with the pain of working for a living. Through sweat and hard work, they spend their time providing for themselves and their families.

The most amazing aspect of the Adamic covenant is God's provision of salvation despite Adam and Eve's sin. We also see God's caring heart in how He provided Adam and Eve with tunics of skin for clothing. He also provided the foreknowledge of His plan of redemption through a coming Messiah, predicted in Genesis 3:15.

God could have rejected humans completely and left us to die without hope, but instead He drove Adam and Eve out of the garden out of love. If they had eaten from the Tree of Life, they would have lived forever with sin. Adam and Eve, and those born after them, would have been unable to physically die.

To be free from sin, physical death is essential. To be free from spiritual death, one needs to become spiritually born again by accepting God's most sacred covenant.[53]

For now, we must look to the third universal covenant established by God, the Noahic covenant.

The Noahic covenant. This covenant is found in Genesis 9:1–19. A span of approximately 1,600 years passes from the beginning of the Adamic covenant to the beginning of the Noahic covenant, allowing for about eighteen generations to live. The population of the earth could have been around five hundred million—or even one billion, considering the long lifespan of humans in those days and the number of children in each family.

---

[52] Ibid., 7.
[53] This covenant will be revealed later in the book.

CHAPTER FOURTEEN: THE HISTORICAL WITNESS

In Genesis 6, we learn that almost one hundred percent of the human race forsook the ways of God and didn't consider Him at all:

> The earth also was corrupt before God, and the earth was filled with violence. So God looked upon the earth, and indeed it was corrupt; for all flesh had corrupted their way on the earth. (Genesis 6:11–12)

How in the world could this have happened? Why didn't the people follow God? You would think they knew about God, that Adam would have taught them about Him and His plan of redemption. But this was not the case.

Not only was God sorry He had made man, but He decided to destroy the entire population of the earth because of their evil intent. They were beyond the point of returning to God.

Of the whole world, only one family kept their faith in God. We can thank God for Noah and his family, because they found grace in His eyes. Why only they followed God is a mystery.

Noah was about five hundred years of age when God began to consider the coming judgment, and he was six hundred when the flooding began. For one hundred years, God waited for the people of the earth to repent of their ways.

Out of obedience, Noah and his family started to build an ark, according to God's instructions, because they knew He was going to send a flood and only they and a selection of animals would be saved. Even those who saw the ark's construction didn't seem too concerned. They most likely thought Noah was crazy to build a giant boat in a place where rain didn't exist. The entire population of the earth rejected Noah's witness and as a result died.

With this covenant, Noah and his family had several assurances:

- They would continue to populate the earth.
- The animals would still be subject to them.
- They could eat the flesh of animals, but not the blood.
- Human life was sacred, even as capital punishment was established.
- God would lift the curse of the ground (Genesis 8:21).
- God would never destroy the earth again by a flood. He displays the rainbow as a testament to this. As long as the rainbow exists, we will know that the Noahic covenant remains in effect.[54]

---

[54] Humbard, *The Prophecy Bible*, 11.

THE THEOCRATIC COVENANTS

Following the universal covenants, God became more specific in establishing His intentions with humanity. However, He had to deal with the fact that the world was becoming too single-minded in fulfilling its own purposes. He decided to establish His rule over the affairs of humanity by implementing five theocratic covenants.

The Abrahamic covenant. This first theocratic covenant occurred about four hundred years after Noah and his family started repopulating the earth. In that time, humanity grew in great number and everyone spoke the same language. No one knows what kind of government was created, but the Bible states in Genesis 11 that the people decided to build the city of Babel on the plain of Shinar, a site most likely located in ancient Babylonia in the southern part of Mesopotamia.

The people also started constructing the tallest tower possible, in order to reach into the heavens solely for the purpose of making a name for themselves (Genesis 11:4). This gave God the opportunity to bring diversity to the human race. He did this by separating the people into groups and supernaturally introducing them to different languages.

The effect was rather ingenious, to say the least. By giving everyone a different language, God caused a scattering effect. Common sense would suggest that because the people couldn't understand each other, they had to move apart in order to live peacefully with each other and avoid conflict with those who were different from them.

As a result, the city of Babel was never completed.

When the time came to introduce the Abrahamic covenant, God needed a man to serve as His representative. This man would become the father of a nation. God needed to set apart a nation to act as His ambassadors to the rest of the world.

He chose Abram from the city of Ur of the Chaldeans. This man of faith was the perfect man for God to establish a covenant with. To make this covenant authentic, God changed Abram's name to Abraham, its meaning changing from "the father is exalted" to "the father of multitudes" (Genesis 17:4–5). To seal the deal, God instituted the custom of circumcision as a sign of this covenant (Genesis 17:10–11).

The Abrahamic covenant is found in Genesis 12:1–3. The heart of this unconditional covenant is founded in the words "I will…" This shows that God freely gave this covenant without obligation. Abraham just had to accept what God offered him. He did and became obedient to whatever God required of him.

In this covenant, Abraham received blessings in three areas:

- Nationally, by making his descendants into a chosen nation.
- Personally, by blessing him in wealth, respect, and honor.

- Universally, by blessing the rest of the world through his seed and legacy. Those who opposed Abraham would be cursed and those who accepted him would benefit, both by God and the coming of the Messiah from Abraham's own flesh.[55]

God confirmed this covenant with Abraham throughout his lifetime: in Shechem (Genesis 12:7), when Abram and Lot separated (Genesis 13:14–17), when Abram worried about his heir since his wife Sarai was barren (Genesis 15:1–21), when God changed Abram's name to Abraham (Genesis 17:1–8), when God instituted the covenant of circumcision (Genesis 17:9–14), when God changed Sarai's name to Sarah and continued the covenant through Isaac (Genesis 17:15–21), and when God tested Abraham's faith through the offering of Isaac as a sacrifice (Genesis 22:15–18).

The Abrahamic covenant is foundational to all the covenants later to come. God declared it an everlasting covenant and an everlasting possession (Genesis 17:7–8, 13, 19). Therefore, God chose Abraham and his seed to be the ones to keep this covenant alive under His guidance.

The Mosaic covenant. The Mosaic covenant is found in Exodus 19:5–8. According to this conditional covenant, the nation of Israel was to be:

- a special treasure to God.
- a kingdom of priests.
- a holy nation.[56]

In Exodus 3:18, God instructed Moses to bring the nation of Israel to Mount Horeb, which included Mount Sinai, so they could worship and sacrifice to their Lord and God. This is where God wanted to introduce Himself to His people.

At the burning bush, Moses and God spoke about to make this introduction:

> Then Moses said to God, "Indeed, when I come to the children of Israel and say to them, 'The God of your fathers has sent me to you,' and they say to me, 'What is His name?' what shall I say to them?"
>
> And God said to Moses, "I AM WHO I AM." And He said, "Thus you shall say to the children of Israel, 'I AM has sent me to you.'"
>
> Moreover God said to Moses, "Thus you shall say to the children of Israel: 'The Lord God of your fathers, the God of Abraham, the God of Isaac, and the God of Jacob, has sent me

---

[55] Ibid., 14.
[56] Ibid., 72.

to you. This is My name forever, and this is My memorial to all generations.'" (Exodus 3:13–15)

This was God's covenant name. Israel later came to know Him by His personal name, Yahweh, which marked them as His possession. He chose them out of all the other nations to be His—and since they were His, He wanted to teach and equip them as His special treasure for all to see.

Once God brought them to Mount Sinai, His intention was to make the people of Israel a holy nation, set apart to serve and represent Him as the One who provides hope and salvation to all. To begin, God gave Moses two sets of tablets, on which were written the Ten Commandments. This began a quest for holiness, with a condition: they had to obey the laws and commandments of God. If they did, He would become their personal God. God wanted them to be keepers of the law, thus establishing the priesthood.

The Palestinian covenant. This covenant is found in Deuteronomy 29:10–15 and 30:11–20. This third theocratic covenant has two aspects to it, both centered around the land of Palestine and its people.

First, there is an important condition:

> Now it shall come to pass, if you diligently obey the voice of the Lord your God, to observe carefully all His commandments which I command you today, that the Lord your God will set you high above all nations of the earth. (Deuteronomy 28:1)

If there was any disobedience, there would come a series of curses (Deuteronomy 28:15–68). On the other hand, with obedience would come a series of blessings (Deuteronomy 28:1–14).

Second, we encounter an unconditional pact in Deuteronomy 30:1–9, whereby God would set apart this land as an everlasting possession for the nation of Israel (Genesis 17:7–8), despite the fact that at certain points in their history the people had failed God by breaking their covenant with Him.[57]

The result was dispersion. One such example can be seen when the people were taken into Babylonian captivity by Nebuchadnezzar. They were restored seventy years later by Cyrus (Daniel 9:2, Jeremiah 29:10).

Throughout their history, the Israelites were fickle. When they followed God, they were triumphant and had peace. When they forsook and disobeyed Him, other nations came to conquer and occupy their land.

---

[57] Ibid., 201.

Thus, this result of the covenant depended on how committed the people were to God. Ultimately, whatever judgment of God befell them, they soon realized they would have to repent and once again faithfully trust in their God to bring them back together when the time was right.

God used Cyrus to restore Israel and her land in 536 B.C., although it wasn't until after World War II, on May 14, 1948, that despite some disputes the people were able to once again return to the land of Palestine, fulfilling God's promise. The United Nations voted in favor of reinstituting Israel as a nation. Nothing would deter God from giving back what He had promised them—their land and their restoration as His people.

The Davidic covenant. The Davidic covenant is found in 2 Samuel 7:4–17. God revealed this covenant to Nathan the prophet in a vision which contained three everlasting promises in 2 Samuel 7:16:

- Your house shall be established forever.
- Your kingdom shall be established forever.
- Your throne shall be established forever.

All three point to Jesus Christ, God's Son, who will forever establish His house, kingdom, and throne as the fulfillment of this covenant. These promises have in mind an individual connection through David, but also a universal connection through his seed, which is fulfilled in Jesus Christ.

David's house is his ancestral line which begins with him and ends with Jesus. Here is how that came about:

> David's particular role is to establish the throne of the Davidic Kingdom forever (v. 13). His throne continues, though his seed is cursed in the person of Jeconiah (Coniah), who was the king under whom the nation was carried captive to Babylon. Jeremiah prophesies that no one whose genealogical descent could be traced back to David through Jeconiah and Solomon would ever sit on David's throne (Jer. 22:24–30). Joseph, the legal, but not physical, father of Jesus traces his lineage to David through Jeconiah (Matt. 1:1–17). David, however, had another son, Nathan. His line was not cursed. Mary, The physical mother of Jesus, traces her lineage back to David, through Nathan (Luke 3:23–38).[58]

---

[58] Ibid., 309.

The result is that Jesus is humanity's everlasting Savior because of His connection to David's house. Jesus also is the everlasting Lord because He will establish the land of Israel universally as His permanent land of residence—but He will also accomplish this individually, within the hearts of those who belong to His kingdom.

Revelation 21:1–3 says,

> Now I saw a new heaven and a new earth, for the first heaven and the first earth had passed away. Also there was no more sea. Then I, John, saw the holy city, New Jerusalem, coming down out of heaven from God, prepared as a bride adorned for her husband. And I heard a loud voice from heaven saying, "Behold, the tabernacle of God is with men, and He will dwell with them, and they shall be His people. God Himself will be with them and be their God."[59]

Jesus will also be the everlasting King because He will rule over everything and everyone. Luke 1:31–33 says it this way:

> And behold, you will conceive in your womb and bring forth a Son, and shall call His name Jesus. He will be great, and will be called the Son of the Highest; and the Lord God will give Him the throne of His father David. And He will reign over the house of Jacob forever, and of His kingdom there will be no end.

The New Covenant. The New Covenant is found in Jeremiah 31:31–34 and confirmed by Jesus in Luke 22:19–20. This fifth and last theocratic covenant is centered around Him, the eternal and permanent fulfiller of everything. He causes us to have abundant and new life with God, transforming us from within so we can receive this New Covenant from God.

The phrase *"after those days"* in Jeremiah 31:33 refers to the restoration of Israel, which is completed through the birth (incarnation), life, ministry, death, and resurrection of Jesus Christ. His atoning work and restoration of all things will be fulfilled. The implementation of this covenant continues with the help of the Holy Spirit.

In that same passage, Jeremiah continues writing about what Jesus will establish:

> But this is the covenant that I will make with the house of Israel after those days, says the Lord: *I will put My law in their minds, and write it on their hearts*; and *I will be their God, and they shall be My people.* No more shall every man teach his neighbor, and every

---

[59] See the description of the New Jerusalem in Revelation 21:9–27.

man his brother, saying, "Know the Lord," for *they all shall know Me, from the least of them to the greatest of them*, says the Lord. For *I will forgive their iniquity, and their sin I will remember no more*. (Jeremiah 31:33–34, emphasis added)

Jesus is the fulfillment of every covenant established by God, allowing us to be restored to right relationship with Him. This is why Jesus is the sacred covenant, without whom all other covenants would be ineffective. Since His time on the earth, more than two thousand years ago, the New Covenant is possible because He accomplished what needed to be done. His life, work, death, and resurrection keep this covenant alive.

This new life with God is now available for us. We just have to believe in Him and what He did for us. When we do, this covenant becomes part of us, which is why the Holy Spirit is so important. He continues to help us benefit from the covenant to have a personal relationship with God.

Throughout history, all the covenants of God have benefitted us. They reveal not only His love for us but show that history would be incomplete without them.

CHAPTER FIFTEEN
THE WRITTEN WITNESS

THE WRITTEN WITNESS is the Holy Bible, the Word of God, which reveals who God is and imparts to us His wisdom, precepts, sovereign ways, and truth. Through the course of time, these insights about God and how He wants us to live have been collected and transmitted, first through the oral tradition and later in writing.

God has used various methods to communicate His words to us. He spoke to people directly, used angels as messengers, gave prophets foretellings, spoke through dreams and visions, and when the time was right directed Moses, the first author of the Bible, to write down His laws so the people could have a record of it (Deuteronomy 31:24–26).

This began the quest of writing down all the words of God, along with the events and circumstances associated with them. These writings have been transcribed in various mediums, including stone, clay, wood, wax, metal, ostraca, papyrus, leather, parchment, and paper. In modern times, the writings are also digital.[60]

Approximately forty different authors had a hand in compiling the books of the Bible in a process that took some 1,600 years to complete. The key in preserving these words of God, especially in the beginning, was through accurate transmission by duplication. This work was done by determined copyists and scribes.

Eventually, the demand for the Bible necessitated that it be translated into different languages. It was written originally in three languages: Hebrew, Aramaic, and Greek. From there, it was translated into Syrian, Coptic, and Latin, and over time it has of course branched out to more modern languages.

Whether the writing style was legislative, historical, poetic, didactic, prophetic, figurative, or narrative, the books of the Bible were inspired both directly and indirectly by God. Jews and Christians value the Word of God as being authoritative, inspired, inerrant, and infallible, explaining why the Bible is one of the most important revelations of God.

SCRIPTURE REFERENCES

- Ephesians 6:17
- 2 Timothy 3:15–17
- Psalm 119:9–16
- Joshua 1:8

---

[60] Neil R. Lightfoot, *How We Got the Bible* (Grand Rapids, MI: Baker Books, 2003), 13–19.

- Proverbs 30:5
- Matthew 4:4
- Hebrews 4:12
- James 1:21–25

QUESTIONS

1. Why did Paul describe the Word of God as a sword in Ephesians 6:17?
2. Is the Bible the authoritative and inspired Word of God? How does the Bible help us in our daily walk with God?
3. Why is it important to read the Bible on a regular basis? How does it cleanse us?
4. How does meditating upon the Word of God help us in our daily lives? Provide examples of certain passages that have helped you.
5. Is the Bible inerrant and infallible?
6. Can you imagine a world without the Bible? Explain what would happen. Is the Bible still relevant today? Does it prove the existence of God?
7. How does the Bible become alive? What makes it living and powerful? How does the Holy Spirit help us understand the Bible?
8. How is the Bible able to save our souls? Why is it so revealing and reflective?

ESTABLISHING TRUTH

Intellectually. A certain realization must take place within us to understand why our existence, our understanding of why we're here, is important. This realization is based on the premise that everything must have been caused by an eternal presence rather than by chance. This original source desired to bring forth the truth to make this reality of ours work. God, therefore, brought forth His written witness so we could live our lives with the understanding that all truth must come from God.

God allowed time to gradually incorporate this truth into our understanding according to our stage of development and what needed to be accomplished. Through inspiration, men wrote down the truth of God throughout history, and these writings demonstrated their commitment to knowing how important God is in the lives of those who want to learn more about Him and His truth. The Bible is a guide to how God revealed Himself and His ways to humanity throughout history.

The Bible was initiated by God and its truth was established before it even existed. It contains many of God's concepts which both describe who He is and inspire us to seek Him out. The Bible is self-authenticating because only an immutable God can permanently establish its truth. In fact, the very first verse in the Bible declares this fact: *"In the beginning God..."* (Genesis 1:1).

How can we deny this? Truth can only come from an eternal source. It cannot begin from nothing and then evolve. It can only have been established by an eternal God.

We also read in John 1:1, *"In the beginning was the Word, and the Word [Jesus, the living Word or living truth of God] was with God, and the Word was God."*

Do we have the right to question what the truth is when we weren't present in the beginning when time began? Since God is a just and personal God, He is the only one who can reveal this truth. And since truth can only come from an eternal source, we must consider that God's hand is reliable.

God sees the complete spectrum of time in one glance. Since His established truth pervades all aspects of time and space, there has to be a logic in how He presents it to us. This can be seen consistently throughout history. It was confirmed, fulfilled, and finalized by the three major revelations of God: His Word, His Son, and the Holy Spirit. All three unite to authenticate God's truth, meaning that we understand God's truth because of them. All of the revelations of God confirm His truth both in the general sense and personally in how He has influenced us.

Traditionally. The Bible is authentic, reliable, and accurate. We can see throughout history how the words of God were transmitted and translated by devoted and determined people who wanted to share the truth with everyone.

Despite inspired words written by flawed humans, God's infallible doctrines of life are well understood and accepted because they reveal His basic principles. No matter how the story is told, these words can't alter His message of truth. Sure, there are discrepancies as to what certain words mean and how they were translated, but they do not alter His ultimate meaning. It is merely a matter of whether someone accepts God and His truth.

The story of how the Bible came about is amazing. Here is what we know about how God preserved the Bible from the very beginning, leading to the document we have today.

The Pentateuch. The Pentateuch, the first five books of the Bible, was written by Moses (Deuteronomy 31:24). God spoke orally to Adam (c. 4004 B.C.), Noah (c. 2948 B.C.), and Moses (c. 1571 B.D.) about His ways. From creation to Moses's death, approximately 2,553 years passed, during which the Word was passed down according to the oral tradition through a series of links:[61]

ADAM →	METHUSELAH →	SHEM →	ISAAC →	LEVI →	AMRAM →	MOSES
687 years	628 years	452 years	77 years	70 years	61 years	

From Joshua to the preexilic period. For twenty-five years, Joshua continued to lead God's people after Moses's death. He kept the tradition of recording the laws of God and the events that happened during his reign: *"Then Joshua wrote these words in the Book of the Law of God"* (Joshua 24:26).

Once the words of God were written down, the additional role of the priests and scribes was to continually preserve these scrolls for the nation of Israel (1 Chronicles 2:55). They preserved these books of the Bible. Since the scrolls didn't last long, perhaps ten to fifteen years, it became essential to duplicate them (Joshua 21:1). For example, Phinehas wrote down everything which was important concerning the nation of Israel and their relationship with God.

Samuel, the priest and fifteenth judge of Israel, became the next most important individual in preserving the Word's path of truth. It is said from the traditions of the Talmud and from oral and other historical writings that he was responsible for gathering the information recorded in the Book of Judges and major portions of 1 Samuel (1 Samuel 10:25).

However, the fact that Samuel's death is recorded in 1 Samuel 25:1 proves that he could not have written all of it. This indicates that a single compiler may have helped to complete the books of 1 and 2 Samuel utilizing information from other texts (1 Chronicles 29:29, 2 Samuel 1:18).

The establishment of royalty helped preserve the words and historical content of the Bible after Samuel's death. Kings utilized their authority through written documents, with the help of priests and prophets who were led by God. David and Solomon published words of revered wisdom and song. Scribes and compilers wrote down the prophetic and historical words of the day.

Evidence suggests that a compiler who had access to historical documents helped to preserve the words of God during various reigns (1 Kings 11:41, 14:19, 14:29, 15:7, 2 Kings 18:18, Isaiah 36–39).

The next key figure was Jeremiah, who was both a prophet and historian. He was called by God to never marry so he could devote his entire life to declaring God's words to Israel in writing. He even had his own secretary, named Baruch, who tran-

---

[61] *The Timechart History of the World*, 4.

scribed everything Jeremiah uttered. While Jeremiah's first scroll was destroyed by the king, his second scroll was even more complete than the first (Jeremiah 36–38). He also may have had a hand in compiling some of the words written in both 1 and 2 Kings.[62]

The majority of the Old Testament books were kept first in the ark of the covenant (1 Kings 8:6–9), and then in the treasury of the temple (2 Kings 22:8). However, the temple was destroyed after Jerusalem was besieged by Nebuchadnezzar in 587 B.C. This resulted in the scrolls being lost. Only the psalms were saved. Through this ordeal, the leaders and priests may have wondered whether the other original books would ever be recovered.

Ezra and the postexilic period. Ezra was a direct priestly descendant of Aaron. He was also an educated scribe (Ezra 7:1–14) and a lover of books who had access to the written documents gathered by Nehemiah (2 Maccabees 2:13–15).

After the people's return from exile, Ezra and an official board of religious leaders collected what was left of the original writings, improved upon them, and added new books in a systematic compilation. The books of the Old Testament were most likely completed in the periods of Ezra and Nehemiah (Ezra 7, Nehemiah 8–10). This finalized canon of the Old Testament, known as the Masoretic Text, became the Hebrew Bible.

Thanks to Ezra and Nehemiah, here is a list of the references in 1 and 2 Chronicles which were utilized to help in the construction of most of the Old Testament:

1. The Book of the Kings of Israel and Judah (1 Chronicles 9:1, 2 Chronicles 16:11, 20:34, 25:26, 27:7, 28:26, 32:32, 35:27, 36:8).
2. A Commentary on the Book of Kings (2 Chronicles 24:27).
3. The Chronicles of Samuel the Seer (1 Chronicles 29:29).
4. The Chronicles of Nathan the Prophet (1 Chronicles 29:29, 2 Chronicles 9:29).
5. The Chronicles of Gad the Seer (1 Chronicles 29:29).
6. The Prophecy of Ahijah the Shilonite (2 Chronicles 9:29).
7. The Visions of Iddo the Seer (2 Chronicles 9:29, 12:15, 13:22).
8. The Records of Shemiah the Prophet (2 Chronicles 12:15).
9. The Records of Iddo the Prophet on Genealogies (2 Chronicles 12:15).
10. The Treatise of the Prophet Iddo (2 Chronicles 13:22).
11. The Annals of Jehu the Son of Hanani (2 Chronicles 20:34).
12. The Acts of Uzziah by Isaiah the Prophet (2 Chronicles 26:22).

---

[62] For example, compare the writing styles of 2 Kings 24:18–25:30 to that of Jeremiah 52.

13. The Vision of Isaiah the Prophet (2 Chronicles 32:32).
14. The Records of the Hozai (2 Chronicles 33:19).
15. The Account of the Chronicles of King David (1 Chronicles 27:24).
16. The Writing of David and His Son Solomon (2 Chronicles 35:4).
17. The Messages and Letters of Sennacherib Pertaining to Genealogies and Documents (2 Chronicles 32:10–17).

During the Maccabean period in the second century B.C., the safety of the Old Testament was again jeopardized. In 167 B.C., Antiochus IV burned the books of the law (1 Maccabees 1:56), trying his best to destroy Israel's sacred writings.

However, after three years of persecution, copies of the Hebrew Bible were procured outside of Judea and saved from destruction.

Many devout Hebrew scholars continued the work of preserving the writings of the Hebrew Bible. The Samaritan Bible, the Septuagint, the Aramaic Targums, the Peshitta, and the Vulgate have all benefitted from the transmission and translation of the Bible. In A.D. 100, Rabbi Aqiba and his colleagues continued to keep the transmission and translation of the Masoretic Text alive and well. They set the standard in preserving the sacred words of God and inspired many devoted scholars to translate the Bible into the different languages of the day.

New Testament transmission and translation. Jesus is key to the entire New Testament. Every book is about Him, His life, His works, and His message of God's truth and how to live before Him. The gospels of Jesus began as an oral tradition and then were written down into simple autographs, which were the authentic originals.

By the second century, the fourfold gospel and Pauline corpus had begun to circulate. Sometime later, the Acts and other epistles began to spread, along with the Book of Revelation.

Four different New Testament texts began to emerge according to their geographical location, including Alexandria, Caesarea, Antioch, and the West. The Alexandrian text gave rise to the earliest manuscripts, which include the Vaticanus (fourth century A.D.), the Sinaiticus (fourth century A.D.), and the Coptic text (also known as the Alexandrinus, fifth century A.D.).

The Vaticanus was used to translate the Textus Receptus Bible in 1515, as well as Luther's German Bible in 1534; although he used the Vulgate translation as well. The Sinaiticus helped to translate Tyndale's English Bible in 1534, the Cloverdales's and Roger's Bible (the Great Bible) in 1539, and then the Bishop's Bible in 1568. From there, the Elizabethan Bible (the Geneva Bible) came about in 1560. And once King James began his reign, his translated version was authorized in 1611.

Most of today's translations and current versions of the Bible come from this historical path of transmission.

From the Western text came most of the Latin versions of the Bible, which include the Codex Amiatinus, Old Latin, and the Vulgate. The Claromontanus manuscript was found in the sixth century, and it contained both Greek and Latin. From the Vulgate text came the first printed Bible, the Gutenberg Bible (1456), and the first English translation by Wycliffe in 1382. Later, in 1610, the Douai-Rheims version came forth as well as the New American Bible by Ronald A. Knox in 1955.

The Antioch early manuscript, or more commonly known as the Byzantine text, focused more on developing the Syriac versions, which birthed the Old Syriac text and the Diatessaron, which eventually developed the New Testament Peshitta. The Caesarea text is mostly a variant text written in a certain *koine* Greek style, but it isn't often found in the other three more commonly recognized New Testament manuscripts.

Today, these New Testament Bibles we possess have come about through a long history of hard work and dedication, even to the point of execution. We must cherish what these early transcribers and translators did for us and reap the benefits of their sacrifices. Their work brings out the best of what Jesus preached, lived, and died for and illuminates the Christian way of life. God preserved every word so we could see His love, plan of salvation, life principles, and truth.

Scientifically. Christianity holds the Bible as the authoritative, inspired Word of God and a major revelation of God. As 2 Timothy 3:16 declares, *"All Scripture is given by inspiration of God, and is profitable for doctrine, for reproof, for correction, for instruction in righteousness."* The Bible declares the truth about God and His ways.

We can prove that individual portions of Scripture are true. In order to prove that the entire Bible is true and logical, only a few facts must be established. The first step pertains to the reliability of Scripture and shows that it has received special divine attention in its preservation and accuracy.

One can determine the reliability of the Bible by using the same method used to authenticate any secular historical document. This method, devised by military historian Chauncey Sanders, consists of three tests: the bibliographical, the internal evidence, and the external evidence.[63]

The bibliographical test. The bibliographical test examines the reliability of existing documents by determining the number of manuscripts used in the transmission process and the time interval between the original and existing copies.

Before discussing how the Bible responds to this test, let's compare what other texts have revealed. The following chart lists the authors of historical documents, the

---

[63] Chauncy Sanders, *An Introduction to Research in English Literary History* (New Yorky, NY: Macmillan, 1952), 26.

year they wrote, the date of the earliest copy, the timespan between those two dates, and the number of copies available.

AUTHOR	WORKS
Aristophanes	Ther Achaemenians, The Knights, The Clouds, Peace, The Birds, The Frogs, Wealth
Aristotle	The Categories, Posterior Analytics, Infinity and the Nature of the Physical World
Caesar	Commentaries on War
Catullus	Archetype
Demosthenes	Speeches, Venetus Marcianus, Monacensis Augustanus, Parisinus
Euripides	The Cyclops, Alcestis, Medea, Hippolytus, The Trojan Woman
Herodotus	Histories
Homer	The Illiad
Livy	History of Rome (Ab Urbe Condita)
Pliny	Natural History
Sophocles	Oedipus the King (Colonus)
Suetonius	The Lives of the Twelve Caesars
Thucydides	History of the Peloponnesian War

AUTHOR	YEAR WRITTEN	EARLIEST COPY	TIMESPAN	NUMBER OF COPIES
Aristophanes	450 B.C.	A.D. 900	1200 years	10
Aristotle	384 B.C.	A.D. 1100	1400 years	49
Caesar	100 B.C.	A.D. 900	1000 years	10
Catullus	54 B.C.	A.D. 1550	1600 years	3
Demosthenes	383 B.C.	A.D. 1100	1300 years	200
Euripides	480 B.C.	A.D. 1100	1500 years	9
Herodotus	480 B.C.	A.D. 900	1300 years	8
Homer	800 B.C.	300 B.C.	500 years	643
Livy	427 B.C.	A.D. 900	1200 years	7
Pliny	A.D. 61	A.D. 850	750 years	7
Sophocles	496 B.C.	A.D. 1000	1400 years	193
Suetonius	A.D. 75	A.D. 950	800 years	8
Thucydides	460 B.C.	A.D. 900	1300 years	8

As this chart indicates, the mark to beat is that of Homer's *Illiad*, which can boast 643 copies, with the first one having been produced 500 years after the original was written. Since this book is accepted so widely today, why not the Bible as well? The Bible should gain recognition purely on the merit of its historical transmission when compared to *The Iliad*.

AUTHOR	YEAR WRITTEN	EARLIEST COPY	TIMESPAN	NUMBER OF COPIES
Homer	800 B.C.	A.D. 300	500 years	643
New Testament	A.D. 100	A.D. 125	25 years	24,000

Not only does the New Testament far outdistance *The Iliad* with respect to the number of copies in existence and the timespan between them and the original, it's also much more accurate. As we read in *A General Introduction to the Bible*,

> There are only 40 lines of the NT that are in doubt whereas 764 lines of the Iliad are questioned. This five percent textual discrepancy compares with only one-half of one percent of similar emendations in the NT.[64]

While the Old Testament cannot match the large number of copies that exist of the New Testament, that in itself bears witness to the high level of perfection achieved by the early transcribers. The earliest of these were the Talmudists, who operated between A.D. 100–500 and developed an intricate system of copying the Scriptures. So exact were their copies that older manuscripts were thought to be even less accurate than the new copies because of the possibility of damage and defacement over time. This tradition of perfection was carried on by the Masorettes from A.D. 500–900.

Although there is no question as to the importance placed on those who transcribed the manuscripts, until the Dead Sea Scrolls were discovered there was still a way to ensure the accuracy of the texts' transmission from the original Hebrew. The high degree of accuracy is shown between a copy of the original Isaiah scroll (125 B.C.) and the Masoretic text of Isaiah (A.D. 916). Of the 166 words in Isaiah 53, there are only seventeen letters in question between the two. Ten of these letters simply present a matter of spelling. Four others represent minor stylistic changes. The remaining three letters (the word translated as "light") do not greatly affect the meaning. Thus, in one chapter of 166 words, one three-letter word is questionable after a thousand years of transmission.[65]

---

[64] Norman L. Geisler and William E. Nix, *A General Introduction to the Bible* (Chicago, IL: Moody Press, 1968), 366.
[65] Ibid., 263.

Both the Old and New Testaments have been preserved remarkably well. One can agree with F.E. Peters that "on the basis of Manuscript tradition alone, the works that make up the Christians' New Testament were among the most frequently copied and widely circulated books of antiquity."[66]

The internal evidence test. The internal evidence test accomplishes much the same task as that of a witness's cross-examination during a trial. It is assumed that the witness is telling the truth unless the cross-examination can prove otherwise.

Since there have been no changes made to the story of the New Testament over the last two thousand years, the only opportunity for error must be with the original story, before any transmission occurred. Determining the reliability of the account must begin with examining the witnesses. For a witness to be valid, he would need to have been both geographically and chronologically near the recorded events when they occurred. The writers of the New Testament certainly fulfill this qualification.

Consideration must also be given to the witnesses themselves.

First, it must be asked if the witnesses are those who might lie based on personal characteristics and past history. If anything, the disciples were painfully simple in their literalness and directness. If a person has no internal defect which would cause a person to lie, the only option would be ascribe to them a motive to falsify—for there is a motive for every act of perjury.

It must then be asked if a witness's specific motive to perjure themselves can be exposed. In the case of the apostles, there are two ways to defeat any accusation of perjury. The first is their obvious lack of gain, either financial or social, by being untruthful. The second is that their Lord commanded them not to lie.

There may still be some who claim to detect discrepancies between the gospel accounts, thus proving their unreliability. However, the opposite is true. Should all four gospel accounts contain the exact same information, there would seem to be a much greater chance of the authors colluding together. The result we see appears to indicate their independent reliability.

The external evidence test. The external evidence test is the reliability of other sources which could refute the internal evidence. Those who would refute the Bible's claim to being historically accurate must show an external source that obviously contradicts information offered by the Scriptures.

The historian Josephus wrote about Jesus Christ as a real person and concluded that He was the Christ. Other external sources include secular historians who acknowledged the written manuscripts pertaining to Jesus and the rise of Christianity. They include Tacitus (A.D. 55–117), Suetonius (A.D. 69–122), Pliny the Younger,

---

[66] F.E. Peters, *The Children of Abraham: Judaism, Christianity, Islam* (Princeton, NJ: Princeton University Press, 2004), 50.

Trajan, Lucian of Samosata, and the lost works of Thallus and Phlegon. These writers all agreed that a movement was happening. They may not have thought the writings of Christianity would amount to anything, assuming instead that this upstart religious would eventually fade away. But that didn't happen, and today Christianity has become the largest religion by adherents around the world.

It can therefore be determined that the people involved with Jesus, including His disciples and those who wrote about Him historically, agree that the gospels and stories told must have been true. As there is so little time between the actual events and the circulation of the written accounts, people would certainly have been alive to either verify or contradict this witness. The very fact that the Bible is still widely circulated today is evidence that these voices did not speak out.

When proving the Bible's reliability, as compared to other historical literature, it can be concluded that it far surpasses the bibliographical test. It also passes the internal evidence test, as its contents and authors reveal no contradictions. And finally, it also passes the external evidence test, as the available critics were silent.

Spiritually. The Bible explains our present predicament and reveals what has happened throughout our history. Think of it as a pathway to God's truth, taking us on a journey of the steps taken from the very beginning to where we are today. God revealed His truth to us through the pages of the Bible, even though they were written by fallible writers. This fallibility reveals the infallible words of God.

As a whole, this is what the Bible reveals:

- God is holy. Therefore, He expects perfection. We were made perfect to have fellowship with Him (Isaiah 6:3, Leviticus 11:44–45, 1 Peter 1:15–16).
- Adam and Eve disobeyed God and were separated from Him (Genesis 2:15–17, Genesis 3:6–7).
- We inherited a sinful nature from Adam and Eve. We died spiritually and gradually die physically (Romans 5:12–14).
- God loved us so much that He wanted us back. He implemented His plan of redemption to restore us to Himself by sending His Son to die for our sinfulness. (John 3:16, Romans 5:15–21).
- Divine Jesus became a sinless human to take on the sins of the world to pay for our unrighteousness (2 Corinthians 5:21).
- By faith we become righteous before God because we belong to Jesus, who died in our place. He prepared the way for us to be restored (Galatians 2:20).

- We can renew our spirit-natures to live abundant lives by accepting Jesus into our lives as Savior and Lord (John 3:3–6).
- We can have fellowship with God today, just like Adam and Eve had before the fall (John 14:20–23, 17:21).
- We have eternal life, living with God forever (John 6:40).

We will find that the main reason for the Bible is to present a Savior for humanity. Every word, story, situation, event, and circumstance points to Jesus as the Messiah and Savior. Most of the discrepancies in transmitting and translating the Bible are due to misinterpreting the truths and principles of God.

Romans 3:23 says that *"all have sinned and fall short of the glory of God."* The fact that we are all going to die proves that we cannot save ourselves. If we were able to save ourselves, we would prevent ourselves from dying. We would prevent ourselves from becoming sick. We would save ourselves from hurting others. Basically, we would be able to resolve our own desire to sin.

If we had sinless spirit-natures, we would already live forever because we would have no contamination. We would be immortal, with no need for a Savior. Since we do eventually die, this means that something happened which we cannot solve. We inherited sinful and dying spirit-natures.

So what does this mean? Our own righteousness cannot save us. Our good works cannot prevent us from being judged by God. Since we cannot do what is necessary to make things right, we cannot save ourselves. Only God can do this work. In other words, we must do things God's way, not our own way.

It seems as though every religion out there, except one, insists that we can save ourselves by our own good works. The Bible, however, says that we cannot, no matter how good we are. Consider the following passages:

> For great is Your mercy toward me, and You have delivered my soul from the depths of Sheol. (Psalm 86:13)

> …for the Son of Man has come to seek and to save that which was lost. (Luke 19:10)

> For God so loved the world that He gave His only begotten Son, that whoever believes in Him should not perish but have everlasting life. For God did not send His Son into the world to condemn the world, but that the world through Him might be saved. (John 3:16–17)

> Nor is there salvation in any other, for there is no other name under heaven given among men by which we must be saved. (Acts 4:12)

> ...even the righteousness of God, through faith in Jesus Christ, to all and on all who believe. For there is no difference; for all have sinned and fall short of the glory of God, being justified freely by His grace through the redemption that is in Christ Jesus... (Romans 3:22–24)

> Therefore, if anyone is in Christ, he is a new creation; old things have passed away; behold, all things have become new. (2 Corinthians 5:17)

> ...knowing that a man is not justified by the works of the law but by faith in Jesus Christ, even we have believed in Christ Jesus, that we might be justified by faith in Christ and not by the works of the law; for by the works of the law no flesh shall be justified. (Galatians 2:16)

> For by grace you have been saved through faith, and that not of yourselves; it is the gift of God, not of works, lest anyone should boast. (Ephesians 2:8–9)

> And this is the promise that He has promised us—eternal life. (1 John 2:25)

> In this the love of God was manifested toward us, that God has sent His only begotten Son into the world, that we might live through Him. (1 John 4:9)

REASONABLE CONCLUSION

To believe in a truth, that truth must pass through a certain level of scrutiny. It must be established as reliable and authentic. We must determine its origin. This is the foundation of any truth. If we look at this reasonably, we must consider three criteria.

It must be reliable. For truth to be acknowledged, it must come from an established source. Something cannot come from nothing. Only then can we settle on a truthful way of life. Truth cannot evolve. It cannot be altered or changed. Laws can change, circumstances can change, and behaviors can change, but truth cannot. It must be established before the beginning, otherwise how can we know what the truth really is?

This is the story of the Word of God. It was inspired and authorized by God, the true original writer of the Bible. He used finite means and methods to reveal His infinite and absolute truth because we needed time to incorporate them into our way of life. What better way for Him to accomplish this but through the use of fallible yet devoted people, chosen through the course of time? These people were inspired and influenced by Him to write down His truth and His ways.

The Bible is our most reliable source of information about God because He is the reason it was written. If you believe in God, you believe in His Word.

It must have purpose. We are only possible because God is possible. Since He is the cause of everything, He is the only one who can explain why things are the way they are. This is why God gave us the Bible: so we could know Him, learn how to live before Him, understand who we are through Christ, and accept the gifts and provisions He has provided for us. Through Him, we can live fulfilling lives that please and honor Him.

The Bible, His written witness, gives us everything we need. It gives us purpose. It is complete, perfect, and foundational to everything we need to know. What would this world be like if we didn't have the Bible? Just imagine not having it around! Our lives would be so misguided. We would be lost without it.

It must prove its worth. How does one prove that the Bible really came from God, that it is more than a collection of books and stories written by mere men? Most truths are accompanied by visible evidence. They are verifiable.

Time is needed to prove a truth's worth. It must be established in the beginning and never altered in any way from its conception. Any truth that comes later is uncertain and the problem becomes one of interpretation.

This is why we must look through the entire Bible to prove that it is consistent in its precepts and doctrines. The Bible is its own best interpreter. Once we gain a clear picture of the truth it discloses, we gain a better picture of who God is and what is expected of us.

For the ideas in the Bible to be consistent and authentic, each author must present them in agreement with every other author of the Bible. Authenticity inspires authenticity!

As a reminder, this is the absolute truth of God:

- God is eternal. His truths, therefore, have been eternally established.

- God is holy. God desires for us to be holy because He is holy.

- God's wisdom far exceeds our own. God's wisdom is established by His sovereignty. He controls everything.

- God's truth is relevant. It has been established since eternity past. God has revealed it to us throughout history.

- God's righteousness matters. It's the only way for us to be restored to right relationship with Him. God implemented His plan to save, redeem us, and restore us through His Son, Jesus.

- God is personal. The Bible is personal because it reveals how personal God can be.

APPLYING TRUTH

Let's turn our attention to the practice of meditating on the Word of God, gaining knowledge through an overview of the books of the Bible and asking ourselves questions. This will involve us not only getting to know the Bible thoroughly but experiencing the truth of God personally and allowing the Holy Spirit to bring to mind what we have learned so we can apply it.

Meditation. How does one meditate on the Bible? There are several key steps.

- Set aside special time, continuous and uninterrupted.
- Before reading, ask God to help you understand it, and thank Him for what He will show you.
- Select a short passage. It shouldn't be more than a few verses.
- Read the passage several times. Then, if available, read it from another translation.
- Write down what the Spirit shows you, taking careful note of any applications He has for your life now. As a guide to what to look for, the following are some suggestions:
    — truth concerning God, Jesus, and the Holy Spirit. What does the text say about them, their character, their ways of working, and their relationship to you?
    — instruction about others and your relationship with them.
    — facts concerning yourself, your life, and how you should live.
    — commands you should obey, examples you should follow, and promises you can claim.
    — sins to forsake, attitudes to change, and errors to either avoid or correct.
- Sometimes these truths will be obvious, but other times you will meditate on them for a while before the Holy Spirit gives you revelation concerning them. Again, be sure to write down what you learn. Record the truth that is impressed upon you by the Holy Spirit.

CHAPTER FIFTEEN: THE WRITTEN WITNESS

- At the end of this time, thank God for His life-giving Word and what you have learned.
- Attempt as soon as possible to start practicing any practical truth you have learned in your time with the Lord through His Word.
- Share it with somebody. Take every opportunity to tell others what God is doing in your life and what you are learning.

Book overview. Before we end this chapter, let's undertake both an overview and comprehensive study of each book of the Bible. This will allow you to know a book of the Bible thoroughly and make it your own, allowing it to become more real to you and inspire you to live according to God's ways.

Here are some key questions to ask yourself of each book of the Bible:

BOOK INFORMATION QUESTIONS

- Who was the author?
- When was it written?
- Where was it written?
- To whom was it written?
- What kind of book is it?
- What language was it written in?
- Why was it written?
- When was it canonized?
- How is Christ presented in the book?

BACKGROUND INFORMATION QUESTIONS

- What period of history does it cover?
- Who were the worldly and religious rulers at the time of its writing?
- What major events were happening at that time?
- Is there any archaeological evidence to support this book?
- Describe the lifestyle and culture of the people living during this period.
- What other background information can you find concerning this book?

PROBLEM AREA QUESTIONS

- What general criticisms can you find concerning the book?
- Are there any theological problems in the book?
- What other problems occur in the book?

Comprehensive Bible study. Finally, let's present an overview of how to study each book of the Bible.

- Bible reading. Read the entire book in one sitting, and if possible in several different translations.
- Conduct a book overview (see above).
    - Book information
    - Background information
    - Problem areas
- Theme divisions. Divide the book into its different sections by theme. Most Bibles already do this.
- Text elaborations. Expand upon any verse that needs to be explained more fully. Use commentaries.
- Personal insights. Write down how a verse has affected you. What personal stories can you share? What does this verse mean to you?
- Christian living. What Christian values or principles are revealed in this verse? Will you incorporate them into your daily life?
- Key verses. What are the key verses in this book? Meditate and memorize these verses.

CHAPTER SIXTEEN
THE LIVING WITNESS

JESUS IS THE reason for everything, including your life, redemption, salvation, restoration, and having a personal relationship with God. It's all possible because of who Jesus is and what He has done for us. He is the living witness of God, having become like us—in the flesh, in a finite moment of time, as a human being.

After His death and resurrection, He personally revealed Himself to us in spiritual renewal. How much more must God do to show that He is real, authentic, and personal? Even when he performed miracles on the earth, people still wouldn't believe in Him. God exercised His supernatural power, wisdom, and love and people chose to reject Him.

Perhaps it seems odd that God would become human. Maybe this deters some from believing in Him. Yet it's important to realize that God had to become human in order to save us from eternal damnation. He was the only one who could do it. God sent His Son Jesus to bring us back to Himself not only as a living revelation, but as an act of love.

How can we deny God's love, mercy, and forgiveness? How can we deny this act of redemption? How can we deny the reality of the divine Jesus, who humbled Himself to be like us so He could restore all that was lost as a result of one act of disobedience in the distant past?

This realization, when we look deep within, should cause us to declare that it is possible—indeed, that it is required—for Jesus to not only be one hundred percent God but also one hundred percent human.

SCRIPTURE REFERENCES

- Genesis 3:15
- Micah 5:2
- Isaiah 7:14
- Isaiah 11:1–2
- Isaiah 53
- Malachi 4:5–6
- 2 Samuel 7:12–13
- Luke 2:26–35
- John 3:16–17
- Matthew 1:18–23

QUESTIONS

1. Did Jesus exist?
2. Did Jesus actually die on the cross? Was this a requirement by God?
3. Is the incarnate conception of Jesus real? Did God become human?
4. Was Jesus only God, or was He only man?
5. Did Jesus rise from the dead? Did He resurrect Himself from the grave?
6. Did Jesus perform supernatural miracles? Does this make Him God?
7. Why did the Pharisees reject Him?
8. Three times, the Father from heaven spoke audibly, calling on us to believe in His Son. Does this prove Jesus's deity?
9. Do the Christian creeds prove Jesus's deity?
10. Do the external witnesses prove that Jesus was real?
11. Does John the Baptist's declaration of Christ prove Him as God?
12. Note how the apostles lived and died. Does this prove Jesus's deity?
13. Do you believe that you can have a personal relationship with Jesus today?

ESTABLISHING TRUTH

Intellectually. When it comes to history, the facts of a person are authenticated by what others say about them. Our actions and words are displayed for all to see.

Jesus is no exception. Christianity was birthed through Him, affected not only by those who lived during His time but people of all times, even today.

The truth of Jesus was declared more than two thousand years ago. The question now is whether we will understand who Jesus really was. We can only decide for ourselves whether to believe. Christianity is more than a religion; it's a relationship worth pursuing, according to whether we believe Him to be who He said He was.

Intellectually, how could you be convinced that Jesus is real and that the truth He declared is worth pursuing and believing? Have you gone by what others have told you, by what you were taught, or by personal experience? Maybe you just can't believe some of the supernatural stories about Jesus, like His incarnation, the resurrection, and the miracles which He performed.

Traditionally. Let's look back through history to see what others have said about Him. Then you can decide whether you believe that this person has told the truth about Jesus.

The Father. Three times in the Bible, the Father spoke audibly about the truth concerning Jesus: at Jesus's baptism, at the transfiguration, and during Jesus's last week.

As for the baptism, Mark 1:11 states, *"Then a voice came from heaven, 'You are My beloved Son, in whom I am well pleased.'"* Regarding the transfiguration, Matthew 17:5 states, *"While he was still speaking, behold, a bright cloud overshadowed them; and suddenly a voice came out of the cloud, saying, 'This is My beloved Son, in whom I am well pleased. Hear him!'"* And pertaining to Jesus's last week, John 12:28 states, *"'Father, glorify Your name.' Then a voice came from heaven, saying, 'I have both glorified it and will glorify it again.'"*

Do you believe that this really happened? Does this cause you to believe that Jesus is God?

The Christian creeds. The early church established three creeds after the resurrection and ascension of Jesus. The apostles, fathers of the Christian faith, and church leaders were affected greatly by Jesus and believed truly that He was God's Son on the earth. They saw the effects of His life, ministry, death, and resurrection. These confessions of faith were declarations of who Jesus was and they followed Him, believing in His truth, because these revelations were authentic and provable. They affected people. They affected them. They affect us.

There are several biblical references to these statements of faith.

For one, Jesus was God in His very nature (Philippians 2:6–11). The church fathers solemnly believed that the following was true about Jesus:

- He was equal with God.
- He revealed God's love.
- He was given a name above every other name.
- By His name, every creature ever created would bow down to worship and praise.
- Every tongue, voice, and those able to confess would declare that He is Lord, above all.

Second, Jesus was the very image of the invisible God (Colossians 1:15–20). Jesus was the restorer, redeemer, and radiance of God, becoming King of Kings and Lord of Lords. One can only declare this if one knows it is true.

Third, Christ's divinity can be confirmed by the oral tradition of countless witnesses (1 Corinthians 15:1–11). The apostle Paul declared a well-known truth, and this became one of the very first creeds ever instituted by the Christian faith. By speaking this truth, he was passing along an oral tradition which has since been forever established by the early church.

This is what Paul declared: *"For I delivered to you first of all that which I also received..."* (1 Corinthians 15:3) This creed was received by Paul within two years of his conversion to Christianity. It was instituted as fact, confirming that Jesus died for our sins, that He was buried and rose from the grave after three days, and that He appeared to Peter, the twelve apostles, more than five hundred fellow believers at once, and then to James and the twelve apostles again.

There are three major creeds: the Apostles' Creed, dating back to A.D. 120–250, the Nicene Creed, dating back to A.D. 325, and the Chalcedonian Creed, dating to A.D. 451.

The Apostles' Creed

I believe in God, the Father Almighty, Creator of heaven and earth, and in Jesus Christ, His only Son, our Lord, who was conceived by the Holy Spirit, born of the virgin Mary, suffered under Pontius Pilate, was crucified, died and was buried; he descended into Hell; on the third day he rose again from the dead; He ascended into heaven, and is seated at the right hand of God the Father Almighty; from there He will come to judge the living and the dead. I believe in The Holy Spirit, the holy Catholic church, the communion of Saints, the forgiveness of sins, the resurrection of the body, and life everlasting. Amen.

The Nicene Creed

I believe in one God, The Father Almighty, maker of heaven and earth, of all things visible and invisible. I believe in one Lord Jesus Christ, the only begotten Son of God, born of the Father, before all ages, God from God, light from light, true God from true God, begotten, not made, consubstantial, with the Father; through Him all things were made. For us men and for our salvation he came down from heaven, and by the Holy Spirit was incarnate of the virgin Mary, and became man. For our sake He was crucified under Pontius Pilate, he suffered death and was buried, and rose again on the third day in accordance with the Scriptures. He ascended into heaven and is seated at the right hand of the Father. He will come again in glory to judge the living and the dead and his Kingdom will have no end. I believe in the Holy Spirit, The Lord, the giver of life, who proceeds from the Father and the Son, who with the Father and the Son is adored and glorified, who has spoken through the prophets. I believe in one, holy, Catholic and apostolic church. I confess one baptism for the forgiveness of sins and I look forward to the resurrection of the dead and the life of the world to come. Amen.

The Chalcedonian Creed

We, then, following the holy Fathers, all with one consent, teach men to confess one and the same Son, our Lord Jesus Christ, the same perfect in Godhead and also perfect in manhood; truly God and truly man, of a reasonable [rational] soul and body; consubstantial with the Father according to the Godhead, and consubstantial with us according to the manhood; in all things like unto us, without sin; begotten before all ages of the Father according to the Godhead, and in these latter days, for us and for our salvation, born of the virgin Mary, the mother of God, according to the manhood; one and the same Christ, Son, Lord, Only-begotten, to be acknowledged in two natures, inconfusedly, unchangeably, indivisibly, inseparably; the distinction of natures being by no means taken away by the union, but rather the property of each nature being preserved, and concurring in one Person and one Subsistence, not parted or divided into two persons, but one and the same Son, and only begotten, God the Word, the Lord Jesus Christ, as the prophets from the beginning [have declared] concerning him, and the Lord Jesus Christ himself has taught us, and the Creed of the holy Fathers has handed down to us.

Josephus. The fact is that history has shown Jesus to be a real person. Josephus, a Jewish historian in the first century, stated this himself. This has become known as the *Testimonium Flavianum*:

Now, there was about this time, Jesus, a wise man, if it be lawful to call him a man, for he was a doer of wonderful works, - a teacher of such men as receive the truth with pleasure. He drew over to him both many of the Jews, and many of the Gentiles. He was [the] Christ; and when Pilate, at the suggestion of the principal men amongst us, had condemned him to the cross, those that loved him at the first did not forsake him, for he appeared to them alive again the third day, as the divine prophets had foretold these and ten thousand other wonderful things concerning him; and the tribe of Christians, so named from him, are not extinct at this day.[67]

Almost every single person who came across the person of Jesus, including historians, comfortably declared that He was a real human being. There is no denying this. The question that comes to many skeptics, however, is that of His deity: was Jesus also God?

Some question how God could become human. Wasn't Jesus born human? Wouldn't it be impossible, even blasphemous, for Him to humble Himself to become human? And who is God that He could be less than Himself, that He could be more than one person, and that He could actually be put to death? It confuses the mind to think of God in this way. It further illuminates the reality of the Trinity.

Aside from Josephus, many secular historians wrote about Jesus and Christianity.

Tacitus, a Roman historian, lived from 55–117 A.D. wrote about Nero blaming the Christians for the fire in Rome in A.D. 64. He mentions Jesus as the Christus.

Then there's Suetonius, a Roman historian and biographer who lived from 69–122 AD. He wrote *The Lives of the Caesars*, in which he mentions the early Christians. He references a figure named Chresto, which may refer to Jesus. The expulsion of the Jews from Rome may be the same event mentioned in Acts 18:2.

Pliny the Younger was governor of the province of Bithynia, which is found in modern-day Turkey. He wrote about the trials of Christians and how they were executed if they believed in Christianity—or, in this case, believed in Jesus, even though he never mentions Him as the Christ.

Trajan, in a letter to Pliny concerning the effects and spread of Christianity, wrote about executing the Christians and their lack of belief in Roman gods.

Lucian of Samosata, who lived from A.D. 125–180, wrote *The Passing of Peregrinus*, in which he wrote: "The Christians, you know, worship a man to this day—the distinguished personage who introduced their novel rites, and was crucified on that account…"

The work of historians Thallus and Phlegon has been lost, but they are quoted in other existing works that reference their reports of a darkness in Judea during the crucifixion of Jesus. For example, they were quoted by Julius Africanus and Origen of Alexandria.[68]

---

[67] Flavius Josephus, *Antiquities of the Jews 18.3*, trans. William Whiston (Grand Rapids, MI: A.M. Kregel, 1981), 379.

[68] "Hostile Ancient Sources Point to Jesus' Divinity," *Christian Apologist*. April 18, 2020 (https://christian-apologist.com/2020/04/18/hostile-ancient-sources-point-to-jesus-divinity).

CHAPTER SIXTEEN: THE LIVING WITNESS

John the Baptist. John the Baptist was a witness of Jesus as the Christ. John 5:31–35 says,

> If I bear witness of Myself, My witness is not true. There is another who bears witness of Me, and I know that the witness which He witnesses of Me is true. You have sent to John, and he has borne witness to the truth. Yet I do not receive testimony from man, but I say these things that you may be saved. He was the burning and shining lamp, and you were willing for a time to rejoice in his light.

The angel Gabriel told Zechariah that his wife, Elizabeth, would bear a son and that his name would be John. This child became John the Baptist, the forerunner of Christ. When Mary visited Elizabeth, the baby within her leapt with joy at Mary's presence. Luke 1:11–17 links this moment with Gabriel's prediction.

Four hundred years earlier, Malachi had testified of this as well, writing that John would be the declarer of light about the coming of the Messiah (Malachi 3:1). Isaiah also confirmed this prophecy (Isaiah 40:3).

When John saw Jesus approaching him to be baptized, he declared,

> I indeed baptize you with water unto repentance, but He who is coming after me is mightier than I, whose sandals I am not worthy to carry. He will baptize you with the Holy Spirit and fire. (Matthew 3:11)

The apostles. The apostles were twelve men of average and simple lifestyles whom Jesus chose as His followers and disciples. They spent three years with Him, learning about a personal God and His way of salvation.

One day Jesus questioned them on who they thought he was.

> He said to them, "But who do you say that I am?"
>
> Simon Peter answered and said, "You are the Christ, the Son of the living God." (Matthew 16:15–16)

We have been influenced by many people in our lives. We learn from them and make positive changes as a result of their instruction, example, and inspiration. Jesus's sole purpose was to bring His understanding of God and salvation to anyone who wanted to know more about God and His living witness.

The twelve disciples were willing to die for their faith in Him, except perhaps for Judas Iscariot, who was more influenced by personal mission than Christ. In the end, however, he was filled with remorse and took matters into his own hands.

Each apostle was changed by Jesus, coming to know God in a real and personal way. They understood what Jesus stood for and what He was about. They discovered how to have a personal relationship with God through their devotion and faith in Jesus, their Savior, Lord, and King.

Let's take the time to consider each of the disciples to learn how their lives were affected by Jesus.[69][70]

Peter, a fisherman and the leader of the twelve, was influenced greatly by Jesus. Even though he denied the Lord three times through fear, he was empowered by the Holy Spirit to perform exploits and miracles. Many were saved through his ministry and he wrote 1 and 2 Peter. After being imprisoned for nine months, Peter was scourged and crucified upside-down.

John, a fisherman and Jesus's beloved disciple, was the brother of James the great. He was one of three in Jesus's inner circle. When Domitian tried to put John to death by boiling oil, John survived and didn't suffer any burns. Thus he was banished to the island of Patmos, where he lived until he was almost one hundred years old. Some claim that he ended up in Edessa in modern-day Turkey and died there. He wrote the books of John, 1, 2, and 3 John, and Revelation.

James the great, brother of John and also a fisherman, was the first of the apostles to be martyred. He was beheaded with a sword by the order of King Herod Agrippa I around 44 A.D. He had such zeal for Jesus and His truth that he loudly proclaimed against Roman gods and idols. His death was a great loss to the early Christians, but his legacy kept the others firm in their faith.

Andrew is the one who introduced his brother Peter to Jesus. He too was a fisherman and after Jesus's ascension into heaven he preached and ministered the gospel to Asia Minor and Thrace, and possibly even in western Greece. The Roman proconsul Aegeates threatened him with death if he continued to preach against the idols they worshiped, but Andrew couldn't stop. He was subsequently tied to a cross with both ends transversely fixed in an X shape. He died two days later.

Philip may have been a disciple of John the Baptist, since he originally lived in the same region as John. He preached in the areas of Greece, Syria, and Phrygia. Tradition says that he was scourged and imprisoned. He was later crucified around 54 A.D.

Little is known about Matthew, whose father was named Alphaeus (Mark 2:14). He was also called Levi. Matthew wrote his gospel some twenty years after the death and resurrection of Jesus. Tradition says that he preached in Jerusalem for fifteen years and afterward spent the rest of his life doing missionary work with the Persians,

---

[69] John Foxe, *Foxe's Book of Martyrs* (Old Tappan, NJ: Jove Publications, 1968), 11–13.

[70] Ryan Nelson, "How Did the Apostles Die? What We Actually Know," *OverviewBible.com*. December 17, 2019 (https://overviewbible.com/how-did-the-apostles-die).

Parthians, and Medes. The details of this are uncertain. Heracleon stated that he died of natural causes, whereas official Roman sources suggest that he was martyred in Ethiopia after being stabbed in the back by a soldier of King Hertacus. Foxe's *Book of Martyrs* supports this view, saying that he was slain by a halberd in the city of Nabadar.

Bartholomew, who is also identified as Nathaneal, is only listed as a disciple in the synoptic gospels (Matthew, Mark, and Luke) and the Book of Acts. Little is known about him. He was martyred for having converted Polymius, king of Armenia, to Christianity. One account of his death has him being crucified. Another describes him being skinned alive and then beheaded.

Thomas Didymus, whose first name is Aramaic and second name Greek, fused the Roman, Greek, and Jewish cultures. This doubting apostle eventually realized that Jesus was both the son of man and Son of God after seeing the resurrected Jesus alive by looking at his pierced hands and side (John 20:24–29). His ministry was focused mainly on the land of India and, to a lesser degree, Greece. Edessene tradition says that he was killed by four soldiers with spears. According to another story from India, he was killed by a Brahmin with a spear in 72 A.D.

There's not much to say about the other James, also known as James the lesser and the son of Alphaeus. We can assume that he was a brother of Jesus or a brother of Matthew. The Bible doesn't specify, so we are left to speculate. Tradition says that he died in the temple at Jerusalem where he preached, first being stoned and then, on the verge of death, being beaten by a fuller's club to the head.

Thaddeus is another obscure apostle known by numerous names, including Jude, Judas, and Lebbaeus. According to extrabiblical literature, he ministered in Armenia, Syria, and Persia and established a church in Edessa. Tradition states that he was either clubbed or axed to death for his faith, or that he was crucified.

Nothing really is known about Simon the zealot and there are no church writings of his ministry. The Golden Legend, a collection of writings that circulated in Europe during the Middle Ages, records that he preached in Egypt and may have partnered with Judas, Jesus's brother. His ministry was mainly focused in Mauritania in West Africa. Later he is said to have been crucified in Britain.

Judas Iscariot is best known for being the one who betrayed Jesus for thirty pieces of silver. As treasurer for the disciples (John 12:6, 13:29), he sometimes used the group's money for ulterior motives to make himself look good. He felt remorseful after turning over Jesus into the hands of the Roman authorities, having thought Jesus would deliver Himself. This remorse grew stronger over time and he eventually tried to return the thirty pieces of silver; when the priests refused it, he threw it in the temple and then hung himself.

Matthias was the new apostle chosen by lot to replace Judas Iscariot. Acts 1:21–22 tells us that he followed Jesus after His baptism and witnessed His ascension. He may have been one of the seventy apostles that Jesus sent out into the world. Tradition suggests that he may have preached in Judea before travelling to Aethiopia in modern-day Georgia. He died—again, according to tradition—either at the hands of cannibals in Aethiopia or from being stoned and then beheaded in Jerusalem. Hippolytus, on the other hand, records that he died in Jerusalem of old age.

Finally, we come to the apostle Paul. After persecuting the early Christians, who didn't believe the truth of the Bible as it was interpreted by Jewish sacred law, Paul changed his ways. Jesus revealed Himself to him through a blinding light, after which he was converted and devoted the rest of his life to sharing the gospel. Twenty-three percent of the New Testament was written by Paul, who was inspired by the Holy Spirit to present the truth of God's ways to Jew and Gentile alike.

Paul had an extensive ministry. After his fifth missionary journey, he was placed under house arrest in Rome and eventually beheaded because of his Christian faith. He died around 67–68 A.D. during the reign of Nero.

Scientifically. There is some physical evidence proving that Jesus lived here on the earth. Plenty of physical artefacts are associated with crucifixion, like the pieces of wood that were used. A few crucified nails containing wood and bone have been found in Caiaphas's tomb. These may be the same nails which were used to crucify Jesus.

According to legend, a robe was found near Jerusalem by Helena, mother of Constantine the Great (in 327 or 328 A.D.), that may have belonged to Jesus. Ancient blood from the time of Christ has also been found on the mercy seat of the Ark of the Covenant. It contained twenty-four chromosomes rather than twenty-three and was analyzed by the late Ron Wyatt, who claimed that it belonged to Jesus. However, he appears to have been an unreliable witness, so we are left to speculate.[71]

Other verified evidence includes the crown of thorns which Christ wore before His crucifixion. Jesus's tomb has possibly been located thanks to the Emperor Constantine's fourth-century declaration of the church of the Holy Sepulcher.

As for the evidence of the shroud of Turin, it can't be related to Christ due to the fact that it has since been dated to have originated in the fourteenth century.

So although there is some evidence, doubt remains. Any of the above could be taken as fact, or not. This is why we must consider the revelations of God, which He

---

[71] John Oakes, "Can We Trust Ron Wyatt's Published Claim..." *Evidence for Christianity*. April 11, 2019 (https://evidenceforchristianity.org/can-we-trust-ron-wyatts-published-claim-that-they-have-discovered-some-of-Jesus-blood-and-that-it-has-24-not-23-chromosomes).

has personally given to us, and compare them to what we have discovered, especially when seeking to prove Jesus's existence.

The proper question to ask, then, is this: why did Jesus have to become human? First of all, Jesus had to become human in order for God's plan to work. And in what manner was He supposed to become human? Did He just appear, as if to say, "Here I am. Believe in me"? One's belief is more convincingly substantiated when it takes into account the whole, from beginning to end. Jesus had to be human all the way through, one hundred percent.

Finally, Jesus had to be personal to us. This is the central message relating to how God views us as people. He loved us so much that He sent His Son to prove that He wanted us back, to belong to Him once again, and this was only possible by becoming human Himself.

Many don't consider Jesus's spiritual aspects to be in the realm of verifiable fact, yet the Bible states that power came out of Jesus when people touched Him, that something invisible and virtuous brought healing to those who stepped out in faith. The healing was made visible (Luke 8:41–48). Can we use this as evidence? Faith must become our reality and the person of Christ, revealed by the Bible, must be considered proof enough for us to believe in Him.

Spiritually. Faith is an arbitrary term to some, yet God states that it is impossible to please Him except through faith. To God, faith is fact. It oozes out of God. It's part of who He is.

The spiritual life is just an extension of faith. Our spirit-natures believe and are influenced by the unseen. This is what faith is.

The Bible includes many stories of Jesus performing miraculous acts that only God could have done. He raised three people from the dead: Jarius's daughter (Mark 5:22–43), a widow's son from Nain (Luke 7:11–15), and Lazarus (John 11:1–44).

He also healed the blind on various occasions: two blind men were given sight (Matthew 9:27–31), the blind and mute demon-possessed man was healed (Matthew 12:22–23), a blind man was given sight when Jesus came to Jericho (Luke 18:35–43), two blind men were given sight by Jesus when he left Jericho (Matthew 20:29–34, Mark 10:46–52), an unknown number of blind people were given sight by Jesus (Matthew 15:29–31, 21:14), a blind man from Bethsaida was healed when Jesus spat in his eyes (Mark 8:22–26), a blind man was healed when Jesus put clay on his eyes and told him to wash it off in the pool of Siloam (John 9:1–41), and Paul's eyesight was healed three days after he was blinded on the road to Damascus (Acts 9:3–18).

Many other miracles are documented in the Bible and other historical writings. It seems that people will believe in an invisible act if the result is profound.

Let's apply this to Jesus's life on earth. Will you trust in what history and the Bible reveals about Him? Will you take the next step of believing that He was resurrected from the grave and now sits in heaven, that He still watches over us and does His work invisibly through the Holy Spirit?

If not, why? Is it because you can't believe in something unseen? Do you need verifiable proof, like Thomas when he saw Jesus's nailed-scared hands and side? Understand that we must utilize our faith both in the physical and spiritual senses. We are, after all, spiritual beings living inside physical bodies. When you use your spiritual faith, your eyes of understanding are opened and you enter a whole new world.

REASONABLE CONCLUSION

How does God reveal Himself to us? Would God create us and then leave us alone? Wouldn't He do something about the sin that has afflicted us, which separates us from Him? Wouldn't He give us a second chance to be saved and redeemed? Isn't this the reason Jesus came to us in the flesh, so we could know more about the reality of God? He paid the price for our sin, overcame death by victoriously arising from the dead, and made atonement and eternal life available to everyone.

Every book of the Bible reveals these facts as a demonstration of His love and kingdom. Jesus stated in John 3:3 that *"unless one is born again, he cannot see the kingdom of God."* We will never understand God and His ways unless we connect to Him through our regenerated spirit-natures. If we don't, we'll be lost and incapable of understanding the reality of Jesus, who demonstrated God to us.

We recognize that Jesus lived on this earth for thirty-three years. We must also realize that He is still alive and available in the spiritual sense. This is the reality we must believe in today. He desires for us to know Him and understand that everything He has done benefits us. God wants us to utilize faith to believe that He is real, through our spirit-natures. This is the only means we have to fully comprehend Him. It will enhance our relationship with him.

If you don't believe this, why? What more must Jesus do to prove He is real? Will you not take this step of faith and believe in the reality of Jesus? If you do, it will change your life.

APPLYING TRUTH

Here is what happens when you believe in the reality of Jesus.

First, you'll realize that Jesus loves you. This was demonstrated when He became human so He could save and redeem us. He paid the price for our sin and took our place in judgment. Romans 5:1–11 explains this love of Jesus and what He had to do to bring us back to God.

You will be forgiven and justified before God. There is nothing worse than being condemned for the rest of your life without hope. Why continue to live with that hanging over your head? With Jesus, there is no condemnation, only forgiveness and love (Romans 8:1).

You will have the assurance of eternal life. John 3:15 says *"that whoever believes in Him should not perish but have eternal life"* — not because of what we have done, but because of what Jesus has done for us. When we accept Him by faith into our hearts, we belong to Him and experience newness of life and the hope of living with Him forever.

Jesus will be with you always. When we have a relationship with Him, we are assured that He will be with us in everything. He said,

> Go therefore and make disciples of all the nations, baptizing them in the name of the Father and of the Son and of the Holy Spirit, teaching them to observe all things that I have commanded you; and lo, I am with you always, even to the end of the age. (Matthew 28:19–20)

You will also have all the blessings you need in order to live a victorious life. Ephesians 1:3 says, *"Blessed be the God and Father of our Lord Jesus Christ, who has blessed us with every spiritual blessing in the heavenly places in Christ…"* Jesus has given us all the tools we need to overcome our circumstances. All we need to do is ask for help and utilize the gifts available to us.

Finally, your life will be changed for the better. We become a new person once Jesus comes into our lives. As 2 Corinthians 5:17 says, *"Therefore, if anyone is in Christ, he is a new creation; old things have passed away; behold, all things have become new."*

Alternatively, here is what happens when you don't believe in the reality of Jesus.

Since Jesus isn't involved in your life, you have to rely on yourself and others for love, acceptance, and fulfillment. But this doesn't take into account the big picture. We need a higher power to have any hope or understanding of life. What hope is there without God? If you believe that the world is purely the result of chance, you'll be left with no hope in the end.

You won't be forgiven or justified. If you don't believe in Jesus, if you deny what He can offer you, you must accept the consequences and realize that you will stand condemned before God in the end. You will live your own way and do the best you can, but by rejecting God's gift of salvation your sins won't be forgiven.

If you don't believe in God, you won't have eternal life. After death, you will live without God and be alone forever. Unfortunately, this is one of the absolute judgments of God: if you deny Him, He will deny you.

Jesus won't be with you in this life either. One of the benefits of having Jesus within you is that He is there to help you along. If you feel that you don't need Him, if having a relationship with Him isn't important, you won't have access to His gifts or His wisdom. You'll have to deal with life on your own and seek out the wisdom of others.

Finally, your life won't improve. You will remain with your unregenerated spirit and deal with sin and whatever else comes along, dealing with the effects of your sinful nature. This means you will answer to Him according to your own selfish wants and desires.

Accepting Jesus into your life. The Bible says that we merely have to ask Jesus to come into our hearts and accept Him as our Savior, Lord, and King. When we realize that we can't save ourselves, we look toward God as the only hope.

We read in John 1:12–13,

> But as many as received Him, to them He gave the right to become children of God, to those who believe in His name: who were born, not of blood, nor of the will of the flesh, nor of the will of man, but of God.

When you accept Jesus, you accept everything about Him. You belong to him and live your life with Him.

1. Admit that you are a sinner and need Jesus as your Savior.
2. Ask Him to come into your life for change and renewal.
3. Develop and mature your new spiritual nature through a relationship with God, church ministry, and daily living.
4. Fellowship with other believers, as the body of Christ, to solidify who you are in Christ, both in ministry and in life.

CHAPTER SEVENTEEN
THE TRANSFORMING WITNESS

THE HOLY SPIRIT executes His transforming power and influence to those who belong to God and do the will of God. He edifies the church, enhances the lives of God's people, and equips them to do service for God.

Observe what happened to the lives of the apostles who were chosen by Jesus. They were simple, ordinary men and women who allowed God to come into their lives and transform them to undertake exploits beyond their imagination. They were given the power to heal the sick, deliver the afflicted from demons, and share the good news. Those who accept Jesus are born into the family of God (Luke 10:1–24).

The Holy Spirit works alongside us. We allow Him to do the work through our lives, witness, and ministry. It's like a symphony, with the Holy Spirit as the conductor. We play our instruments through giftings and obey the moving of His promptings to fulfill the will of God by storing up treasures in heaven and expanding His kingdom for all of eternity.

It begins with your commitment to become a follower of Christ. Jesus must be your focus; when He is, He will give you a new nature, establishing your spiritual connection and relationship with Him. The Holy Spirit then dwells within you to enhance your life in so many ways. He becomes your helper and comforter, giving life meaning and purpose. The proof of this change is seen in how our lives are transformed.

In this chapter, we will look at how the Holy Spirit transforms us. We start by examining how the Holy Spirit works through us and then explore our spiritual journeys and ministries.

But first let us read some verses pertaining to this witness and ask key questions.

SCRIPTURE REFERENCES

- John 3:5–8
- John 7:37–39
- John 14:26
- John 15:26–27
- John 16:7–15
- Acts 1:8
- Romans 8:15–17
- Romans 12:4–8
- 1 Corinthians 12:1–11

- Galatians 5:22–25
- Ephesians 4:11–12

QUESTIONS

1. Do you believe that the Holy Spirit is the third person of the Trinity?
2. Is the Holy Spirit real?
3. Have you felt His presence in your life?
4. Are you born again?
5. What gifts has the Holy Spirit given you?
6. Has your life been transformed because of the Holy Spirit?
7. Share how the Holy Spirit has revealed Himself to you. How has He impacted your life?

HOW THE HOLY SPIRIT WORKS INSIDE US

The very first step in understanding how the Holy Spirit does His work is to obtain a new spiritual nature from God. In other words, you must be spiritually born again (John 3:3). This begins with your conversion, when you accepted Jesus into your heart, giving you a personal relationship with God.

Once you have this spiritual connection with God, the Holy Spirit dwells within you. Not only does He become your helper and comforter, but you become His servant in acting for God, encouraging others, and ministering salvation. He guides you to do His work through your presence, ministry, and gifts.

The Holy Spirit gets involved in your life by prompting you. For example, while out for dinner you may suddenly feel compelled to do something—perhaps to write down an inspiration, help someone in need, minister either personally or corporately, or go somewhere to meet someone. This is the Holy Spirit. Once you familiarize yourself with His voice through the utilization of your gifts, you will begin to build on that trust and rely on Him. These promptings must be followed obediently, but make sure you know that these promptings come from God.

Writer Tim Augustyn explains that these promptings must be discerned. He states that they are a common experience for the Christian believer. Here are some examples from the Bible:

- Simeon was moved by the Spirit to go into the temple where Joseph and Mary were dedicating Jesus (Luke 2:27).
- Jesus was led by the Spirit into the desert to be tempted by the devil (Luke 4:1).
- Paul was compelled by the Spirit to go to Jerusalem (Acts 20:22).

It's important to remember that there are other kinds of promptings we can experience besides the leading of the Holy Spirit. For example,

- Your heart can prompt you to give (Exodus 25:3).
- Your sin can also prompt you to speak (Job 15:5).
- Your troubled thoughts can prompt you to answer (Job 20:2).
- The devil even prompted Judas to betray Jesus (John 13:2).

Becoming a Christian doesn't ensure that all your promptings come from God. According to the apostle John, *"Beloved, do not believe every spirit, but test the spirits, whether they are of God"* (1 John 4:1).

In the Bible, some promptings came from the Spirit of God. Others came from inside people themselves, and still others originated with the devil. It's important to distinguish where promptings really come from.[72]

There is another important factor in terms of how the Holy Spirit does His work through us. We are to make ourselves continuously available and make sure we are open to allowing Him to work through our daily lives. This is what a servant does. A servant waits to be called, to be available to do his master's bidding, and to do the work well in obedience.

As a Christ-follower, do you have the Holy Spirit working in your life? Are you willing to be obedient to His promptings?

This is the beauty of having a personal relationship with the Holy Spirit. There are so many different ways in which to minister to others, so many different gifts to be utilized in sharing the gospel and helping those who are in need. Using your spiritual gift is both a personal blessing and an enhancement of your witness of God to others.

What a special privilege it is to be used by the Holy Spirit! He wants to be personally involved in your life so you can be sure that God personally loves you and wants you to be blessed beyond anything else.

SPIRITUAL LIFE AND MINISTRY

When the Holy Spirit is with you, not only will He lead and guide you but He will share Himself with you in moments when you're in need. Here are some examples:

- He will make the Word of God real to you.
- He will utilize your spiritual gifts in life and ministry.
- He will share His heart with you through prayer.
- He will speak words of wisdom and give insight.

---

[72] Tim Augustyn, "How to Discern Promptings from the Holy Spirit," *Open the Bible*. July 19, 2013 (https://openthebible.org/article/how-to-discern-promptings-from-the-holy-spirit).

- He will always bring you to Jesus.
- He will enhance your relationship with God.
- He will give revelations of encouragement and confirmation throughout your life.

Your Christian life can be divided into two areas: your spiritual life and your ministry. They complete who you are in Christ and can be synonymous. Your life can be your ministry and your ministry can be your life.

For instance, a prophet has his own unique personality and mannerisms. He shares his prophetic ministry through words and deeds. He also lives his regular life as a child of God.

In a way, we are all prophets. Even though most don't devote their lives to a call of ministry, we must have spiritual lives that are devoted to God. Whether we realize it or not, our lives can be a ministry. People watch how we live for God.

Establishing your spiritual life. Your spiritual life is a personal journey in living for Christ. It comes with its ups and downs, its ebbs and flows, its successes and failures. But with the help of God in your life, you will be encouraged to keep growing and maturing in Him. In this personal relationship, Jesus becomes the focus of your life—and this focus is sharpened by the Holy Spirit. He always leads us to Jesus so we can live as He lived, with love, commitment, and dedication.

The Holy Spirit will guide you and confirm your faith in God by giving you revelations of encouragement. This is done at different moments. For example, the Holy Spirit may tell you to remember a particular person. Or it could be a specific event. Later, you find yourself suddenly remembering that person or event. This moment of reflection is the Holy Spirit confirming to you that He was with you in the past and continues to guide your life.

Personal reflections. In order to provide insight into these revelations of the Holy Spirit, let me share some reflections from times in my own life when the Holy Spirit guided me.

I received a unique revelation of God when I was eight years of age. I couldn't sleep one night, because questions about God filled my mind. I couldn't figure out the eternalness of God.

So I went to my mom and asked her, "Where did God come from?"

I kept asking her questions. This was the Holy Spirit wooing me, causing me to appreciate who God is. He wanted to have a relationship with me. I was overwhelmed by the love He shared with me that night. Afterward, I couldn't help but accept Jesus as my Lord and Savior.

Later, when I was a teenager, my parents were struggling to pay the bills, so they asked me to pray. We owned two houses, and I prayed for God to help us sell one of them to help us meet our obligations. I prayed for a whole hour.

The next morning, I got up an hour early, got on my knees, and prayed again. Once finished, I went to school.

When I arrived home later that day, my parents couldn't contain themselves: they had received offers on *both* houses. My prayers had been answered!

On another occasion, the Holy Spirit helped me to recall a certain pastor who was involved at a church I occasionally attended. After a few years, our family moved to another city where we started going to a different church. And wouldn't you know it—there he was, the same man whom the Holy Spirit had prompted me to remember! It turned out that he had moved to this same city and become the new youth pastor at our new church.

This man, Pastor Colin Wellard, mentored me through a discipleship program. He has had such an impact in my Christian walk with God.

After getting into a car accident in 2011, an amazing feeling of unconditional love overwhelmed me. While driving that day, a spirit of anger and rebellion had risen up within me. The poor winter conditions hadn't deterred me from driving a little bit too fast. As a result, I lost control while taking a turn and hit an oncoming vehicle head-on. I asked for God's forgiveness and asked Him to help me get through this. That's when I felt Him touch me with his hand.

As I mentioned in Chapter Eight, I received a supernatural revelation of God at the time of my dad's death. This was a God-moment that confirmed to me how the Holy Spirit not only graciously guided me through a traumatic event but had a plan and purpose for my life.

One day, while at the bank to deposit a cheque, I found out that God had given me the gift of word of knowledge. I wasn't sure what was happening, but I suddenly felt the unction to speak this word to the teller. I told her that her husband would pass away and for her to be ready. When I saw her again the next month, she told me that her husband had been killed in a car accident only a few days after I was given that revelation.

Spiritual pilgrimage graph. Realizing that everything happens for a reason, know that the Holy Spirit is guiding you as a shining light and transformed witness to those around you. To understand the beauty of this, recognize how God continues to work within you.

The best way to understand this is to draw a graph showing how God has worked in your life, highlighting the revelations and experiences of Him being there for you. This graph reveals your spiritual pilgrimage in a glance.

DISCOVERING THE REVELATIONS OF GOD

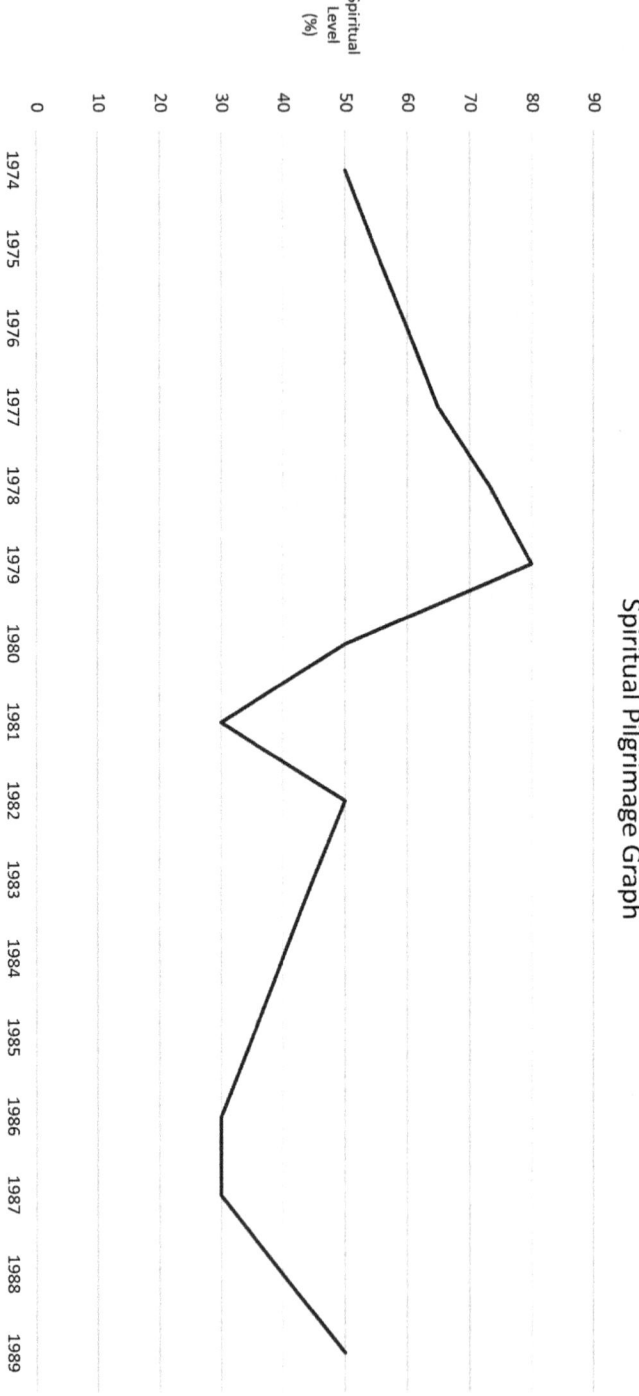

This graph provides an honest outlook of the most pertinent events of your life and how they have affected you spiritually.

The vertical axis measures your spiritual level, measured as a percentage. How committed are you to God? How complete are you as a Christian?

When you're in the eighty to one hundred percent range, that means you are in the perfect will of God. You pray daily, your focus is on God continuously, you're utilizing your gifts in ministry, and you regularly attend church services to worship and serve God and others.

When you're in the sixty to eighty percent range, you have an above average commitment. However, you experience lapses in dedication. This is normal in life. Sometimes our focus isn't fixed on God.

When you're in the forty to sixty percent range, your commitment is average. You are sometimes committed, but then you waver due to circumstances in your life. You rely on your own strength to get through.

When you're in the twenty to forty percent range, you aren't very committed to God. You're not developing your spiritual life. You pray occasionally and attend church mostly just to be there. Your focus is on the world as opposed to God. You don't involve yourself much in ministry and your devotion to God is low.

When you're in the zero to twenty percent range, you are in a backslidden state of spiritual depravity. Your commitment to God is nonexistent. You don't pray or attend church. You have become carnal and neglected the development of your spirituality. You have become worldly in your ways and conduct.

The horizontal axis indicates the year and your age.

To complete the graph, think back on your life and remember all the incidences when the Holy Spirit has been there for you. Recall those times when He has guided you through your circumstances. Realize that this is a confirmation of the Holy Spirit revealing Himself to you.

You are special to God and unique in your ways and personality. Your life matters! The graph will highlight those moments when the Holy Spirit was with you. Just note that a normal graph will reveal a very up-and-down type of spiritual experience over time. Whereas, a seasoned Christian will display a spiritual life of consistency and steadiness.

Here are some important key factors to remember:

- God is with you even when you are at your lowest.
- Your life may reflect a mixture of experiences, but God is guiding you.

- Write about those moments when you felt that your relationship with God was growing. Then write about those times when your faith declined.
- Don't be afraid to acknowledge the sins in your life. Learn from them.
- God has accepted you, both the good and the bad. He will never leave you.
- The Holy Spirit is there for you. Don't neglect Him and His workings throughout your life.
- The Holy Spirit will give you glimpses of Himself, confirming your direction and leading and strengthening your faith in God. These confirmations demonstrate that you are living according to His will.

Establishing your ministry. As a Christ-follower, you are in a relationship with God. Not only that, but you have been adopted into the family of God. You are now involved with the body of Christ, His church. It is a living organism and you are very important to it. You establish your ministry by enhancing the lives of God's people.

The church can be considered the tenth witness to God's existence; this revelation encompasses all the other nine, utilizing them to reveal God's truth, love, and salvation to others. We are the keepers of God's truth. The church is:

- The external witness of God's movement and direction (Matthew 16:18–19, 24:14, Ephesians 3).
- The conscience of God (John 17:20–26, 2 Corinthians 5:16–21).
- The continuing presence of God throughout history (Acts 17:26–27, Ephesians 1:4–5).
- The Word of God written in the hearts of His people (Jeremiah 31:31–34, Hebrews 8:7–13).
- The bride of Christ (Revelation 19:7–9, Ephesians 5:23, 1 Corinthians 12:17, Ephesians 1:22–23).
- A living and transformed organism being led by Jesus as the head of the church through the Holy Spirit (Ephesians 1:1–14).
- A place where God moves specifically in the lives of His people to meet their needs, bring healing, and give purpose to their lives (2 Chronicles 7:14–16)

- A place of worship and prayer where God meets with us personally. He is there with us (Matthew 18:20).
- A glorious church without spot or wrinkle, washed in the blood of the Lamb (Ephesians 5:25–27).

Realize that your ministry can be divided into three areas: spiritual life, full-time ministry, and lay leadership.

Spiritual life. After giving your life over to God, your goals change from what they were in your former life. You now lead a more spiritual life, growing and maturing to become more Christ-like.

Paul says in 1 Corinthians 12:12–27 that the body is one, even though it has many members. We are all part of the church, each of us endowed with individual gifts and personalities. We join to become the body of Christ: to worship and glorify Him, fellowship together in enjoying who we are in Christ, and share the truth with those outside the church who are seeking God. We celebrate God's goodness together and hurt together when one member is in pain. We build each other up and encourage one another in every aspect of life.

This is what the spiritual life is. This is church life! It's God being with us as we gather as a united family, enjoying His presence together.

Once you commit to attending a church, you begin to see ways to involve yourself in certain areas of ministry, whether it's full-time or as a layperson. This process develops every aspect of who you are and how you glorify God throughout your life and ministry. God wants you to experience the joy of being involved in His kingdom and purposes. He wants you to be attentive to His ways and honor him with a Christ-like attitude.

What kind of attitude must we evince in every aspect of our lives and ministry for God? Our attitude must be prayer-like:

> May I be mindful of You and Your ways, Father God. May I follow and serve You, Jesus, my Savior, Lord, and King. May I be obedient and sensitive to You, Holy Spirit, as the One who guides my life and gives glory to God.

Full-time ministry. Ephesians 4:11–12 explains the spiritual gifts of leadership. Are you a natural leader? Are you being called to full-time ministry? Here are some questions you should ask yourself.

- What do you believe God is calling you to do?
- Who will be your focus of ministry?

- Outline the confirmations of your calling for ministry.
- Which ministries would you like to commit to?
- Do you have any ministry experiences that confirm your calling?

Once you've established this calling in your life, ask yourself how you are going to get there.

The Bible, in 1 Timothy 3:1–13, also indicates that there are four offices of leadership:

- The elder: one who teaches and governs the church.
- The bishop: one who oversees the care and spiritual well-being of the church.
- The pastor: one who shepherds the flock, guiding the church to spiritual renewal and maturity so more sheep can be added to God's kingdom.
- The deacon: one who ministers to the needs of the church.

The Holy Spirit will confirm your calling in various ways: answered prayer, conversion, inspiration through others, supernatural revelation, inner promptings, resources and availability, circumstances, visions and dreams, prophecies, angel messengers, and hearing God speak either inwardly or outwardly.

Please note that your calling is specific and according to who you are as God's servant. Your ministry will always be comfortable, and you will feel a sense of continuance throughout your involvements. If you feel no such peace, it may indicate that a change is warranted.

Lay leadership. The apostles understood the importance of ministry. They also understood how church leaders and believers could work together, distributing the work to get everyone involved and fulfilled in their proper roles. Acts 6:1–4 states,

> Now in those days, when the number of the disciples was multiplying, there arose a complaint against the Hebrews by the Hellenists, because their widows were neglected in the daily distribution. Then the twelve summoned the multitude of the disciples and said, "It is not desirable that we should leave the word of God and serve tables. Therefore, brethren, seek out from among you seven men of good reputation, full of the Holy Spirit and wisdom, whom we may appoint over this business; but we will give ourselves continually to prayer and to the ministry of the word."

It is important to lessen the workload of leaders in the church so they can focus on studying the Word of God and spending time in prayer for God's guidance and leading. In this way, they can share with the people their insights.

Note that there are many roles for lay leadership in the church, including:

- Music ministry (worship/singing, piano and instrumental support, technical support/sound, advertising).
- Community ministry (witnessing, discipleship, and the ministry of helps).
- Teaching ministry (Sunday school, Bible studies, and special sessions and retreats).
- Support ministry (giving/tithing, exhortation, prayer and prophecy, hospitality, administration, special needs and groups, and fellowship gatherings).

CHAPTER EIGHTEEN
THE GIFTS OF THE HOLY SPIRIT

AFTER BECOMING PART of God's family through relationship and ministry, the Holy Spirit will give you a spiritual gift—maybe even more than one. Not only are all the spiritual blessings available for Him to use us for His purposes (Ephesians 1:3), but we will be given special gifts that will enhance our lives and ministry even more for God's glory.

In this chapter, we will delve into the gifts of the Holy Spirit, which we previously discussed in Chapter Seven.

MANIFESTATION GIFTS (1 CORINTHIANS 12:4–11).

These gifts are used by all of the people some of the time. There are three gifts of utterance: prophecy, speaking in various tongues, and the interpretation of tongues. There are also three gifts of power: faith, working miracles, and healing. Finally, there are three gifts of revelation: the word of wisdom, the word of knowledge, and discerning of spirits.

Those who have been gifted in this way will utilize them some of the time, when they are prompted to be used for God's purpose. These gifts are manifested through the Holy Spirit and He uses people who have been authorized by Him to use the gift to minister, exhort, and help.

Do you have any of these gifts? Sometimes it will be obvious, but other times you will have to experience and experiment to find out. Ask the following questions to see if you are gifted in these areas.

> 1. The gift of prophecy. This gift is a divinely anointed utterance from the Holy Spirit, usually given spontaneously, conveying His prophetic words to God's people.
>   a) Do you feel the prompting to speak words that have been given to you by God? Yes_____ No_____
>   b) Do you love to read and study God's Word? Yes_____ No_____
>   c) Do you regularly spend time in prayer? Yes_____ No_____
>   d) Do you have the gift of exhortation? Yes_____ No_____
>   e) Are you unafraid to speak the accurate words of God even if they're condemning? Yes_____ No_____
>   f) Do you see any personal gain from the use of your gift of prophecy? Yes_____ No_____

CHAPTER EIGHTEEN: THE GIFTS OF THE HOLY SPIRIT

2. The gift of tongues. This is a divinely anointed utterance of the Holy Spirit, given at a special moment in time. He utilizes your tongue and speech to speak in an unknown or heavenly language, either to groups, individuals, or even when you're alone in prayer.
    a) Do you have the gift of allowing the Holy Spirit to use your tongue to speak in an unknown language? Yes_____ No_____
    b) Is it easy for you to continually walk in the Spirit, communicating constantly with God? Yes_____ No_____
    c) Do you love to share God's Word? Yes_____ No_____
    d) Do you love to encourage and exhort those around you? Yes_____ No_____
    e) While speaking in tongues, do you have the ability to multitask, such as speaking and reading at the same time? Yes_____ No_____

3. The gift of interpretation. At the moment of hearing a prophetic gift of tongues, you know the intent of the message or can state the message verbatim.
    a) Do you have the ability to interpret any message in an unknown tongue? Yes_____ No_____
    b) Do you ask the Holy Spirit to give you the interpretation of any message you hear in an unknown tongue? Yes_____ No_____
    c) Are you spiritually attuned to know what to say after hearing a message in an unknown tongue? Yes_____ No_____
    d) Do you receive promptings from the Holy Spirit to interpret any message in an unknown tongue? Yes_____ No_____

4. The gift of faith. At a particular moment in time, or seen far in advance, this gift is used to reveal the workings of God, with the sure knowledge that He is going to carry out the work.
    a) Do you understand how to utilize faith in your life? Yes_____ No_____
    b) Are you able to step out of your comfort zone and utilize your gift of faith to believe that God will answer your prayer? Yes_____ No_____
    c) Do you like to pray for people, knowing that God is going to do something special? Yes_____ No_____

d) Do you have a deep trust in God no matter the circumstance? Yes_____ No_____

5. The gift of working miracles. God does something beyond what is normal and expected, such as when He calmed the sea during a storm. The gift is mostly supernatural, but it can also be a natural blessing on occasions when He uses someone to fulfill a need.
    a) Have you seen God perform a miracle in your life? Yes_____ No_____
    b) Have you prayed for God to do something profound and He answered your prayer? Yes_____ No_____
    c) Do you sense that God is going to use you for a special purpose to help the church or others who are in need? Yes_____ No_____
    d) Is your life filled with unexplained miracles, like those that might be performed by a prophet? Yes_____ No_____

6. The gift of healing. God uses you to bring healing to someone's life, whether it's physical, psychological, or spiritual.
    a) Have you felt the call to pray for people? Yes_____ No_____
    b) When you pray with someone, do you know for sure that God is going to heal them? Yes_____ No_____
    c) Are you free from any sin that hinders your ministry? Yes_____ No_____
    d) Is your faith able to overcome any circumstances or problems in your life? Yes_____ No_____
    e) Have you ever felt God's power pass through you as you prayed for healing? Yes_____ No_____

7. The gift of a word of wisdom. You have the wisdom to accomplish a specific task even when you don't know how to do it; you know an answer when faced with the question. This can come to mind spontaneously as the Holy Spirit illuminates your understanding.
    a) Have you been given the wisdom to understand something at a specific moment in time? Yes_____ No_____
    b) Have you felt the Holy Spirit give you an answer through His prompting? Yes_____ No_____

c) Have you been given the expertise to understand how a specific task or skill should be performed? Yes_____ No_____

8. The gift of a word of knowledge. You have the ability to speak words that have come to mind through the promptings of the Holy Spirit.
    a) Have you been given words to say to someone while being prompted to do so? Yes_____ No_____
    b) Can you clearly recognize the voice of the Holy Spirit? Yes_____ No_____
    c) Have you ever been given an exact vision of what will happen to someone and wondered if you should speak to them about it? Yes_____ No_____

9. The gift of discerning of spirits. You know and recognize the actions of the spirit world at any given time.
    a) Do you have the ability to discern someone's inner motivation or intent? Yes_____ No_____
    b) Can you recognize a demon-possessed person? Yes_____ No_____
    c) Do you have the ability to live your life in the spiritual sense? Yes_____ No_____
    d) Do you have the ability to speak directly to spirits? Yes_____ No_____
    e) Do you have the ability to sense what is going to happen? Yes_____ No_____

MINISTRY GIFTS (EPHESIANS 4:11–12)

These are used by some of the people all of the time. These special gifts are extended to apostles, prophets, evangelists, pastors, and teachers. They are usually used in leadership roles for the equipping of the saints for the work of ministry and the edification of the body of Christ.

Do you have any of these gifts? Are you being called to become a leader or pastor of a church or ministry? If so, this is a special calling which the Holy Spirit will lead you into. It will encompass all that you are in your abilities, personality, and situation. Answer these questions:

1. Do you feel that you have been called to become a leader?
2. Which area of ministry will be your focus?
3. Have you received a supernatural or special revelation from God?
4. Do you love studying and sharing the Word of God?
5. Are you able to wear different hats and act confidently in your dealings with people?
6. Do you pray often?
7. Have others said that you should be in the ministry?
8. Is your house and life in order?

MOTIVATIONAL GIFTS (ROMANS 12:4–8)

These are used by all the people all the time. The characteristics of these gifts can be described as: the perceiver, the server, the teacher, the exhorter, the giver, the administrator, or the compassionate person.

To discover your motivational gift, examine each of the following descriptions and characteristics to see if you can find the traits that describe your character. They will be revealed by how you conduct yourself with people and difficult situations on a daily basis.

The perceiver. The perceiver will have good spiritual insight. They will be outspoken and action-committed. They are very perceptive and can read others very well. They will know exactly where you stand on any issue, pursue their agenda with conviction, and be very principled. When it comes to fulfilling a task, they will be bold, do their best, and be persuasive when it comes to the tasks they are given to perform. They can perceive evil and live for God at all costs.

The server. The server will excel in the ministry of helps. They have the gift of serving others and see where they can be of assistance. They automatically set up chairs and tables when they see others doing it. When they see a need, they meet it. They have a courteous attitude and a heart of gold. They deem serving to be a priority and get upset when others don't think it's important.

The teacher. The teacher will have a certain culture and eloquence. They study knowledge and tend to be very intelligent. They also have a conviction that learning is valuable and precious. They have a teaching gift, which is seen in how passionately they express themselves. They present truth accurately and logically, absorbing new truth and sharing it with others. They validate truth with facts and get excited at the prospect of learning more truth.

The exhorter. Exhorters are encouragers. They are positive influencers and encourage others to live victoriously. They work with people, counseling them and watching them succeed. They tend to be very positive and optimistic and don't like it when others get down on themselves. They see the good in any situation and get excited when people receive good news. Their purpose is to leave a legacy by enhancing people's lives and leaving them better off than they were before.

The giver. The giver has the resources to give both materially and personally, specially by being generous with their time. They have a natural business sense, an industrious mindset, and seek the needs of others before their own. They freely give to support and bless people, quickly volunteering to help when they perceive a need. They pursue excellence and give joyfully through tithes and offerings. They believe that God is the source of provision and will deal with any financial obligation with honesty and transparency.

The administrator. The administrator is a visionary with many ideas. They set long-term goals, endure criticism in order to accomplish tasks, and take responsibility. They are good at accessing resources. They are highly organized and motivated, preferring to operate under another's authority in order to focus on the task at hand. They tend to do jobs themselves rather than delegate because they want to make sure it's done right.

The compassionate person. The compassionate person is like the Samaritan in Luke 10:30–37 who worked hard to save and help the man who was beaten by robbers. Their compassion dictates their attitude and actions. They have a sense of pity and put others' needs before their own. They detect others' pain and take steps to relieve that pain. They give wholeheartedly of their time, resources, and energy to make sure that others are blessed.

What are your top three motivational gifts?

CHAPTER NINETEEN
THE SPECIAL WITNESS

LET'S REVIEW WHAT we know thus far about the first six revelational witnesses of God, with the church serving as the tenth, or consummation, of them all.

They are subject to personal opinion and interpretation. You either believe in God or you don't. You either believe that God has revealed Himself through these revelations or you don't. You therefore interpret them according to what you believe is true and what you have experienced:

- The external witness: God created everything or He didn't.
- The internal witness: God gave us a conscience or He didn't.
- The historical witness: God was involved in our history or He wasn't.
- The written witness: God inspired the writings of the Bible or He didn't.
- The living witness: Jesus is deity or He isn't.
- The transforming witness: the Holy Spirit is real and alive to transform lives or He isn't.
- The church: God has guided His people through history as the keepers of His truth or He didn't.

Now we come to the remaining three revelations of God. These are more personal, individual, specific, unique, and intimate. If you aren't convinced that the first six revelations are associated with God, then these last three should bring you to a place of reckoning. You will have to make a final decision about God.

We will begin with the special witness of God. These are your God-moments, occasions when you've personally met God in various ways: prayerful self-searching, conversion encounters, miracles, and other unexplained occurrences.

When Adam and Eve heard the voice of the Lord God in the garden in the cool of the day (Genesis 3:8), it meant that they recognized that God was approaching them in person. This is how He wants us to know that He will continually have encounters with us in whatever way He decides.

After reading a few verses and answering some questions, we will examine some of these occurrences when God specially reveals Himself to us.

SCRIPTURE REFERENCES

- Psalm 8:3–9
- Psalm 20:1–9
- Psalm 46:10
- Proverbs 3:5–6
- Proverbs 8:17
- Daniel 2:28
- John 14:12
- Romans 8:26–30
- 1 Corinthians 2:7–11
- Philippians 3:20–21
- Hebrews 2:1–4
- 1 Peter 3:15–16
- 1 John 5:1–13

QUESTIONS

1. Have you experienced occasions when God answered your prayers?
2. Have you been converted or born again?
3. Has God revealed Himself to you supernaturally?
4. Have you received a miracle in your life?
5. Has God healed you in any way?
6. Do you receive promptings from the Holy Spirit?
7. What other God-moments have you encountered in your life?
8. Has God delivered you from any infirmities, sicknesses, addictions, or sin?

ANSWERED PRAYER

This witness comes from your personal relationship with God and it's founded on a committed prayer life. Do you make it a habit to spend daily time in prayer with Him? If you do, this is when God will seek your heart and deepest desires. He will begin to work for you and with you, developing your spiritual life and filling you with faith.

In essence, God wants to be sure that your heart and purpose are in sync with His. Once you have that assurance, He is going to be there for you. That's when you know something special is going to happen.

The Bible declares, *"The effective, fervent prayer of a righteous man avails much"* (James 5:16). When results happen, you will know that God has affirmed Himself with you and agreed with your prayers. These special God-moments are a catalyst for establishing the will of God in your life.

Not only does prayer change the situation, it changes you. It causes you to focus on the heart of God. It focuses you to seek what is most important. It unites and releases the power of God and reveals His will.

Here are some examples from the Bible:

- Elijah cried out to God in prayer, asking Him to bring a certain woman's son back to life. After her son came back to life, she said, *"Now by this I know that you are a man of God, and that the word of the Lord in your mouth is the truth"* (1 Kings 17:24).
- A barren Hannah asked God to give her a son. God answered her prayer (1 Samuel 1:9–20).
- Solomon asked for wisdom and God granted his request. (1 Kings 3:9–13).
- David, after the wives and children of those with them were kidnapped, asked the Lord how they should proceed. God gave him insight and David rescued all who had been taken (1 Samuel 30:8–19).
- Paul prayed for the healing of Publius's father and all those who came to him. The man was healed, along with many others (Acts 28:8–9).

Write out all those moments when God answered your prayer. Does this convince you that God is real and personal? Yes_____ No_____

CONVERSION

The moment when you're converted is an acknowledgment that God has met you personally and that you need Him to be involved in your life. You come to the realization that God is real and wants a personal relationship with you. You decide to accept Him and His way of life through the revelation of Jesus Christ, God's Son.

Conversion is associated with salvation. The bottom line is that humanity, from its depth of despair and hopelessness, couldn't save itself and needed a Savior. When Adam and Eve disobeyed, we all inherited the consequence of their sin, which separates us from God. But God provided a way to deliver us from evil and eternal damnation.

Sin, death, and sickness are part of the world we are born into. We have no control over them, but they bring us to a state of humility. In that state, we surrender ourselves to a higher authority. Once we come to realize that the only answer to our quandary is God, through Jesus Christ, everything makes sense. We need Jesus. We need Him to be our Savior.

Conversion is a God-moment when we encounter His presence. He meets with us in unique ways, tugging at our hearts and prompting our minds so we make the critical final decision about the reality of God. Once we decide to believe, spiritual change occurs within us.

Jesus conquered sin, death, and sickness on our behalf and conversion instills this understanding within us. Because of what Jesus did, we allow Him to change us, convert us, deliver us, and bring us hope. You will cherish this experience for the rest of your life.

Receiving the gospel of salvation can happen through various ways such as healing, deliverance, inspiration from others, miracles, unexplained acts, prophetic messages, or even encounters with the Holy Spirit. Jesus spiritually woos us to accept Him as our Savior, Lord, and King.

Our conversion—believing in what He has done for us and accepting our need of Him—is so important. This inward transformation is our ticket to an amazing relationship with God, and to eternal life with Him.

Here are some examples from the Bible:

- In the gospels, Jesus and the disciples performed many miracles, healings, and deliverances. They spoke hope and salvation and deeply affected those who sought God and His truth—and those who believed were converted.
- Crispus, a Gentile, was converted along with his family (Acts 18:7–11).
- After Paul preached to the Athenians on Mars Hill, some believed and were converted. Among them were Dionysius and Damaris (Acts 17:16–34).
- A jailer was converted after a supernatural earthquake set Paul and Silas free by opening the prison cell doors and releasing their chains. The jailer asked them, *"Sirs, what must I do to be saved?"* (Acts 16:30).
- Philip witnessed to the Samaritans. Through miracles and healings, they were converted. The treasurer was especially convinced after Philip shared with him the meaning of Isaiah's prophecy. Through a supernatural event of the Holy Spirit, he received the gospel, was baptized, and became converted (Acts 8:5–40).

Share your own conversion story. Does this convince you that God is real and personal? Yes_____ No_____

SUPERNATURAL REVELATION

God spoke to many people directly, including Adam, Noah, Moses, and Abraham. A voice from heaven was even heard by some of the disciples. Peter, James, and John watched the transfiguration of Jesus. They heard the Father's voice: *"This is My beloved Son, in whom I am well pleased. Hear Him!"* (Matthew 17:5)

Not only does God provide what we need in the natural sense, but He occasionally reveals Himself to us supernaturally. These special supernatural appearances always display God's transparent heart and fill us with divine purpose. They grab our attention even if we don't realize that it's God Himself, or an angel, appearing to us in person.

God's appearances are unique to us. We will either be oblivious or filled with curiosity. The event will be like no other we have faced before, and afterward we will question ourselves about what happened and why. As soon as we realize that God was involved, we'll have to decide whether to obey Him.

These encounters become lifelong remembrances. Because of them, we must dedicate ourselves to fulfilling the purpose that God has revealed to us.

Here are some examples from the Bible:

- God appeared to Moses at the burning bush (Exodus 3:1–6).
- Elijah and Elisha encountered God in the whirlwind (2 Kings 2:1–4).
- Shadrach, Meshach, and Abed-Nego were supernaturally delivered from the hot furnace (Daniel 3:19–30).
- Daniel was protected from harm inside the lion's den (Daniel 6:16–24).
- Jesus calmed the sea in the midst of a storm (Matthew 8:23–27, Mark 4:35–41, Luke 8:22–25).
- Jesus multiplied food in order to feed a large crowd (Matthew 14:13–21, Mark 6:32–44, Luke 9:12–17, John 6:1–14).
- Jesus walked on the water (Matthew 14:22–33, Mark 6:45–52, John 6:15–21).
- Jesus turned water into wine (John 2:1–10).
- Philip was supernaturally transported (Acts 8:26–40).
- Peter, James, and John witnessed the transfiguration of Jesus (Matthew 17:1–13, Mark 9:1–13, Luke 9:27–36).

If you have received a supernatural revelation from God, explain what happened and its purpose. If you haven't received one, then pray with an honest and transparent heart for God to give you one. Will you commit yourself to seek such a revelation? Does this convince you that God is real and personal? Yes_____ No_____

MIRACLES

Jesus was available to perform miracles in people's lives while He was on the earth. When they wanted healing, deliverance, or answers, Jesus granted their requests, especially when they believed and stepped out by faith.

Even though Jesus healed many people, however, there were those who were not healed because of their lack of faith.

While Jesus was always available to demonstrate the power and love of God through healing and ministry while He was on the earth, is He still available to us now that He's in heaven? Does He still work miracles today, even while the Holy Spirit continues to do the work of Christ in our lives? The answer is simple: "Yes, He does!"

Those believers who have the gift of performing healing and miracles have an unwavering faith in God, knowing that He will deliver in any situation. And receiving a miracle is always a special God-moment. It can be about so much more than a physical healing. It can be an occasion when God provides something you need, like food, guidance, wisdom, or finances.

There are many examples of healing in the Bible.[73] Healing often came about directly because of Christ:

- Jesus was anointed by the Holy Spirit to heal (Luke 4:8).
- We read that by His stripes, we are healed (1 Peter 2:24).
- Jesus bears our infirmities (Isaiah 53:4–5).
- Healing is always performed in the name of Jesus (Acts 4:30).
- All the fullness and power of the Godhead dwell in Jesus, giving us power over illnesses (Colossians 2:9).

We also read that Jesus has power over all manner of diseases, including fever (Matthew 8:14–15), leprosy (Matthew 8:2–3), paralytics (John 5:1–9), a withered hand (Luke 6:6–10), palsy (Luke 5:17–26), blindness (Mark 10:46–52), hemorrhaging (Luke 8:43–48), nervous conditions (Matthew 15:21–28), deafness (Matthew 11:5), muteness (Luke 11:14), seizures (Matthew 17:14–20), crippling spirits (Luke 13:10–17), dropsy (Luke 14:1–6), a severed ear (Luke 22:49–51), unclean spirits (Luke 6:18), and demon possession (Luke 8:36).

---

[73] Humbard, *The Prophecy Bible*, 1347–1349.

The gospels reveal to us that Christ's followers were also given power to perform miracles:

- Jesus told His followers to heal the sick (Mark 3:15, Luke 9:1–2).
- Jesus said that certain signs would follow those who believe in Him (Mark 16:18).
- The early believers practiced prayer for the sick, who were healed (Acts 3:1–11, 9:33–34, 8:6–7, 14:8–11, 19:11–12, 28:8–9).
- God has given gifts of healing to those in the church (1 Corinthians 12:9, 28).
- Jesus promised that we would do greater works than He (John 14:12).

So what is the formula for healing? This is also revealed in the Bible. We are to call for the elders of the church (James 5:14–15), anoint the person with oil (Mark 6:13), lay hands on those who are sick (Acts 28:8), and pray in the name of the Lord (James 5:14–15).

Further, when we minister to those who are sick, we are told that we are ministering personally to Christ (Matthew 25:36–40).

But the Bible also tells us of those occasions when healing doesn't go entirely according to plan. Not all people receive healing (Hebrews 9:27, John 11:4). When this happens, we must realize that God sees all things much better than we do (Romans 9:14, 16).

The truth is that some human and spiritual causes of illness must be corrected before healing is able to come (John 9:31, 1 Corinthians 11:30–31, James 5:16).

Despite these problems, God nonetheless desires for us to be prosperous and healthy.

Have you experienced a miracle of God in your life, whether directly or indirectly, at some point in your life? Describe what happened. Does this convince you that God is real and personal? Yes_____ No_____

ANGEL ENCOUNTERS

Throughout the Bible, there are almost three hundred references pertaining to the appearances and activities of angels.[74] They are God's messengers and our helpers, when directed by God, in time of need.

We are told about guardian angels (Matthew 18:10, Psalm 34:7, 91:11), celestial angels (Revelation 4:4), powerful angels (Revelation 12:7–9, 2 Thessalonians 1:7–10, Revelation 9:1, 20:1–3), herald angels (Luke 1:26–35, Acts 8:26), praising angels

---

[74] Lockyer, *All the Doctrines of the Bible*, 128.

(Luke 2:13–14), singing angels (Revelation 5:11–12), delivering angels (Acts 12:7–10), revealing angels (Matthew 1:20–24, 2:13–19), judging angels (Genesis 19, Matthew 13:41–42), and special angels like those who are specifically called to fulfill certain tasks (Genesis 3:24, 2 Kings 6:13–17).

We can't be sure whether they resemble humans, but they have been creatively designed by God with peculiar appearances. Some have eyes surrounding their bodies while others may feature symmetrical appendages. Most with wings. Ezekiel 1:4–28 describes multiple creatures being connected as one.

Angelic revelations can be startling. Some who encountered angels in the Bible were initially filled with fear. Once they realized what was happening, though, they were assured that the angel was there to fulfill God's will and declarations.

Good angels, those who have not fallen, are our friends. They protect, direct, and guide us. They provide for and encourage us, giving us prophetic words about what will happen in the future.

Sometimes we aren't even aware of their activities and involvements with us, but they come to cater to our needs and fulfill God's purpose in our lives. Angels are among the most unique and amazing revelations of God.

Here are some examples from the Bible:

- Angels appeared before Abraham at the announcement of Isaac's birth, as well as at the judgment of Sodom and Gomorrah (Genesis 18:2).
- Angels appeared to Lot (Genesis 19).
- A unique angel wrestled with Jacob at Peniel (Genesis 32:1).
- The angel Gabriel announced to Mary that she would give birth to the Messiah (Luke 1:26–35).
- An angel appeared before Zacharias (Luke 1:16–23).
- Angels appeared before Jesus to strengthen Him during His wilderness experience (Matthew 4:11).
- When Jesus was in agony in the Garden of Gethsemane, angels were there to support Him (Luke 22:43).
- Angels appeared before the sorrowing women at Christ's tomb (Matthew 28:1–8, Luke 24:22–24, John 20:11–18).
- Angels performed miracles (Acts 5:19, 8:26, 10:30–32, 12:7–11, 27:23).
- Angels also minister to the saints (1 Corinthians 11:10, Hebrews 1:14).

Have you experienced a revelation or encounter with an angel? Describe the moment. Does this convince you that God is real and personal? Yes_____ No_____

REASONABLE CONCLUSION

Enjoy your encounters with God. Enjoy the journey of experiencing these God-moments in your life, especially the supernatural revelations which are so personal, memorable, and intimate. God gave you these revelations for a reason. Please don't neglect them. Develop and pursue them in obedience so that God may be glorified in your life and ministry, and that others may share in the joy of what you have experienced.

Ultimately, these witnesses are about storing up treasures in heaven. We can watch others grow in Christ, experience Him, and expand God's kingdom through the conversion of new believers and followers of Christ. This is worth more than all the wealth and power in the world.

Encourage others to pray that they may receive these special moments of God. Encourage the people in your life to be patient to pursue God with heartfelt devotion and commitment so they can become the complete person God wants them to be. These God-moments reveal a life of divine purpose and they are special, between God and you.

CHAPTER TWENTY
THE PERSONAL WITNESS

EVERYONE HAS A story to tell. We have unique lives to live, wondering what each day will bring and what challenges we'll face. Will we overcome what life has given us or will we fall short? Will we be successful in our endeavors or experience failure? And when difficulties come our way, will we curl up in a ball and give up? Will we run and hide? Will we succumb to the world's influences? Or will we fight with determination and utilize our inner strength, gifts, and motivations to overcome?

Life isn't easy. It can be hurtful and cruel. It can squeeze everything out of us to the point that we can hardly breathe, think, or figure out what to do.

So we ask, "Why, God? Why have You allowed me to go through this? Why am I facing these difficulties and impossible situations? Why?"

SCRIPTURE REFERENCES

- Deuteronomy 32:39
- Job 5:18
- Psalm 23:3
- Psalm 30:2
- Jeremiah 18:1–6
- Romans 8:28–30
- Proverbs 3:5–6
- John 15:1–5
- Ephesians 2:10
- 1 John 3:1–3
- Romans 12:1–2
- 2 Corinthians 5:17
- 2 Corinthians 12:9

QUESTIONS

1. Why do we go through difficulties in life?
2. Do you wish you had a different life?
3. Do you suffer from an addiction?
4. Do you live with a disability?
5. Does it seem like nothing ever goes right?
6. Do you give up easily?
7. Do you have dreams and goals, and do you pursue them?

8. Do you know who you are in Christ?
9. Do you feel appreciated by others?
10. Do you do your best in every situation?
11. Do you like who you are?
12. Do you blame God for what has happened in your life?
13. Do you accept what has happened in your life?
14. Are you allowing God to refine you?
15. Will you build yourself up when others don't?
16. Will you believe and trust in God?
17. Will you pursue who you are as you were meant to be?
18. Will you be a personal witness to those around you?

CHALLENGING CIRCUMSTANCES

The Bible contains so many stories about people struggling through great calamity and emerging victorious despite them.

The apostle Paul tells us about all the troubles he went through to share the gospel with others. But he knew his purpose in life and was willing to die for it, which he eventually did (2 Corinthians 11:23–33).

Naaman was the commander and general of the king of Syria. He obtained many victories despite being a leper. He was later healed of leprosy by the prophet Elisha (2 Kings 5:1–19).

Job lost everything in his life. Despite all the suffering and pain he went through, he still trusted God through it all. Eventually God restored everything back to Job (Job 1:1–2:1–10, 42:10).

In 1 Chronicles 11:22, Benaiah went down into a pit with a lion on a snowy day. How much worse could this day get? There he was with one of the most ferocious animals, amidst some of the worst weather conditions, in one of the least escapable spaces possible. Yet Benaiah was resilient and overcame all these obstacles.

In the modern world, too, people endure extreme difficulties. Let's take a glimpse at some of this suffering.

Approximately six to eight percent of American adults are addicted to sex. That's about twenty-four million people.[75]

The United Nations has estimated that 271 million people between the ages of fifteen and sixty-four has used drugs in 2017. A study conducted in 2017 estimated that there were 585,500 deaths from drug use that year.[76]

---

[75] "Does Society Have a Sex Addiction Problem?" *Mayo Clinic*. December 6, 2022 (https://news-network.mayoclinic.org/discussion/does-society-have-a-sex-addiction-problem).
[76] "World Drug Report 2019, Executive Summary," *United Nations*. Date of access: November 3, 2023 (https://wdr.unodc.org/wdr2019/en/exsum.html).

CHAPTER TWENTY: THE PERSONAL WITNESS

The World Health Organization says that three million deaths occur each year, worldwide, from the harmful use of alcohol.[77]

It is estimated that 1.6 billion people are homeless around the world, and this includes those who report having inadequate shelter.[78]

The world has 253 million people with impaired vision, thirty-six million of whom are totally blind.[79]

As of 2010, there were an estimated thirty-eight million deaf people in the world.[80]

One billion people in the world live with a disability.[81]

One in fifty people live with some kind of paralysis.[82]

About 9.3 percent of the world's population lives in extreme poverty.[83]

The global unemployment rate is 5.77 percent, which account for 210.94 million people.[84]

In 2017, 9.6 million people are estimated to have died from various forms of cancer.[85]

One in four people worldwide at some point in their lives are affected by a mental or neurological disorder.[86]

The average global murder rate in 2017 was 6.1 homicides per 100,000 people. The rate is highest in the Americas at 17.2.[87]

---

[77] "Alcohol," *World Health Organization*. May 9, 2022 (https://www.who.int/news-room/factsheets/detail/alcohol).

[78] "First-Ever United Nations Resolution on Homelessness," *United Nations*. March 9, 2020 (https://www.un.org/development/desa/dspd/2020/03/resolution-homelessness).

[79] Peter Ackland, Serge Resnikoff, and Rupert Bourne, "World Blindness and Visual Impairment: Despite Many Successes, the Problem Is Growing," *Community Eye Health Journal*. Date of access: November 3, 2023 (https://www.cehjournal.org/article/world-blindness-and-visual-impairment-despite-many-successes-the-problem-is-growing).

[80] "The Global Deaf Population: 38 Million and Counting," *International Congress of Phonetic Sciences 2019*. November 6, 2022 (https://icphs2019.org/the-global-deaf-population-38-million-and-counting).

[81] "Factsheet on Persons with Disabilities," *United Nations*. Date of access: November 3, 2023 (https://www.un.org/development/desa/disabilities/resources/factsheet-on-persons-with-disabilities.html).

[82] "Paralysis in the U.S.," *Christopher & Dana Reeve Foundation*. Date of access: November 3, 2023 (https://www.christopherreeve.org/todays-care/paralysis-help-overview/stats-about-paralysis).

[83] "Poverty," *The World Bank*. Date of access: November 3, 2023 (https://www.worldbank.org/en/topic/poverty/overview).

[84] "Unemployment Worldwide: Statistics and Facts," *Statista*. August 31, 2023 (https://www.statista.com/topics/9225/unemployment-worldwide/#topicOverview).

[85] Hannah Ritchie, "How Many People in the World Die from Cancer?" *Our World in Data*. February 1, 2018 (https://ourworldindata.org/how-many-people-in-the-world-die-from-cancer).

[86] "Mental Health: The Silent Crisis," *International Baccalaureate*. Date of access: March 25, 2017 (https://blogs.ibo.org/2017/03/25/mental-health-the-silent-crisis).

[87] "Countries by Murder Rate: Ranked," *The Facts Institute*. June 17, 2020 (https://www.factsinstitute.com/ranking/countries-by-murder-rate).

Wow! How brave these people are, and how personal and unique their stories must be. Do we get the picture? Do we understand why we shouldn't condemn others, especially when they're just trying to live their lives as best they can?

Sometimes, though, judgment is warranted. Even when suffering occurs, we hope that good comes of it in the end. Yet there are some who would say that if something bad happens, the person who suffers may have deserved their particular fate.

So many people are living with addictions, disabilities, illnesses or chronic conditions, and poverty.

On the other hand, a large number of people are also living with purpose. In this chapter, we will focus on how our lives can change when we allow God to influence us. Let's see how God personally witnesses to us.

LIVING WITH ADDICTIONS

Even though we are creatures of habit, we have all experienced an addicted way of life in some form or another. Like anything else, that addiction can be positive or negative. It can be related to our behavior, what we consume, what we indulge in, and how we treat others.

There are so many substances or activities we can be addicted to, including:

- Caffeine
- Gambling
- Compulsive shopping
- Internet browsing
- Addiction
- Sex
- Alcohol
- Smoking
- Stealing
- Drugs (including prescription drugs
- Video Games
- Abusive and deceptive conduct

Howard was a hard-working tradesman. He had a servant's heart of gold and would do anything for a friend in need. He was the strong, silent type, fairly tall at six-two, and athletic. In his spare time, he played sports. He loved keeping fit and ran on a regular basis.

Yet everyone wondered why he kept to himself and never had a relationship, despite the fact that he was good-looking, personable, and successful. He seemed to have it all.

He grew up in a very strict religious home but then found God at an early age and was born again, accepting Jesus as His personal Lord and Savior. He went to church on a weekly basis, got involved in ministry, and shared his gift of teaching the Word of God.

Still, even though many women showed interest in him, he seemed not to return their affection. He showed no desire to involve himself in a relationship.

In a moment of counsel, Howard revealed to me the reason he couldn't seem to share his life with anyone. He had kept the secret to himself: he was a sex addict. To fulfill his hypersexual need for gratification, he regularly sought to have sex with the most desirable and attractive women he could find. He didn't understand why he couldn't seem to get emotionally attached to any of these women; all he wanted was a sexual connection.

He struggled with this addiction for a very long time, unable to overcome it. And despite being involved in ministry, he couldn't find a solution.

How do you view Howard? Do you think he's a bad person? Is he living a life of hypocrisy? Is he truly a born-again Christian despite being controlled by his carnal nature? Why isn't he able to overcome his addiction, especially when he appears to have it all together as a devout Christian?

And what about the other listed addictions we've mentioned? Will you condemn those who consume caffeine? Those who smoke, use drugs, drink, shop compulsively, gamble, browse the internet continuously, play video games all night, steal, and conduct themselves abusively? What would you say to them? "You really aren't a Christian! Why are you doing this?"

Perhaps you aren't affected by any of these addictions. Or maybe you don't deem all substance abuse to be dangerous, for example, creating enmity and separation between you and God. But addiction is no laughing matter. Just look at how easy it was for Satan to deceive Adam and Eve.

Each addiction we face is a lesson in how to overcome. God has allowed us to go through these struggles as a way for Him to work in our lives—bringing us closer to Him and focusing our attention on Jesus, who gave us the means to overcome addictions.

We've been given the tools to overcome temptation, too, for when we are spiritually renewed from above we have the ability to overcome lusts and desires through Jesus Christ.

Howard hadn't learned to utilize these spiritual tools to overcome his addiction, but he should be given the time and support he needs to keep up his daily fight.

So how are we to help these people? How are we helping Howard? Why do we condemn them? Their struggle is part of their personal witness of God. We must realize that those who have been allowed by God to go through addictions need our support, not our condemnation. We need to be there for them even when they don't want us to be there. God wants to transform them to be more like Jesus.

Consider those who have overcome addiction. It takes a lot of work to live for Christ on a daily basis. This is what having a personal witness of God is all about. It's about showing others how God is at work in our lives and what He has done to help us overcome sin. We must allow Christ to motivate us. We must look to Him for help.

In this way, our lives reveal God. It's not easy. It's hard work. It's a continuous endeavor to allow God and others to help us through our personal situations. We must humble ourselves and admit our faults (James 5:16).

If you do suffer from an addiction, realize that you aren't alone. People are there to help. Don't be embarrassed and ashamed to ask.

The wakeup call arrives when we realize that we can't overcome an addiction on our own. We must admit our problem and accept God's grace. Through addiction, we reject ourselves and come to believe that we're no good, that we have no value, but this is not the case. Addictions *can* be defeated. We grow more powerful when we understand that addictions are a way for us to place our trust in the right people. We have learned to trust in the addiction as the thing that will make us happy, but it really doesn't.

This is easier said than done, of course. Addictions are very controlling. Healing comes through the renewing of our minds and understanding how addictions affect our brains. To experience freedom, we must release ourselves and our situations over to someone else, not only to those professionals who understand how addictions work but to God.

Romans 12:2 says that we have been spiritually transformed by God, and physiologically transformed by rearranging the pathways in our brains. This is done by changing our behavior, substituting our addiction with more beneficial beliefs, and gradually developing a healthy lifestyle, all of which takes time.

LIVING WITH DISABILITIES

Those with disabilities are more dependent upon others for support, provision, and guidance. For those looking in from the outside, it can seem as though life is unfair to those with disabilities, and that God shouldn't have allowed such impairments and limitations to occur. This is because we feel sad for those who are afflicted in such a manner.

However, we forget that this revelation of God is what makes disabled people so special. We contemplate how these exceptional people inspire us by what they have to deal with and yet still manage to live happy, fulfilling lives.

A disability can be defined as any condition that makes it more difficult than usual for a person to perform certain activities or effectively interact with the world around them, either socially or materially. These conditions, or impairments, may be cognitive, developmental, intellectual, mental, physical, sensory, or a combination of multiple factors. Impairments causing disability may be present from birth or acquired during a person's lifetime.[88]

Before we go further, take a moment to reflect honestly on the following scenarios and how you view them:

- a person with no legs or arms, in a wheelchair.
- a person who is both autistic and blind.
- a person who is paralyzed.
- a person with Down syndrome.
- a person who is deaf.
- a person with a mental disorder.

People without disabilities often view those with disabilities as enigmas. Sometimes we don't know what to say, how to act, or how to deal with them. They can make us uncomfortable. Yet we are amazed at how they persevere. How do they continue to strive forward?

And how can we improve their way of life so they can feel appreciated, fulfilled, and valued? By giving them the opportunity to experience life in a variety of ways. We have braille and sign language to help communication. We also have sports opportunities designed for the disabled among us, such as the Special Olympics and the Paralympics. There are hockey leagues, basketball leagues, and even organized foot races for those with special needs, such as the blind or people in wheelchairs.

There are so many opportunities today for a person with a disability to pursue their passion. They just want to be treated like anyone else—to utilize their gifts, chase their dreams, and build their careers. Their true selves are contained within impaired bodies with greater limits than the rest of us, but they are nonetheless human beings. They want their independence and the opportunity to experience life to the fullest extent.

Accepting a disabled person brings out the best in us because we want the best for them. We can appreciate who they really are inside without judging them by their limitations. They too are able to be transformed by the revelation of God. He is what makes life worth living.

---

[88] "Disability," *Wikipedia*. Date of access: October 12, 2023 (https://en.wikipedia.org/wiki/disability).

A disabled person pursues their own personal witness of God. Their relationship with Him is the same as ours. They can worship, give thanks, and accept Him as their personal Lord and Savior. They can get involved in ministry, work a career, have a family, and feel accepted by those around them. We just have to accept their amazing and inspirational journeys.

LIVING WITH ILLNESSES OR CHRONIC CONDITIONS

Living with an illness or chronic condition, even old age, can be a challenge too, but it's something we all have to face at some point in time. We live our normal lives in our comfort zones, going about our business, until something life-altering stops us in our tracks. Confronted with the unfamiliar, we have to re-evaluate ourselves.

This is yet another opportunity for a personal witness of God.

As we've discussed, He allows us to go through struggles because He is always seeking our highest good. Does this mean that He purposely gives us illnesses? It can seem like a bewildering concept, because no one wants to get sick. No one wants to deal with something that makes life harder. When we have a disease, we want a cure. When we face a difficulty, we want a solution. We want our problems to go away so we can feel normal again.

The apostle Paul asked the Lord about this. He was infected with a so-called "thorn in the flesh." We don't know what the real issue was, but Paul wanted to be free of it:

> And lest I should be exalted above measure by the abundance of the revelations, a thorn in the flesh was given to me, a messenger of Satan to buffet me, lest I be exalted above measure. Concerning this thing I pleaded with the Lord three times that it might depart from me. And He said to me, "My grace is sufficient for you, for My strength is made perfect in weakness." Therefore most gladly I will rather boast in my infirmities, that the power of Christ may rest upon me. (2 Corinthians 12:7–9)

If God doesn't heal someone, it means He's giving them the grace to accept and deal with what they're facing. Paul understood that life happens and sometimes we can't change it. So we must change our attitude and accept what's happened. We must adapt ourselves to understand what God is trying to say to us.

So how are you dealing with these things?

When Jane Marczewski, also known as Nightbirde, auditioned for *America's Got Talent*, she shared her story of facing a type of cancer with a two percent chance of survival. She sang an incredibly inspirational original song, "It's Okay." That song told her life story and the attitude she held, that her life was about so much more than the bad things.

She later passed away from cancer, but she has left behind a legacy that will continue to resonate with people who learn of her.

Likewise, another singer on *America's Got Talent*, Cody Lee, affected the audience by performing his rendition of Donny Hathaway's "A Song for You." Despite being autistic and blind, he ended up winning the contest and having his own show in Las Vegas. What an inspiration!

We must realize that God has allowed us a certain amount of time on this earth (Hebrews 9:27). He has given us a purpose so we can live our lives to the best of our ability. We become revelations of God because our lives have meaning and we share what God has done for us as a way to inspire others to live purposefully and glorify God.

Please accept your current condition as a source of inspiration for others, one that points them to God as the sustainer, helper, healer, deliverer, and Savior. This is one of the most amazing revelations of God, because He works through us as a way to show Himself to others.

LIVING WITH POVERTY

What would it be like to not have enough money to eat? How would you deal with that? Almost nine percent of the world's population lives in extreme poverty. They haven't eaten in days, have no extra clothes, and most likely walk barefoot and live on the streets. One cannot imagine how they continue to hold onto the hope that perhaps things will get better one day.

Money seems to be the way of the world. Those who have it are free to choose what they want to do. They can buy anything to suit their uninhibited desires. Those who don't have money, however, have nowhere to go. They're stuck and often have no hope at all.

In 2012, according to the Organization for Economic Cooperation and Development (OECD), the top 0.6 percent of the world's population, or the forty-two million richest people, held 39.3 percent of the world's wealth. The next 4.4 percent (311 million people) held 32.3 percent of the wealth. The bottom ninety-five percent held 28.45 percent.[89]

Likewise, the Global Wealth Distribution found that individuals worth more than $1 billion, constituting just 1.1 percent of the world's population, held 45.8 percent of

---

[89] "Distribution of Wealth," *Wikipedia*. Date of access: October 10, 2023 (https://en.wikipedia.org/wiki/Distribution_of_wealth).

global wealth, whereas the lower fifty-five percent of the population owned only 1.3 percent of global wealth.[90]

It seems a little unfair that a chosen few can dictate where the world's wealth goes, how to control it, and how to spend it. They consider it as their very own possession and no one else is allowed to have it. The world deems this appropriate, yet most can't understand God's concept—that all the wealth of the world belongs to Him. He has allowed us to use His wealth and possessions for the betterment of ourselves and others. Instead of trusting in our own money and wealth, we should accept the concept of letting go of our possessions and being owned by God.

A rich man was once asked how much money would be enough for him to feel secure. His answer? He would need $170 million.

There is a biblical concept that says a person cannot serve both God and money at the same time (Matthew 6:24). It's a matter of trust; we either trust in our money or in God.

So will it be possible for those who have money to start distributing their wealth more freely? This seems to be difficult for some, yet there are those who have established charities and foundations to give to those who are in need.

This is a godly concept birthed in the heart. It goes with the understanding that God gave us money so we could learn how to give. He blesses us so we can bless others. This is an effective way to reveal God to others and deliver to people the hope that God does love and care for them. When we do this, we share God. If we hold onto our wealth and hoard it, we give people the impression that God isn't there, that He doesn't care.

We read in 1 Timothy 6:10, *"For the love of money is a root of all kinds of evil..."* Why is this true? Because when we hoard money, we focus only on ourselves and no one else. We must not pursue money as our highest priority.

When we give of ourselves, especially our finances, we reveal God to everyone around us and can be blessed beyond anything we could have imagined. We can delve deeper to understand the heart of God.

If you're living in poverty, please understand that you can give of yourself even if you don't have much money. It's a matter of attitude and trust. Even those who are poor will spend eternity with Him.

Faith plays an important role, because the greatest hope we have is in God. Money disappears and we can't take it with us after this life is over, but God is always there. He is faithful in everything concerning us. When we have a relationship with Him, He stays with us through everything we face.

---

[90] Anshool Deshmukh, "This Simple Chart Reveals the Distribution of Global Wealth," *Visual Capitalist*. September 20, 2021 (https://www.visualcapitalist.com/distribution-of-global-wealth-chart).

This is what our life revelation is founded upon: God working through us. We reveal Him to others with our lives, by what we do and how we give.

LIVING WITH PURPOSE

Each of us has been allowed by God to go through challenging circumstances, although they vary in the type of condition, how they affect us, how prepared and adaptable we are in facing them, how dependent we are on others, or how much they rely on us, and how we provide for ourselves and the ones we love.

This is all part of our revelation of God and it's an aspect of our relationship with Him. When we understand this, we better appreciate our lives and see the benefits of what others have gone through. It inspires us.

In any event, we need to appreciate everyone we meet, because they all have a story to tell. This is how God becomes more personal to us. Our lives matter to Him. He has the foreknowledge of what we will face in life, and in turn we glorify and trust Him through it.

Before we conclude this chapter, let's turn our attention to a few helpful truths.

You reap what you sow. Any tool we use can be for good or bad. For instance, we can use a knife to cut up pieces of meat. Yet some may use that same knife to harm others. It can be used as a weapon. Likewise, using the right amount of medication is good, but abusing it can do us harm. We can spend our money on frivolous things or use it to pay rent or buy groceries. And we can use sex as a means to fulfill us in the context of committed relationships, or we can use it to commit lustful infidelity.

It all comes down to our choices. Will we glorify God? Will we better ourselves and be productive? Or will we falter and allow ourselves to act destructively?

> Finally, brothers and sisters, whatever is true, whatever is honorable, whatever is right, whatever is pure, whatever is lovely, whatever is commendable, if there is any excellence and if anything worthy of praise, think about these things. (Philippians 4:8, NASB)

When you do good, you become good. When you focus on what's important and meet your own needs, you become happier and more satisfied. Likewise, as Christians, when we allow God to work through our lives and display Him as our own, others will see it. We share God with others by how we choose to live. People are affected by these revelations.

Accept yourself. It all begins with accepting yourself as having been created in the image of God. Fearfully and wonderfully, we were created for His pleasure, to have fellowship with Him, and to socialize with those around us. We are all part of

God's family and have different roles, abilities, gifts, and purposes which make the body of Christ a treasure. God is working in each of our lives. We appreciate each other because of this.

Accepting yourself means accepting God. Even though we can't understand why we go through certain issues in life, and we don't always know why God seems absent, we must realize that this life on earth is temporary. God sees the bigger picture: our home is in heaven. Once we understand this, we can understand ourselves as revealing God through our lives. It's a lifelong journey of trust.

Put God first. Even though we face addictions, disabilities, illnesses, and poverty, we must realize that God knows all. How we live is important to Him. So don't give up. Don't blame God. Don't blame yourself or others. Instead look to God first as the one who holds the answers.

Jehoshaphat, king of Judah, understood this when the Moabites, Ammonites, and Meunites decided to make war against him. Even though he was afraid, he sought God first (2 Chronicles 20:1–5). He called an assembly of the people and proclaimed a fast. He urged the people to pray and seek God. All of Judah stood before the Lord with their wives and children (2 Chronicles 20:13). When the battle began, it was God who won the war.

Likewise, when we face difficulties, it is God who brings us victory, especially when we seek Him first.

Remember that the battle is the Lord's. You are not alone. God is with you and He will give you answers when you're ready and the time is right.

Despite what's happening in your life, let God shine through. We are all ambassadors of Christ, who uses us to witness to others about God's greatness, provision, deliverances, guidance, redemption, and salvation.

Whatever you're facing right now, make it your life revelation of God. Let Him shine through you to inspire others. Not only will this become your purpose in life, but it will cause others to seek God.

CHAPTER TWENTY-ONE
THE PROPHETIC WITNESS

THE PROPHETIC WITNESS is a profound and unique revelation of God. Some call it a premonition, a prompting, a prediction, or a sign of some sort. Regardless of how it's presented, God uses creative ways to let us know about future events or circumstances He wants us to be ready for.

God can appear before us and speak to us directly, or He can speak quietly in our hearts, like He did with Abraham (Genesis 12:7). He can also speak a prophetic word through another person, who may speak in tongues or give a word of edification. Or he can speak to us verbally from heaven, like He did with Hagar (Genesis 21:17).

Many people in the Bible also received visions and dreams, like what happened with Peter and Cornelius (Acts 10:9–16). Angels can be sent to declare God's message, such as when the angel Gabriel spoke to Mary about her conception of Jesus.

God can even use an animal to declare a prophetic message. Balaam's donkey spoke to him about how stupid he was for not noticing the angel of the Lord, and not realizing that a donkey was actually talking to him! (Numbers 22:21–35)

Other methods can be symbolic. Numbers can be used as signs of affirmation or insight. During David's time, lots were cast to select the high priest. The apostles selected Matthias to replace Judas Iscariot by the same method. Gideon used a fleece to signify God's direction. Stars can represent significant events, like the star that led the wise men to the birthplace of Jesus. It has been said that a blood moon serves as an indication of turmoil.

Supernatural and natural God-moments can also be used as a prophetic witness. They occur when our relationship with God is built on trust, and when He wants to give us divine purpose. And when we don't understand an occurrence or situation, do we declare what happens to us as fate or as a sign of God's leading? Wherever we're at, in whatever situation we're in, we need to understand the will of God in our lives.

This chapter will look at the nine revelational witnesses of God—as well as the church, as the tenth and final witness—to discuss how their past, present, and future aspects affect us. We will also review what we've learned about these witnesses in earlier chapters.

According to Revelation and the prophetic message of Jesus in Matthew 24, we are now in the last days. Those texts prophesy that the history of humanity on this earth is nearing completion.

SCRIPTURE REFERENCES

- The Book of Revelation
- 1 Thessalonians 4:16–17
- 1 Peter 1:19–21
- 2 Thessalonians 2:3–12
- Matthew 24:3–31
- John 14:1–4
- Daniel 7–8
- Zechariah 14:4
- Daniel 9:26–27
- Matthew 25:31–46
- Daniel 12:4
- 2 Peter 3:10–13
- 2 Timothy 3:1–4
- Luke 12:40
- Luke 21:25–28
- Jeremiah 30:3, 7
- 1 Timothy 4:1
- 1 Corinthians 15:52

QUESTIONS

1. Have you ever received a prophecy concerning your future?
2. Have you given a prophecy to someone else?
3. Do you believe that your life has been designed by God and that He guides us through prophetic signs and inner promptings? Explain why.
4. Do you believe that the book of Revelation is literal, figurative, spiritual, or just a symbolic narrative?
5. Do you believe that we are in the last days?
6. Is Jesus about to return in His second coming?
7. Do you believe in the pre-, mid-, or post-tribulation rapture?
8. Does the Bible give you guidance and revelation?
9. Does the Holy Spirit speak to you concerning what you should do?
10. Is the rapture going to happen? Are you ready for it?
11. Describe the Antichrist. What does the Bible say about him?

12. Are you looking forward to the millennial reign of Christ?
13. Is the prophetic witness a revelation of God? Explain why you feel this way.

TIME IS THE CONTROLLING MECHANISM

Was time created by God, or is it the product of its environment? We can see and experience the passage of time in how precisely the seasons turn, for example. Time is the correlation between the rotation of the earth and its orbital position from the sun. It is difficult for us to understand, since we have no control over this. We wouldn't experience life as we know it without time, though, because of the way we age. And how could time have evolved by chance? Also, the fact that we have hope for the future serves as a proof of both time and God's creation of it.

God has established the continuum of time, space, and matter as the foundation of bringing our existence into reality. Genesis one declares this fact: "In the beginning...[that's time], God created the heavens… [there's space], and the earth [there's matter]."

God, therefore, cannot be limited by this continuum because He is outside of this realm. If He was limited by time, space, and matter, then He would not be God. He declared the continuum as an established decree so that everything will be fulfilled according to His will. Just like holding a ruler in His hands, God knows how time begins and how it ends. Since God is existing in the past, the present, and the future at the same time, He knows what the future is like. It has already happened in His view. It is therefore logical to conclude that time, through God's design, is the controlling mechanism behind the universe – and time is under His control. Time proves God's existence as the master designer.

This is why the prophetic witness is an authentic revelation of God. He created the full continuity of time, from the beginning to the present moment and into the future, including its ending. He knows what's going to happen, which is why He is able to give us prophetic messages.

THE SIGN OF THE TIMES

Can prophecy be proven scientifically? Yes. If the prophecy becomes true and fulfills itself, we would consider it to be proven fact. We must realize that only God can reveal future events. How else would events fall into place unless God exercised control?

Not only does the Bible contain many prophecies which have been fulfilled, it also tells us how the end will play out. Let's begin our discussion by addressing the prophetic signs of the last days, as predicted by Jesus in Matthew 24:

> Do you not see all these things? Assuredly, I say to you, not one stone shall be left here upon another, that shall not be thrown down...[91]
>
> For many will come in My name, saying, "I am the Christ," and will deceive many. And you will hear of wars and rumors of wars. See that you are not troubled; for all these things must come to pass, but the end is not yet. For nation will rise against nation, and kingdom against kingdom. And there will be famines, pestilences, and earthquakes in various places.
>
> Then they will deliver you up to tribulation and kill you, and you will be hated by all nations for My name's sake. And then many will be offended, will betray one another, and will hate one another. Then many false prophets will rise up and deceive many. And because lawlessness will abound, the love of many will grow cold. (Matthew 24:2, 5–7, 9–12)

Do we see these things happening today? Yes, we do! Even Paul predicted what these times would be like, in regards to how far we have fallen away from God and His way of life.

Consider what 2 Timothy 3:1–4 says regarding people's attitudes becoming more selfish and hateful:

> But know this, that in the last days perilous times will come: For men will be lovers of themselves, lovers of money, boasters, proud, blasphemers, disobedient to parents, unthankful, unholy, unloving, unforgiving, slanderers, without self-control, brutal, despisers of good, traitors, headstrong, haughty, lovers of pleasure rather than lovers of God...

We are surely in the last days, for it's amazing how accurately this describes the world today. We have become godless, no longer fearing Him or seeking His purposes. We seek our own agendas, our own pleasures, our own goals and desires. We have taken God out of the picture and replaced Him with ourselves.

THE GENERAL REVELATIONS OF GOD

In this next section, we will examine each of the revelational witnesses of God in terms of how they relate to the last days. We begin with the three general, extrinsic

---
[91] Note that the temple was destroyed just one decade later, approximately, in A.D. 70.

revelations: nature (from what we see externally), conscience (what we perceive inwardly), and history (what we perceive about the human story throughout time).

Nature. *The past.* The Bible says that God created everything, including the earth. Psalm 24:1 says, *"The earth is the Lord's, and all its fullness, the world and those who dwell therein."* The reason God decided to do this is found in Revelation 4:11: *"You are worthy, O Lord, to receive glory and honor and power; for You created all things, and by Your will they exist and were created."*

God wanted us to have the gift of life so we could enjoy who we are and experience the blessings of what this world brings, including the joy of having personal relationships with family, others, and God.

The present. By using common sense, we first realize that something can only come from something, and that this something must be eternal in order for existence to function. Only God is eternal. He is the only one with the intelligence, creativity, and ability to bring everything into existence.

Why does the universe operate so precisely and logically? It can only be explained by an intelligent designer. How could natural processes conduct themselves on their own without some form of intelligence behind them? The fact that we have the ability to reason and explain what we observe of the world proves that we were given the gift of understanding through the eyes of God.

The future. Our earth is becoming more prone to destruction, devastation, and defects as time passes. It is aging and falling apart. Diseases are becoming more prevalent, weather patterns more destructive, and volcanic eruptions and earthquakes more frequent. Climate change is increasing the temperature. The human heart, too, is becoming colder and more selfish.

The prophecy. The end of history seems to be imminent. Revelation 21:1 says, *"Now I saw a new heaven and a new earth, for the first heaven and the first earth had passed away. Also there was no more sea."*

The external witness. The universe is continually expanding. How can there be more room? Since God is boundless, this proves that He is infinite and eternal. Nature and the universe display God's characteristics and traits. How can we not see this?

Do you believe that God is revealed through nature? Yes_____ No_____ Explain why.

Conscience. *The past.* How did Cain feel after he took the life of his brother Abel? And how did Adam and Eve feel after they ate from the tree of knowledge of good and evil? We can be sure to have this same feeling after we're caught stealing, lying, or doing anything else that's contrary to the law.

We were made in the image of God. He designed us so we'd know Him and understand how to live before Him. God gave us a copy of Himself, and this is shown by our conscience.

The present. This world appears to be out of control. We don't seem to live with integrity anymore, and people are forcing their own purposes and desires over everyone and everything else. Murderers often walk into public places and start shooting people without thought or remorse. It just doesn't make sense.

But when we don't care about anything, when we ignore God's witness within us, we must realize that we are capable of doing hurtful things.

The future. God is holy and has communicated His standards to us. We know what's important to Him and can read about it in Leviticus, which tells us how to conduct ourselves sexually and socially.

What we read in Leviticus is quite different from the world we see now and in the future. It seems that every generation more liberally explores these forbidden subjects. That which was once considered taboo has been normalized. When God isn't present in our lives, we lose our consciences.

The prophecy. As referenced earlier, 2 Timothy 3:1–4 tells us what will happen in this type of society.

The internal witness. Christians are now being persecuted, as the Bible predicted in Matthew 10:22, for upholding the holiness of God. Since it appears that people no longer listen to their own conscience in regards to how to conduct themselves, we are being told by the world that God's truth doesn't matter anymore. And since God is left out, Christians are also left out.

For the most part, people understand how the conscience works and the importance of it. It's the few who don't seem to care that we must watch out for.

Do you believe that God is revealed through the conscience? Yes_____ No_____ Explain why.

History. *The past.* There are different views on this, because science usually pegs the earth as being 4.5 billion years old. Creationists view the earth as being relatively young, at just ten thousand years of age. Old earth creationists, however, settle on an age in the millions of years.

If we rely on God and what the Bible says, we can interpret science differently, proving that the earth is young and noticing the effects of a worldwide flood.

We should confirm whether the stories of the Bible are provable by the scientific evidence, such as through archaeology. Then we must discuss the reality of Jesus being the Son of God and son of man simultaneously; this must become part of our view of God guiding His truth throughout history.

Is there enough evidence to prove the reality of Jesus's life, death, and resurrection? Yes, even though there is much speculation in this regard. There is ample physical evidence proving that what the Bible says about Jesus is true.

The present. The historical truth of the Bible can be seen with the discovery of Noah's ark at Mount Ararat. Archaeologists have discovered a structure there that has the shape of a large ark, fitting Noah's description (Genesis 6:14–16). This proves that a worldwide flood did occur.

We also have evidence in the form of the crown of thorns Jesus wore during His crucifixion (Matthew 27:29, Mark 15:17, John 19:2). Along with many other treasures of the church, it was transferred to the Byzantine Empire between the fourth and tenth centuries. Its preservation was confirmed by St. Paulinus of Nola, who mentioned the veneration of the crown of thorns in Jerusalem in 409 A.D.[92] Through many transfers and relocations of this item, it eventually moved to the Notre Dame Cathedral in Paris. When fire broke out there on April 15, 2019, the crown of thorns was saved. Afterward, the crown was returned to its former place as proof of Christ's crucifixion.

The future. The future of human history is dependent upon God and the Bible reveals what will happen. The following is a general guideline of what we can expect:

- The establishment of a world order and revealing of the Antichrist (Daniel 7–9, Revelation 13:1–18, 2 Thessalonians 2:1–12, Revelation 17:7–14, 19:20, 20:10).
- The rapture will take place, either before the tribulation (pre-trib), middle of it (mid-trib), or after it (post-trib) (1 Thessalonians 4:16–18, 5:1–8, John 14:3, Matthew 24:31, 1 Corinthians 15:51–53, Mark 13:24–27).
- Believers in Christ will be judged at the bema seat of Christ immediately after the rapture of the church (1 Thessalonians 4:14–17, 1 Corinthians 15:51–53, John 14:3).
- The church will attend the marriage supper of the Lamb right after the bema seat judgment in heaven, before Jesus's second coming (Revelation 19:7–10).
- On the earth, the tribulation period will last seven years (Revelation 7:14, Matthew 24:21, 1 Thessalonians 5:2, Daniel 9:27, 1 Thessalonians 4:16–17, Daniel 12:1, John 16:33, 2 Peter 3:10).

---

[92] Patricia Kasten, "Where Is the Crown of Thorns Today?" *The Compass*. April 6, 2017 (https://www.thecompassnews.org/2017/04/crown-thorns-today).

- The Armageddon conflict will take place, with certain nations fighting against Israel. (Revelation 16:12–16, 19:11–21, 17:14, Daniel 11:40).
- At the second coming, Jesus will come down from heaven with His saints to defeat the enemies of Israel (Acts 1:9–11, 1 Corinthians 15:51–53, Revelation 1:7, 1 Thessalonians 5:1–3, 5:23, Matthew 24:42, Luke 12:40, 1 Thessalonians 4:16–17).
- In the millennial reign, Jesus will preside over the earth for a thousand years, during which time Satan will be bound at the same time (Revelation 20:1–10).
- The final judgment, the great white throne judgment, will take place (Revelation 20:11–13, Hebrews 9:27, 1 Peter 4:5).
- The new heaven and new earth will be established (Revelation 21:1).

The prophecy. The history of humanity will end when God decides to end it. Matthew 24:36 says, *"But of that day and hour no one knows, no, not even the angels of heaven, but My Father only."*

The historical witness. It is said that history keeps repeating itself. What has happened before will happen again and again, as if we never learn anything in life. Yet we must be aware of the times, because eventually history will come to an end. God warns us about this. So we must be prepared in terms of our relationship with God.

Know that God has everything under His control and that you are secure in Him. The end-times must come. They are inevitable. But God has been faithful to all of humanity by guiding His truth throughout history, from beginning to end. Why would God not give us insight into how the end will come about?

Do you believe that God is revealed through history? Yes_____ No_____ Explain why.

THE MAJOR REVELATIONS OF GOD

Next, we will turn our attention to the three major revelations of God: the Bible (God in writing), the Son (God in the flesh), and the Holy Spirit (God in the spirit).

The Bible. *The past.* God is a revealing God. The revelational witnesses prove this. When we read the Bible from beginning to end, we can see how God has been active in guiding His truth throughout history, giving us the knowledge and understanding to live before Him.

It therefore can be concluded that God's words are life to us. John 8:31–32 says,

CHAPTER TWENTY-ONE: THE PROPHETIC WITNESS

> Then Jesus said to those Jews who believed Him, "If you abide in My word, you are My disciples indeed. And you shall know the truth, and the truth shall make you free."

The present. God directs our paths in our daily lives through His Word. Hebrews 4:12 says,

> For the word of God is living and powerful, and sharper than any two-edged sword, piercing even to the division of soul and spirit, and of joints and marrow, and is a discerner of the thoughts and intents of the heart.

We also keep God's Word in our hearts so we may not sin against Him (Psalm 119:11). We read His Word to walk before Him with integrity (Psalm 119:105, Proverbs 3:5–6).

The future. God inspires and equips us to be righteous in every way and to live our future days in this manner so everyone around us will profit from the words of God. 2 Timothy 3:16–17 says,

> All Scripture is given by inspiration of God, and is profitable for doctrine, for reproof, for correction, for instruction in righteousness, that the [people] of God may be complete, thoroughly equipped for every good work.

Even though all things will pass away, God's Word and the truths contained within it will never pass away (Matthew 24:35).

The prophecy. We read in 1 Peter 1:23–25,

> …having been born again, not of corruptible seed but incorruptible, through the word of God which lives and abides forever, because "All flesh is as grass, and all the glory of man as the flower of the grass. The grass withers, and its flower falls away, but the word of the Lord endures forever." [Isaiah 40:8] Now this is the word which by the gospel was preached to you.

The written witness. Imagine not having the Bible at all today. How would we live our lives? We can't live in this world without the Word of God. The Bible reveals how holy God is, including His standards for how we are to conduct ourselves. It also reveals how He has guided His people throughout history, from the beginning of history to the present and even understanding what the future holds. The Bible is also powerful in spiritual warfare and enlightenment, sharing the love of God, who gives us what we need and guides us along the steps to receive redemption and salvation.

Do you believe that God is revealed through His Word, the Bible? Yes_____ No_____ Explain why.

Jesus. *The past.* Jesus has been involved with humanity through every moment of time since the beginning. Not only did He desire to create beings who would have fellowship with Him, but He has guided His people into knowing Him and living their lives according to godly principles. Once we realize this, we become justified because we accept Him as our Savior.

Jacob declared Jesus as the angel of the Lord (Genesis 48:15–16). John the Baptist prepared the way of the Lord after four hundred years of silence (Isaiah 40:3, Matthew 3:3). The disciples knew Jesus as God in the flesh (John 1:14). From amongst those who witnessed Jesus's life, death, and resurrection, no reaction was more emotional and profound than when the Roman centurion declared, *"Truly this was the Son of God!"* (Matthew 27:54)

The present. Jesus said in Matthew 28:20 that He is with us always, and in Matthew 18:20 we read that He is in our midst when two or more are gathered together in His name. Jesus is the reason for our lives. When we struggle in our daily walk, we know that we can come to Him for help along the way. We are sanctified before Him because He is working in us to make us more like Him.

> Who shall separate us from the love of Christ? Shall tribulation, or distress, or persecution, or famine, or nakedness, or peril, or sword? ...For I am persuaded that neither death nor life, nor angels nor principalities nor powers, nor things present nor things to come, nor height nor depth, nor any other created thing, shall be able to separate us from the love of God which is in Christ Jesus our Lord. (Romans 8:35, 38–39)

The future. We know that Jesus now sits at the right hand of God, making intercession for us (Romans 8:34). He is watching over us and leading us in our daily walk with Him as our King forever.

We also know that Jesus is the same yesterday, today, and forever (Hebrews 13:8). He is the author and finisher of our faith (Hebrews 12:2). No one can come to the Father but through Him (John 14:6). God has highly exalted Him and given Him a name which is above every name, and at the name of Jesus every knee shall bow and every tongue confess that Christ is Lord (Philippians 2:9–11).

The prophecy. The angel Gabriel announced to Mary that she would give birth to Jesus:

> Then the angel said to her, "Do not be afraid, Mary, for you have found favor with God. And behold, you will conceive in your womb and bring forth a Son, and shall call His name Jesus. He will be great, and will be called the Son of the Highest; and the Lord God will give Him the throne of His father David. And He will reign over the house of Jacob forever, and of His kingdom there will be no end." (Luke 1:30–33)

The living witness. What more can we say about Jesus? He is the reason for everything. Not only did He show us the way to God, He personally meets with us in person: in the flesh, when He died for us, and now in the spirit so we can live with Him forever (John 10:28, John 3:16).

Do you believe that God is revealed through His Son, Jesus? Yes_____ No_____ Explain why.

The Holy Spirit. *The past.* Humanity's first experience with the Holy Spirit came on the day of Pentecost. The disciples and those Christ-followers who gathered in the upper room were waiting for God's presence to come. And when He came, they were all filled with the Holy Spirit:

> When the Day of Pentecost had fully come, they were all with one accord in one place. And suddenly there came a sound from heaven, as of a rushing mighty wind, and it filled the whole house where they were sitting. Then there appeared to them divided tongues, as of fire, and one sat upon each of them. And they were all filled with the Holy Spirit and began to speak with other tongues, as the Spirit gave them utterance. (Acts 2:1–4)

The present. The Holy Spirit is our helper and comforter:

> But when the Helper comes, whom I shall send to you from the Father, the Spirit of truth who proceeds from the Father, He will testify of Me. (John 15:26)

The Holy Spirit teaches and transforms us daily.

The future. The Holy Spirit is continuously guiding us to do the will of God and live before Him righteously. We read in 2 Peter 1:19–21,

> And so we have the prophetic word confirmed, which you do well to heed as a light that shines in a dark place, until the day dawns and the morning star rises in your hearts; knowing this first, that no prophecy of Scripture is of any private interpretation, for prophecy

never came by the will of man, but holy men of God spoke as they were moved by the Holy Spirit.

The prophecy. The Holy Spirit will transform us to do the will of God and share Him with all the world. Acts 1:8 says,

> But you shall receive power when the Holy Spirit has come upon you; and you shall be witnesses to Me in Jerusalem, and in all Judea and Samaria, and to the end of the earth."

This power is one of transformation.

The transforming witness. Have you ever known a person who is always disruptive and carnal in conduct? They do whatever they feel is okay and don't care about anyone else. Then, after not seeing this person for a few years, imagine meeting him again and discovering that he is a completely different person. To your amazement, he's changed. Suddenly his conduct and demeaner is full of integrity and courtesy.

After being told that he found Jesus and was filled with the Holy Spirit, it all makes sense. God is so powerful! Through the Holy Spirit, he can change the most sinful, selfish, and unlikely person.

Do you believe that God is revealed through the Holy Spirit? Yes_____ No_____ Explain why.

THE MINOR REVELATIONS OF GOD

Now let's discuss the three minor revelations of God, specifically: the special witness (through God-moments in our lives), the personal witness (through personal moments) and the prophetic witness (through predictive moments).

God-moments. *The past.* On many occasions, according to the Bible, God has intervened in people's lives, giving them guidance, encouragement, and purpose. Earlier we discussed three God-moments relating to Moses, Paul, and Elisha. Each of these three men were affected by God's supernatural appearance. Deuteronomy 29:29 says,

> The secret things belong to the Lord our God, but those things which are revealed belong to us and to our children forever, that we may do all the words of this law.

The present. God is continually watching over us at every moment in life. Psalm 32:8 says, *"I will instruct you and teach you in the way you should go; I will guide you with My eye."* Our steps are also directed by God: *"The steps of a good man are ordered by the Lord, and He delights in his way"* (Psalm 37:23).

The future. God will be there for us in the future. Jeremiah 29:11 says, *"For I know the thoughts that I think toward you, says the Lord, thoughts of peace and not of evil, to give you a future and a hope."*

The prophecy. We read in Acts 17:26–28,

> And He has made from one blood every nation of men to dwell on all the face of the earth, and has determined their preappointed times and the boundaries of their dwellings, so that they should seek the Lord, in the hope that they might grope for Him and find Him, though He is not far from each one of us; for in Him we live and move and have our being… (Acts 17:26–28)

The special witness. God will give us a special revelation of Himself when we're committed to Him and ready to receive His plan for our lives. He is purposeful in this way so we may have confidence in doing His will and stepping out by faith to declare His message to others.

> …[God] has saved us and called us with a holy calling, not according to our works, but according to His own purpose and grace which was given to us in Christ Jesus before time began… (2 Timothy 1:9)

Do you believe that God is revealed through God-moments? Yes_____ No_____ Explain why.

Personal moments. *The past.* We have been predestined and chosen by God to experience life and know Him. Ephesians 1:3–6 says,

> Blessed be the God and Father of our Lord Jesus Christ, who has blessed us with every spiritual blessing in the heavenly places in Christ, just as He chose us in Him before the foundation of the world, that we should be holy and without blame before Him in love, having predestined us to adoption as sons by Jesus Christ to Himself, according to the good pleasure of His will, to the praise of the glory of His grace, by which He made us accepted in the Beloved.

The present. God is working in our lives to make us the best version of ourselves so we can be more like Jesus:

> But we all, with unveiled face, beholding as in a mirror the glory of the Lord, are being transformed into the same image from glory to glory, just as by the Spirit of the Lord. (2 Corinthians 3:18)

The future. Our lives are in the hands of God. No matter what we go through in life, He is there to guide us, give us encouragement, and provide answers to all we need to know. We just have to put our trust in Him, because we are special and unique treasures, belonging to a God who loves us.

> But you are a chosen generation, a royal priesthood, a holy nation, His own special people, that you may proclaim the praises of Him who called you out of darkness into His marvelous light. (1 Peter 2:9)

The prophecy. We know that God allows us to go through struggles in life so we may glorify Him in return and inspire others to follow Him:

> And we know that all things work together for good to those who love God, to those who are the called according to His purpose. For whom He foreknew, He also predestined to be conformed to the image of His Son, that He might be the firstborn among many brethren. (Romans 8:28–29)

The personal witness. It's amazing what people in this world go through. We marvel at how they overcome it all. Somehow they have the necessary strength and courage, inspiring us as they show us how to trust in a higher power, in a higher faith, in a God who reveals Himself through people's circumstances.

Do you believe that God is revealed through people's personal lives? Yes_____ No_____ Explain why.

Predictive moments. *The past.* Colossians 1:15–18 explains that Jesus is the reason we exist and have our being:

> He is the image of the invisible God, the firstborn over all creation. For by Him all things were created that are in heaven and that are on earth, visible and invisible, whether thrones or dominions or principalities or powers. All things were created through Him and for Him. And He is before all things, and in Him all things consist. And He is the head of the body, the church, who is the beginning, the firstborn from the dead, that in all things He may have the preeminence.

The present. Jesus is our foundation, our salvation, and our fortress. He seeks us daily and wants to be there for us. Proverbs 3:5–6 says, *"Trust in the Lord with all your heart, and lean not on your own understanding; in all your ways acknowledge Him, and He shall direct your paths."*

The future. God is working in our lives so we can become more like Jesus. Philippians 1:6 says that we are to be *"confident of this very thing, that He who has begun a good work in [us] will complete it until the day of Jesus Christ."* God also gives us a heavenly inheritance:

> Blessed be the God and Father of our Lord Jesus Christ, who according to His abundant mercy has begotten us again to a living hope through the resurrection of Jesus Christ from the dead, to an inheritance incorruptible and undefiled and that does not fade away, reserved in heaven for you (1 Peter 1:3–4).

The prophecy. Jesus is our example and inspiration. 1 John 3:2 says,

> Beloved, now we are children of God; and it has not yet been revealed what we shall be, but we know that when He is revealed, we shall be like Him, for we shall see Him as He is.

The prophetic witness. God continually gives us wisdom and insight into what's going to happen in our lives. No matter how this is revealed, it comes from the revelations of God. They intertwine to let us know that our future is in God's hands and that He cares for us. All their prophecies are signs that God is directing our paths each step of the way.

Do you believe that God is revealed through prophetic moments? Yes_____ No_____ Explain why.

THE CHURCH

Finally we come to the tenth and final witness, the consummation of all the others: the church. What is the church? It is comprised of Christ-followers, the keepers of God's truth and members of His family. God is revealed through His people, to whom He has gifted His power.

The past. Jesus is building the church to become His inheritance and ultimate witness. Matthew 16:18 says, *"And I also say to you that you are Peter, and on this rock I will build My church, and the gates of Hades shall not prevail against it."*

The present. God has given us everything we need as His church through the knowledge of His will, wisdom, and spiritual understanding:

> …that you may walk worthy of the Lord, fully pleasing Him, being fruitful in every good work and increasing in the knowledge of God; strengthened with all might, according to His glorious power, for all patience and longsuffering with joy; giving thanks to the Father who has qualified us to be partakers of the inheritance of the saints

in the light. He has delivered us from the power of darkness and conveyed us into the kingdom of the Son of His love, in whom we have redemption through His blood, the forgiveness of sins. (Colossians 1:10–14)

The future. Paul gives us a mystery, a prophetic happening which will change us completely.

> …in a moment, in the twinkling of an eye, at the last trumpet. For the trumpet will sound, and the dead will be raised incorruptible, and we shall be changed. For this corruptible must put on incorruption, and this mortal must put on immortality… But thanks be to God, who gives us the victory through our Lord Jesus Christ. (1 Corinthians 15:52–53, 57)

The prophecy. Jesus gave Himself for the church so He could cleanse it and sanctify it *"that He might present her to Himself a glorious church, not having spot or wrinkle or any such thing, but that she should be holy and without blemish"* (Ephesians 5:27).

The final witness. We are God's people, His saints. We are the final revelation of God, sharing God with others, including His truth, love, and mercy. We share what He has done for us and share His prophetic message of the future. We are His hands and feet, His message of hope. We are the carriers of His truth and reveal who He is.

Do you believe that God is revealed by the church? Yes_____ No_____ Explain why.

CONCLUSION
KNOWING THE WILL OF GOD

WHAT A REMARKABLE journey you have just experienced through reading this book! You have found that God is truly a revealing God. The revelations He has given to us can easily be seen and understood now that you have looked at yourself to realize that this truth you believe in is so trustworthy, valuable, intimate, and personal.

The world questions this truth because they don't understand this God we hold in such high regard. The only way they could believe in Him would be for Him to visibly reveal Himself. They want to see Him with their own eyes, to hear His voice from heaven. But God is wise and full of understanding, knowing that for us to believe in something it must be deeply rooted in our most inner being. This comes through faith.

We must experience Him through these revelations and witnesses of God. They confirm our faith, establish our truth, and cause us to live before a God who truly loves us.

So please, study this conclusion to confirm your faith so that you may inspire others to pursue Him… because He wills for everyone to find Him and know Him.

THE REVELATIONAL WITNESSES

External witness. There will be a new heaven and a new earth (Revelation 21:1). God gave you a purpose on this earth and placed you at the exact location where He wanted you to be. He gave you parents or guardians (and maybe siblings), gifts and abilities, and the ability to experience the wonders of nature and His presence. Know that He has everything under His control and is sovereign in every respect when it comes to what occurs on this earth. We are to trust Him no matter what happens. Put your faith in that.

Internal witness. We will be free from sin and become perfect (Romans 6:22). Keep your conscience pure and your focus on God and the things of God. This world keeps trying to hide and ignore the truth of God, encouraging us to stray from His standards. He gave us a moral replica of Himself so we could get to know Him personally, live with integrity, and honor Him with our lives.

Historical witness. Our days are numbered, and then comes judgment (Acts 17:26, Hebrews 9:27). Please realize that this earth is temporary and that you must make the best use of your time, for it is limited and we don't know when it will end. God is continually directing us throughout our lives from beginning to end. The Bible has given us great examples of how God led His people throughout history.

Written witness. God's Word will abide forever (1 Peter 1:23–25). Keep the Word of God in your hearts and live them to the fullest, for they are everlasting. They will never change and never end. Live the Bible daily, learn its truths, and know the heart of God. These words of God are life to us.

Living witness. Jesus becomes our Savior, Lord, and King (Philippians 2:9–11). The Father loved us so much that He sent His very own Son to show us the way, die for us, and rise again so we could live with Him forever. He is our example of how to live… and how to love. What a privilege it is to have a personal relationship with Him.

Transforming witness. The Holy Spirit dwells within us to righteously transform us (2 Corinthians 5:17). The Holy Spirit continually shows us how to do things in the right way. Allow Him to direct your life in every respect. Allow Him to change your ways and transform you so you can become more Christ-like, for we are His inheritance.

Special witness. God directs our path and reveals Himself to us (Proverbs 3:5–6; Hebrews 13:20–21). He has a special plan for your life. Seek it out and find it. Test it and experience it. When the time is right, He will make it known to you. It all begins with you being faithful to Him and spending time with Him in prayer. Once He reveals this special witness to you, be obedient and pursue it with divine passion. Never lay it aside or neglect it.

Personal witness. Jesus is building our home in heaven by what we go through (John 14:1–3). You have a personal calling and a story to tell. How are you living for God by what you experience in life? God allows these circumstances in order to show us more of ourselves, and more of Him. He has given us the tools we need to overcome our troubles through His Word, through Jesus, and through the Holy Spirit. Your life is a personal testimony to show others how great and loving God is.

Prophetic witness. For in Christ we live and move and have our being (Acts 17:26–28). We seek to plan our lives and rely on our own wisdom and strength, expecting everything to turn out the way we intend it to. But God intervenes on our behalf and gives us timely answers when we need them most. We therefore must understand His prophetic messages from a divine perspective, to help us understand how the future will affect us.

Final witness. We are a glorious church without spot or wrinkle, washed in the blood of the Lamb (2 Corinthians 3:18). From glory to glory, God is changing us so we can share Him with the world. We are His hands and feet. We hold His truth and His ways so others can see them. Be witnesses of God by making disciples and followers of Christ, teaching them all things pertaining to the rule and glory of God.

BIBLIOGRAPHY

Augustyn, Tim, "How to Discern Promptings from the Holy Spirit," *Open the Bible*. July 19, 2013 (https://openthebible.org/article/how-to-discern-promptings-from-the-holy-spirit).

Brown Jr., Walter T., *In the Beginning…* (Phoenix, AR: Center for Scientific Creation, 1986), 2.

Ackland, Peter, Serge Resnikoff, and Rupert Bourne, "World Blindness and Visual Impairment: Despite Many Successes, the Problem Is Growing," *Community Eye Health Journal*. Date of access: November 3, 2023 (https://www.cehjournal.org/article/world-blindness-and-visual-impairment-despite-many-successes-the-problem-is-growing).

"Alcohol," *World Health Organization*. May 9, 2022 (https://www.who.int/news-room/factsheets/detail/alcohol).

Anshool Deshmukh, "This Simple Chart Reveals the Distribution of Global Wealth," *Visual Capitalist*. September 20, 2021 (https://www.visualcapitalist.com/distribution-of-global-wealth-chart).

"Countries by Murder Rate: Ranked," *The Facts Institute*. June 17, 2020 (https://www.factsinstitute.com/ranking/countries-by-murder-rate).

"Dark Energy, Dark Matter," *NASA*. Date of access: November 13, 2023 (https://science.nasa.gov/astrophysics/focus-areas/what-is-dark-energy).

"Distribution of Wealth," *Wikipedia*. Date of access: October 10, 2023 (https://en.wikipedia.org/wiki/Distribution_of_wealth).

Douglas, J.D., *The New Bible Dictionary* (Grand Rapids, MI: Eerdmans, 1962), 478.

"Does Society Have a Sex Addiction Problem?" *Mayo Clinic*. December 6, 2022 (https://newsnetwork.mayoclinic.org/discussion/does-society-have-a-sex-addiction-problem).

Evans, Sophie, "How Mere Humans Manage to Comprehend the Vastness of the Universe," *Scientific American*. October 11, 2019 (https://blogs.scientificamerican.com/observations/how-mere-humans-manage-to-comprehend-the-vastness-of-the-universe).

"Factsheet on Persons with Disabilities," *United Nations*. Date of access: November 3, 2023 (https://www.un.org/development/desa/disabilities/resources/factsheet-on-persons-with-disabilities.html).

Finlayson, R.A., *The Holiness of God* (London, UK: Westminster Chapel, 1955), 530.

"First-Ever United Nations Resolution on Homelessness," *United Nations*. March 9, 2020 (https://www.un.org/development/desa/dspd/2020/03/resolution-homelessness).

Foxe, John, *Foxe's Book of Martyrs* (Old Tappan, NJ: Jove Publications, 1968), 11–13.

Geisler, Norman L. and William E. Nix, *A General Introduction to the Bible* (Chicago, IL: Moody Press, 1968), 366.

"The Global Deaf Population: 38 Million and Counting," *International Congress of Phonetic Sciences 2019*. November 6, 2022 (https://icphs2019.org/the-global-deaf-population-38-million-and-counting).

Haber, Audrey and Richard P. Runyon, *Fundamental of Psychology, Second Edition* (Manila, Philippines: Addison-Wesley, 1978), 9.

"Hostile Ancient Sources Point to Jesus' Divinity," Christian Apologist. April 18, 2020 (https://christian-apologist.com/2020/04/18/hostile-ancient-sources-point-to-jesus-divinity).

Humbard, Rex, *The Prophecy Bible* (Akron, OH: Rex Humbard Ministries, 1985), 38.

Huse, Scott M., *The Collapse of Evolution, Third Edition* (Grand Rapids, MI: Baker Books, 1997), 23–24.

Josephus, Flavius, *Antiquities of the Jews 18.3*, trans. William Whiston (Grand Rapids, MI: A.M. Kregel, 1981), 379.

Kasten, Patricia, "Where Is the Crown of Thorns Today?" *The Compass*. April 6, 2017 (https://www.thecompassnews.org/2017/04/crown-thorns-today).

Koukl, Gregory, "Why I'm Not an Evolutionist," Ambassador Basic Curriculum, CD #3, 2003 (https://www.str.org/greg-koukl/topics).

Larson, Bob, *Larson's Book of Cults* (Wheaton, IL: Tyndale House, 1984), 47.

Lightfoot, Neil R., *How We Got the Bible* (Grand Rapids, MI: Baker Books, 2003), 13–19.

Little, Paul E., *Know What You Believe* (Wheaton, IL: Victor Books, 1987), 33.

Lockyer, Herbert, *All the Doctrines of the Bible* (Grand Rapids, MI: Zondervan, 1964), 152.

"Mental Health: The Silent Crisis," *International Baccalaureate*. Date of access: March 25, 2017 (https://blogs.ibo.org/2017/03/25/mental-health-the-silent-crisis).

Nee, Watchman, *The Spiritual Man* (New York, NY: Christian Fellowship Publishers, 1968).

Nelson, Ryan, "How Did the Apostles Die? What We Actually Know," *OverviewBible.com*. December 17, 2019 (https://overviewbible.com/how-did-the-apostles-die).

Oakes, John, "Can We Trust Ron Wyatt's Published Claim…" *Evidence for Christianity*. April 11, 2019 (https://evidenceforchristianity.org/can-we-trust-ron-wyatts-published-claim-that-they-have-discovered-some-of-Jesus-blood-and-that-it-has-24-not-23-chromosomes).

"Paralysis in the U.S.," *Christopher & Dana Reeve Foundation*. Date of access: November 3, 2023 (https://www.christopherreeve.org/todays-care/paralysis-help-overview/stats-about-paralysis).

Patzia, Arthur G., *The Making of the New Testament* (Downers Grove, IL: InterVarsity Press, 1995), 40.

Peters, F.E., *The Children of Abraham: Judaism, Christianity, Islam* (Princeton, NJ: Princeton University Press, 2004), 50.

"Poverty," *The World Bank*. Date of access: November 3, 2023 (https://www.worldbank.org/en/topic/poverty/overview).

Reno, Cora A., *Evolution on Trial* (Chicago, IL: Moody Press, 1970), 103.

Ritchie, Hannah, "How Many People in the World Die from Cancer?" *Our World in Data*. February 1, 2018 (https://ourworldindata.org/how-many-people-in-the-world-die-from-cancer).

Sailhamer, John H., *Christian Theology* (Grand Rapids, MI: Zondervan, 1998), 29.

Sanders, Chauncy, *An Introduction to Research in English Literary History* (New Yorky, NY: Macmillan, 1952), 26.

Sarfati, Jonathan, *Refuting Evolution* (Green Forest, AR: Master Books, 2000), 16.

Shelley, Bruce L., *Church History in Plain Language* (Nashville, TN: Thomas Nelson, 1995).

The Timechart History of the World (London, UK: Parkgate Books, 1997), 4.

Thiessen, Henry C., *Lectures in Systematic Theology* (Grand Rapids, MI: Eerdmans, 1979), 10.

"Unemployment Worldwide: Statistics and Facts," Statista. August 31, 2023 (https://www.statista.com/topics/9225/unemployment-worldwide/#topicOverview).

"Universe Facts," *National Geographic Kids*. Date of access: November 13, 2023 (https://www.natgeokids.com/nz/discover/science/space/universe-facts).

"The Universe Is Expanding Faster than Scientists Thought," *Science in the News*. October 30, 2019 (https://sitn.hms.harvard.edu/flash/2019/universe-expanding-faster-scientists-thought).

"World Drug Report 2019, Executive Summary," United Nations. Date of access: November 3, 2023 (https://wdr.unodc.org/wdr2019/en/exsum.html).

Wysong, R.L., *The Creation-Evolution Controversy* (Midland, MI: Inquiry Press, 1981), 308.

www.ingramcontent.com/pod-product-compliance
Lightning Source LLC
Chambersburg PA
CBHW071656090426
42738CB00009B/1554